Envisionary Management

Envisionary Management

A GUIDE FOR HUMAN RESOURCE PROFESSIONALS IN MANAGEMENT TRAINING AND DEVELOPMENT

William P. Anthony,
E. Nick Maddox,
and
Walter Wheatley, Jr.

QUORUM BOOKS

NEW YORK • WESTPORT, CONNECTICUT • LONDON

101510

Library of Congress Cataloging-in-Publication Data

Anthony, William P.
  Envisionary management.

  Bibliography: p.
  Includes index.
  1. Management. 2. Imagery (Psychology) I. Maddox,
E. Nick. II. Wheatley, Walter. III. Title.
HD38.A6256   1988   658.3   87–7373
ISBN 0–89930–257–2 (lib. bdg. : alk. paper)

British Library Cataloguing in Publication Data is available.

Library of Congress Catalog Card Number: 87–7373
ISBN: 0–89930–257–2

First published in 1988 by Quorum Books

Greenwood Press, Inc.
88 Post Road West, Westport, Connecticut 06881

Printed in the United States of America

(∞)™

The paper used in this book complies with the
Permanent Paper Standard issued by the National
Information Standards Organization (Z39.48–1984).

10 9 8 7 6 5 4 3 2 1

To
Catherine and Sarah
Eric
Catherine, Gretchen, and Valarie

CONTENTS

ILLUSTRATIONS

Figures

Exhibit

PREFACE

As human resource professional, you are concerned with helping your organization achieve excellence. One way you can help improve your organization's managerial performance and your own personal effectiveness is to practice a technique widely used in sports, counseling, and other fields. This technique is known as mental imagery or visualization, and this book tells you how to use it to help people become more effective managers.

Management is an abstract action for many people. The management functions of planning, staffing, leading, and controlling are difficult for many people to visualize concretely. And yet, in order to be effective, managers must perform desirable behaviors just as an athlete must perform a set of desirable behaviors required for managerial effectiveness.

By using mental imagery we can clearly see in our mind how we should perform in a particular situation for maximum effectiveness. We can mentally rehearse the desired behaviors prior to performing them. We can anticipate possible problems that can emerge and prepare for them in anticipation. We can prepare contingency plans. We can learn from possible mistakes before we make the mistake.

In short, mental imagery allows us to adopt a whole new approach for practicing management. It forces us to take a performance orientation and requires us to think through the specific behaviors required for top performance. It allows us to develop positive mental scripts, which can serve as guides to enhance our self-confidence. It allows us to learn about management through mental practice as well as through actual practice.

The application of mental imagery to management is a rather new endeavor. Most of us probably use certain types of imagery as managers from time to time: as we prepare a presentation, as we are about to deal with an angry employee, or as we attempt to prepare a forecast for a strategic plan. The technique is not completely foreign to us; but few of us use imagery on a regular and systematic basis. We have yet to tap the full power of imagery. This book will help you to help your organization tap this power for its managers.

We have conducted experiments both in and out of the classroom in applying mental imagery to management. Thus far the experiments have been very encouraging. However, more work needs to be done. As you try the various imagery exercises in this book, we would like to hear from you regarding your experiences with the technique. (Please respond to any one of us.) In a later edition of the book, we will report some of these experiences.

So for now, relax, open your mind, and be receptive to a new and exciting management technique, which should enhance your effectiveness and that of the managers in your organization.

ACKNOWLEDGMENTS

We wish to acknowledge the numerous individuals who have helped us with the book. Jane C. Wager read and edited a large portion of the book. We appreciate her views since she is a professional human resource specialist with Wicat International. Pam Perrewe of Florida State University also provided editorial assistance on a number of chapters. Brenda Moore and Kelly Shrode did an excellent job with the typing and artwork. Lisa Myers and Susan Landfried helped with the indexing and copyediting.

We also wish to acknowledge the numerous managers and human resource professionals on whom we have tested not only our ideas but also the scripts and exercises contained in the book. This real world testing helped us to make the material more relevant and effective.

Finally, we owe a debt of gratitude to the scholars and writers cited in our bibliography. Our material is well grounded in the theory and research provided by numerous individuals in the fields of psychology, education, medicine, and counseling. Their work has provided us with a solid foundation in imagery which we have used to build human resource management applications.

We are grateful to all of these people for their assistance. Of course we take responsibility for any errors in the manuscript.

1

THE MIND'S EYE

Visualize this: you are at the beach. The sun feels warm on your shoulders. The sand is soft on your feet. There is a nice cool breeze off the water gently blowing in your face. There are white puffy clouds in the sky. You have all afternoon to lie on your blanket, rest, and relax. You hear the waves gently break on shore. Children laugh and shout in the distance. Their voices mix in with music from a radio. You are very relaxed.

The creation of this restful scene in your mind is an example of a technique that can be used to improve management performance. The technique, known as imagery, establishes a scenario in one's mind that clearly depicts a set of desired circumstances. By creating a mental image of a desired situation we can better set goals and determine ways of achieving them. As a human resource professional, you can act as a catalyst to introduce imagery in your organization as a part of a total management education and development program.

Imagery has been part of human existence from the earliest times. Primordial humans depicted nature scenes and godly images on cave walls, tombs, and pottery. Literature and art abound with rich imagery. Memory, learning, and creative thinking depend to a large extent on imagery. Almost all active human functioning involves an imaginal aspect that helps us anticipate, rehearse, or plan for the experiences we have. More recently, imagery techniques have been used to improve sports performance, reduce pain and phobias, counsel individuals with problems, and in career development. However, until now imagery has seen little use in management. That is the purpose of this book—to show

Figure 1-1
The Guided Imagery Process

| Outside Cues | → | Sensory Perception of Cue | → | Associations of Cue with Stored Images | → | Creation of Mental Image | → | Action or Response |

you how you can use various imagery techniques to improve the performance of managers in your organization and to improve your own personal effectiveness as well.

THE IMAGERY PROCESS

Imagery goes by several names. Common names include *visualization, conceptualization,* and *mental picturing.* These terms refer to essentially the same process—creating a mental picture or image of a situation in your mind's eye. In fact, some experts have called imagery "seeing with the mind's eye."

The form of imagery we discuss primarily in this book is guided imagery. This form of imagery involves guidance and scripting from either an outside person, such as yourself, a book, or a set of facts to create desired mental images and experiences as shown in Figure 1–1. These outside factors are cues to stimulate the creation of a mental image. The beach image created previously in your mind was elicited because of the words you read and the associations you made between those words and similar experiences you have had. A similar image could have been created had these words been spoken to you. Perhaps the smell of the salt air or the feel of sand on your feet could have also created the beach image.

With guided imagery, we use a specific sequence of cues or a script to create a desired imaginal set. In the beach scene, our image of calmness, restfulness, and peacefulness were the desired result of your imagery. The goal was to have you actually place yourself on a beach experiencing the soft breeze and the warm sun. Authors of fiction use this technique throughout their books. In fact, when we read we actually place ourselves in the imaginal context of a story and thus experience the lives of the various characters.

The image created can serve to promote a desired response. After visualizing the beach scene, the desired response was one of relaxation and calm. Imagery can also be used to create responses of fear, anxiety, understanding, revulsion, or movement. In sport, high jumpers, such as Dwight Stones, actually visualize themselves approaching the runway and sailing over the bar. Basketball players prior to shooting visualize the ball swishing through the hoop. Students understand a complex math problem when it is depicted with pictures. In this book, we promote imagery, a powerful technique, to enhance performance and to help you establish effective management behavior and habits in your organization.

The more complex and abstract the desired response, the more difficult it is to create the desired image; yet, it is precisely with this type of response that imagery can have its greatest payout. For example, think of the task of calming an angry subordinate. Imagery can be used to create a scene in your mind that both helps you to understand the factors involved in an angry confrontation and to use the effective managerial behaviors needed to deal with it. Thus, you might visualize yourself remaining calm in the face of the onslaught while shaping your subordinate's actions so that he/she also becomes calm.

IMAGERY AND THE BRAIN

Imagery is associated with the right side of the brain. Research on the brain shows that the right and left sides of the brain perform separate or distinct functions. As shown in Exhibit 1–1, the right side of the brain is connected to the left side of the body. The left side of the brain is connected to the right side of the body. The right side of the brain deals with spatial and relationship functions. It specializes in memory and recognition of objects. It normally tends to specialize in intuition and is the seat of passion and dreams. It is the crucial side for artists, crafts people, and musicians. It is this side of the brain where imagery functions lie.

Reasoning, verbal, and mathematical functions and logic lie in the left side of the brain. This side processes information in a linear manner. This is the crucial side of the brain for wordsmiths, mathematicians, and scientists.

IMAGERY AND THE SENSES

Although most of the work in psychology and related disciplines has been focused on visual imagery, we explore the four other types of imagery as well: hearing, taste-smell, feel-touch, and movement. Each of these forms of imagery has a role to play in various parts of the management process. Visual imagery is important and much of this book explains how to use visual imagery techniques in management. But it is also important to hear, taste, feel, and experience movement in various parts of the management process.

For example, when using imagery as a technique of calming an angry employee, we should not only be able to visualize the conversation we plan to have, but also to hear what we plan to say, and what the other

Exhibit 1-1
The Properties of Both Hemispheres

The Left Side	The Right Side
Connected to the right side of the body, and the right side of each eye's vision.	Connected to the left side of the body, and the left side of each eye's vision.
Deals with inputs one at a time.	Demands ready integration of many inputs at once.
Processes information in a linear manner. Has a lineal and sequential mode of operation.	Processes information more diffusely. Has a nonlineal and simultaneous mode of operation.
Deals with time. Responsible for the faculty of verbal expression, or language.	Deals with space. Responsible for gestures, facial and body movements (or "body language"), tone of voice, etc.
Responsible for verbal and mathematical functions.	Responsible for spatial and relational functions; awareness of our bodies; for sports and dancing; our orientation in space; recognition of faces; artistic endeavor; musical ability and recognition of pitch.
Specializes in memory and recognition of words or numbers.	Specializes in memory and recognition of objects, persons, and places, music, etc.
Normally tends to specialize in logic and analytical reasoning or thinking.	Normally tends to specialize in intuition and holistic perception or thinking.
The seat of reason.	The seat of passion and of dreams.
The crucial side of the brain for wordsmiths, mathematicians, and scientists.	The crucial side of the brain for artists, crafts people, musicians.

Source: Robert E. Ornstein, *Psychology of Consciousness* (New York: Harcourt Brace Jovanovich, 1973).

person will say. We may wish to imagine ourselves shaking hands (touching) with the other person. We may wish to imagine the smell of the office where we plan to hold our conversation. We may wish to let ourselves rehearse body movements (e.g., hand and facial gestures) that we plan to use in talking with the employee.

By using the senses, we can create a full range of experiences in using imagery and thereby enrich the value of the technique. It will allow us to be more realistic in using imagery to create desired scenarios in management. Figure 1–2 shows that these five senses will be used to create rich imagery scenarios.

Figure 1-2
Imagery and the Senses

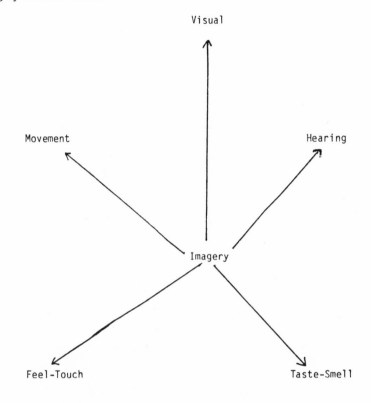

FORMS OF IMAGERY

As we have noted, there are several forms of imagery, although primary focus is on guided imagery and the several forms in which it may be used. Note that guided imagery can be other-directed or self-directed. In other-directed imagery a coach, group leader, or script writer guides you to create the desired imagery scenario. In self-directed imagery, you assemble the needed data and cues to create your own image set. For example, in self-directed imagery, you may go to a quiet room, shut the door, put on some soft music, dim the lights, and reflect on a problem you are having at work in hopes of being able to create an image to help you solve it. In this book, the format most commonly used is other-directed guided imagery with you as the facilitator. That is, this book will help you to implement imagery in your organization.

There is also static and dynamic imagery. In static imagery, a set picture is created, such as a snapshot. Visualizing the face of a loved one, such as a spouse, child, or parent is an example of a static image. A dynamic image is akin to a movie in which you picture a sequence of events occurring. When this sequence of events is created over and over again in your mind you are engaging in mental rehearsal, a form of dynamic imagery. Mental rehearsal can be used to deal with difficult anticipated future events, such as giving a speech on a controversial topic before an important group. In your mind, you would rehearse the speech, and your presentation style, while anticipating comments and how you will respond to them. You would repeat this scenario several times prior to the speech so that you'll feel fully prepared to manage the experience. You would actually visualize yourself in front of the group, making the speech and responding to questions and comments.

When we rehearse several different sequences we are engaged in mental scenario rehearsal, in which we create "if-then" situations in our mind. We frequently use this technique when considering a sensitive issue with a close friend, spouse, or subordinate. We create "if-then" situations—"if she says A, then I'll say B. However, if she says C, then I'll say D." We mentally rehearse alternative conversations in order to prepare ourselves for the anticipated interaction.

Fantasy and dreaming are two additional forms of imagery in which we let our imaginations roam, often free of our conscious control. With a fantasy, we imagine that we are in an unusual or unique situation that is not likely to happen, such as being President of the United States or running nude through church. When we daydream, we let our mind spontaneously focus upon a pleasant experience, such as being at the beach, sailing, or skiing. Dreaming while asleep is quite vivid for many of us and is usually uncontrollable, although some people can influence what they dream and, after practice, can wake themselves from a dream.

Because imagery is often associated with fantasy and dreaming, it sometimes carries a "flaky" connotation. This is unfortunate, because as we shall see, guided imagery when properly practiced can be a very effective technique for self-enhancement. Consequently, our approach and the approaches successfully used in the past, will emphasize guided imagery instead of fantasy and dreaming forms of imagery.

THE DEVELOPMENT OF IMAGERY AS AN IDEA

Imagery has its cultural roots in the early art forms of our prehistoric ancestors; in the analysis of dreams, first popular many years ago; in literature, folklore, fables, and story-telling; and in the development of cultural symbols and artifacts such as totem poles archetyes and adornments. It serves as a basis for such relatively modern works as Dr. Norman Vincent Peale's *The Power of Positive Thinking*. Interest in and the use of imagery is not new, but there is a renewed interest in the technique because of its recent successful applications in sports, medicine, learning, and counseling.

For years, imagery has been neglected by science because of the difficulty in measuring it. Obviously, it's difficult to measure any internal state. Observable behavior that was subject to quantification became popular with psychologists instead of cognitive theories that dealt with hard-to-measure processes of the mind. However, by measuring the results of imagery, such as improved performance in sports or reduced fear, scientists are once again interested in the technique.

In the next chapter, we'll see that imagery is being used in many fields today. However, its roots lie in the study of the mind, consciousness, and thought. This study of thought has occupied psychologists for many years. The imagery process is not the only way of explaining how the mind works, but it is important, and worth reviewing in detail.

Since psychologists have had much to tell us about effective management behavior over the years, we should be interested in imaginal techniques that hold so much promise for improved management behavior. Yet this important psychological technique has not been readily applied to management.

Our focus in this book is toward the many practical applications of imaginal technoloiges. We want to focus on the question of how imagery can be used to improve the behavior of managers in your organization.

IMAGERY AND HUMAN RESOURCE PROFESSIONALS

As a human resource professional, you may already be familiar with imagery. Many human resource professionals study the process in counseling and education courses. If you have played sports, your coach may have used the technique. However, even though you might be familiar with the technique, it is unlikely that you are familiar with its application to management, since there simply have been so few applications made; in fact, that is the purpose of this book.

In applying imagery to management in organizations, human resource professionals have a unique opportunity. Regardless of whether you are a training director, personnel manager, employee relations supervisor, or human resource vice president, you have the unique opportunity of helping your organization better tap into its human resource potential. The role often played by many human resource professionals is that of a coach. Imagery is one new and creative way this potential can be unleashed, particularly among managers and supervisors in your organization.

As you explore these imagery applications in this book, you will also see how they apply to yourself. By using imagery techniques discussed in the book yourself, you will enhance your own personal effectiveness.

As we discuss elsewhere in this book, not all organizations are ready to embrace imagery as a development technique. Consequently, the ease with which you can introduce the technique in your organization will depend on a number of factors—all have a bearing on how imagery should be introduced: your familiarity with the topic, your belief in the efficiency of the technique, your credibility, your organization's previous experience with imagery, and your organization's culture.

In some instances you may wish to proceed slowly, on an experimental basis with just a few managers to "test" the technique. You may act as the facilitator or bring in an outside professional. In other cases, you may wish to tie imagery to an already existing training and development program, such as one in leadership development, strategic planning, or communications enhancement. The specifics of introducing imagery are covered in Chapter 9 of this book.

IMAGERY AND MANAGEMENT

Reflect for a moment on all the various activities involved in the management process: managers establish and implement policy, they make decisions, they solve problems, they handle arguments and manage conflict, they assign and appraise work, they plan what is supposed to happen, and they try to ensure that it does happen, they lead and influence others, they motivate and communicate. The list could go on and on. Management is truly a very complicated and challenging profession.

Every time a manager faces a situation where action is needed, a decision must be made as to what to do. Sometimes the decision is simply to do what has always been done in similar situations in the past; at other times, it requires trying something new. How does a manager decide what to do?

Consider this situation. Suppose one of your organization's manager's subordinates comes to him with this problem: she has just witnessed two of his employees having a heated argument in the office in front of the rest of the employees. She tells him that not only are the two employees very upset, but so is the entire office. She wants him to do something. Should he? If so, what should he do? As a human resource professional, what would you advise in this situation?

Or consider this situation. A department manager in your company is reviewing the department's performance against quarterly goals. She notices that very few goals are being met. This is the first time so many have been missed. What would you advise her to do?

Finally, consider this situation. You come in to work one morning and there is a handwritten note on your desk from your secretary indicating that she has resigned. She is not at her desk. What action do you take?

In each of the above examples, the person involved has the choice of either taking action or doing nothing. Most of us would first try to get more information before we decide what to do. Then we would mentally evaluate alternative courses of action we could take. Most likely we would reflect on whether we had experienced a similar situation in the past and, if so, how we had handled it. We might also check company policy to see if it offers some guidance. We may even talk with others to get advice. Then at some point we must decide what to do. It is at this point that imagery can play a significantly active role in decision making.

By using the imagery process in each of the above situations, we can form a clear picture of the situation and mentally visualize the actions we might take and the possible consequences of the actions. The clearer the picture we can form in our mind's eye, the more likely it is that the course of action we decide on will be the right one. We try to "see" a solution to the problem before we act.

The Angry Employees

For example, in the first case, we might advise that the manager leave his office and walk to the place where the argument occurred to see what happened. Let's suppose that when he got there, the two arguing employees are no longer present. The office is buzzing with talk of the occurrence. The manager asks someone—those who witnessed the argument—what happened. After hearing their story and determining whether it is essentially the same story that was originally brought to his attention, he decides to locate each of the two parties involved to discuss the matter with them.

At this point he has several choices. Should he set up a meeting and talk with them together or see each one privately? Should he see them in his office, their offices, or on some neutral ground? Should he walk to their office or call them? Or should he send each a memo to set up the meeting? Once he determines how and where he wants to meet with each, what should he plan to say to each of them?

No doubt what you advise him to do and say will depend upon what you and he know about each employee involved. Have they argued before? Is one of them "hot tempered"? Is one of them particularly sensitive? Do other matters have a bearing on the situation such as the race, sex, or age of each party involved? Of course once the manager involved talks to them (or even before he does), he must decide whether to say anything to the entire office staff that witnessed the argument.

No doubt, much of what you advise in this situation will be influenced by the manager's overall style of management. Does he feel comfortable in confrontational situations? Does he like to go to employees or does he prefer them to come to see him? How many other pressures does he feel in his job, and what priority does resolving employee conflicts have?

However, even though a manager's basic style of management will likely influence what he may do, he will have freedom to maneuver. Most managers are not so rigid that they have an automatic, knee-jerk response to situations faced. They exercise judgment and latitude in deciding what to do.

Let's suppose you advise the manager to talk with each employee involved alone in their respective offices. Here's where imagery has a role to play. Before going to each person's office, the manager can mentally rehearse what he plans to say and what the employee's reaction will be. He can then go through a process of if-then statements: "If he says this, then I'll say this." He can actually visualize himself sitting or standing in the office talking with the employee and responding to what the employee says. If he thinks the employee may become angry or defensive, imagery will allow him to actually visualize what the employee's face will look like—eyes bulging, face red, veins in neck standing out, fists slammed on desk. If this happens how should he respond?

The manager involved can mentally practice this until he feels comfortable that he has rehearsed what might happen compared to what he actually wants to have happen; that is, until he can "see" the optimal solution. All this *mental rehearsal* (one form of imagery) may only take a few minutes. Then he is ready to proceed to the employee's office to bring his imagery into action.

The advantage of using imagery in this and many other situations is that it helps the manager to prepare in a very clear way for an experience he is about to have. Just as an actor rehearses prior to a performance, the manager rehearses in his own mind what he plans to do and say. This process is called *covert learning*, because the individual is learning not by actually experiencing an event, but by experiencing it in the mind. The sequence of events that will likely happen is visualized and responses are practiced by the individual before he actually experiences the event; by learning prior to the event, and most people will most likely do a better job.

Mental rehearsal is so critical in many things that we do, and most of us probably already practice it to some degree. We practice a speech before we deliver it. We practice what we'll say to our spouse if we plan to raise a sensitive issue. We visualize ourself in a new car before we buy it. What we are suggesting is that managers should make a conscientious effort to practice imagery in various situations that they encounter.

GOAL PERFORMANCE

Let's look at the second situation and see how imagery might apply. This is the situation where a department is not meeting its quarterly goals. The first thing that must be determined is whether the variance of performance from goals is really significant. Then it must be determined whether the goals were realistic to begin with. Finally, the cause of the variance must be determined so a solution can be developed.

Once again imagery can be a useful tool. Let's consider the realism of goals; sometimes they can be stated in such a way that they are abstract and difficult to visualize. We don't understand what they mean. For example, President Kennedy could have announced in 1962 that he wanted the United States to have the best space program possible; but he did not. Instead, he said he wanted the United States to land a man on the moon and return him safely by the end of the decade. This is certainly much easier to visualize than having the best space program.

Our organization's goals may not be easily visualized. Too often we develop goals of good service, high employee morale, strong profits, or quality products without really knowing what these terms mean. Goals need to be specific and visualizable. We need to be able to actually envision what it means to accomplish the goal. We need to see the man on the moon.

Imagery can help us visualize the performance necessary to achieve our desired goal. Even if we have a clearly visualizable goal, we need to also be sure that the *path* to this goal is clearly visualizable. Let's take opening a new restaurant as an example; managers and subordinates need to be able to clearly see the sequence of steps actually involved, for example, can they actually see themselves going through the activities of opening the restaurant? Mental imagery practice in this situation involves people explicitly picturing themselves in scenes as if in a movie dealing with the subject. They see themselves working with subordinates and others to complete the furnishings. They see the new restaurant nicely landscaped and ready for customers. They see themselves training new employees, planning the opening night, placing advertisements, ordering the food inventory, holding practice dinners and doing all the various activities involved. People can rehearse this process in their minds to try to anticipate any blockages or problems.

If we have never been involved with a restaurant opening, we will have some difficulty visualizing the activities. We may talk with others, read manuals, or go through a training session until we become familiar with the process. At some point, we will begin to develop a clear set of images of the activities involved. To the extent that we can play these images in our mind, we will be prepared for a successful opening.

Problem-Solving

Let's look at the last situation. Here, you have just come into your office, and there is a note on your desk indicating your secretary has resigned. What do you do?

If you're like most people, your immediate reaction will be one of shock. You have *no* clear images, only confusion (or a jumble of confusing images). However, you'll ask others if they knew anything about her decision. Depending on what you find out, you may try to call her to see what is going on. Here is an opportunity to use mental imagery prior to calling by rehearsing the conversation you will likely have. Is it the one you want to have? If not, now can you guide the conversation along the lines you desire?

Forming a clear image of her on the phone while you are talking even to the point of visualizing her facial expressions and reactions, and imagining the tone of voice will help you to prepare for the phone call in this delicate situation. You can mentally rehearse your conversation and her possible answers so that you play out in your mind all possible scenarios. Then you can practice this conversation in order to be in the best position to guide it so that it will turn out as you desire.

Of course the actual actions you would take in the case would depend upon the circumstances. But for most of us, her leaving would create a problem that imagery could help us solve by allowing us to mentally rehearse how we will handle the situation.

These examples are but three common situations among many where the technique of mental imagery can be used to enhance managerial performance and efficacy. Imagery is a powerful technique that you are familiar with and use in other parts of your life; but actually using it in management in a systematic and conscientious way is probably new to you.

ONE CAUTION

Some people believe imagery to be a flaky, pseudo-scientific, or mystical technique. It is not. Even though it has not yet been fully applied to management, it is widely used and studied in other fields, which is discussed in the next chapter. The widespread use of imagery in so many arenas has served to legitimize it. There is no need for an apologetical for the use of the technique. Imagery works and it can be widely and intelligently used in management. To learn about imagery, you must have an open mind. You must be willing to experiment with a technique you probably practice every day but do not systematically or consciously use on the job. Imagery is not a magical technique, but it is one that can work for you if you're willing to become aware of your inner experiences and use them to make yourself more effective. In the next section, we see some of the potential applications imagery has in management; each of which is discussed in more depth in the chapters that follow.

Figure 1-3
The Management Process

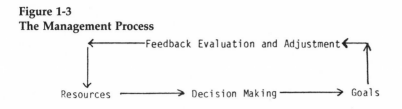

MANAGEMENT PERFORMANCE: PROCESS AND ROLES

Process Approach

There are two common ways of depicting the process of management. The first, and oldest way, is to show it as a process involving four basic components and five basic functions. The four basic components of the process are usually shown as follows in Figure 1–3. Here managers make decisions about the best way to obtain and use resources in order to achieve desired goals. The prudent manager evaluates and adjusts performance as necessary in order to achieve goals. Goals are the focus.

Using this model, an office manager makes decisions in using people, materials, equipment, and other resources in order to obtain desired goals of letter, memorandum, report, and filing output levels. A plant department head makes decisions on the use of people, equipment, raw materials, and other resources to achieve desired production output goals.

The five basic decision functions of managers are usually depicted as follows: (1) planning decisions; (2) organizing decisions; (3) staffing decisions; (4) leading decisions; and (5) controlling decisions. These five decision functions are viewed as being critical and universal for all levels of managers, from supervisor to CEO in all types of organizations—business, government, educational, charitable—of any size. This is usually called the universality of management. The basic process of management is the same, even though the context within which it is practiced is very different from management level to management level and from organization to organization.

Roles Approach

A second, more recent, way of depicting management is the roles approach, developed by Henry Mintzberg. He observed a sample of high-level managers for a period of time to determine what they actually did as managers. He concluded that all managers play three very important and distinct role sets as follows: (1) interpersonal roles; (2) informational roles; and (3) decisional roles.

Interpersonal roles involve dealing with other people. There are three key interpersonal roles: figurehead, leader, and liaison. The figurehead role occurs when the manager represents the organization or the unit to others. The manager serves as both the actual and ceremonial head. The leader role occurs when the manager guides the unit toward established goals. Finally, the manager plays the liaison role when he or she serves as an interface point between his or her unit and other units including that of his/her boss.

There are also three key informational roles: monitor, disseminator, and spokesperson. The manager monitors the communication within his or her unit as well as that in other units. He or she also disseminates information from above or information which is self-generated. Finally, he or she serves as a spokesperson for the unit when dealing with other units inside or outside of the organization.

The last set of roles played by the manager—decisional—involve four major subroles: entrepreneur, disturbance handler, resource allocator, and negotiator. The entrepreneur gets things started; he or she generates new ideas and takes risks. The disturbance handler tries to resolve conflicts among people in the unit. The resource allocator allocates scarce resources, such as money or help, among various people in the unit. And, finally, in the negotiator role the manager makes requests of people in the unit and bargains to try to get them carried out.

We can show how the functional and roles view of management relate as seen in Figure 1–4. Interpersonal roles relate to organizing, staffing, and leading. Each of these functions requires a manager to perform activity with transmitting, or using information. Managers play decisional roles when they deal with other people. Informational roles relate to planning, leading, and controlling. When managers are planning, organizing, and staffing, they make key decisions.

Our thesis is that by using imagery, managers can improve their performance of management functions while carrying out their multiple roles.

For many people, the process of management is rather abstract because it is difficult to visualize what is meant by "planning decisions," or "organizing decisions," or "decisional roles." This is more difficult than visualizing what we mean by the activities of other professions. We can see a lawyer arguing a case in court. We can see a surgeon operating. An auto mechanic working under a car hood presents a vivid image in our mind's eye. But what do we visualize when we think of a manager who is at work planning? Do we have an image in our mind? Most of us do not.

In this book we make it easier to visualize the job of management in the mind's eye. This will help to show more clearly the actions required in order to manage most efficiently and effectively. By clearly visualizing these actions, managers can practice them in their mind. They can see

Figure 1-4
Roles and Functions of Managers

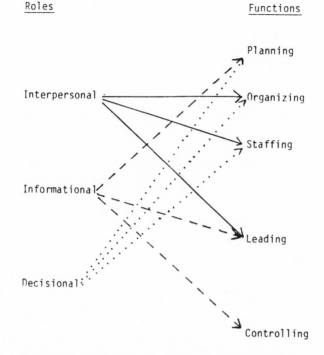

Source: Dan Wren and Dan Voich, *Management*, 3rd ed. (New York: Wiley, 1984), p. 7. Copyright © 1984 by John Wiley & Sons, Inc. Reprinted by permission of John Wiley & Sons, Inc.

the desirable action and rehearse in their mind's eye until they think they can perform them properly. Just as a golfer visualizes the proper swing and then practices the body movements in his mind's eye, managers, too, can visualize the planning process and other management processes and practice them, thus improving performance.

Each of the remaining chapters in the book is summarized in the remainder of this chapter. This gives you an idea as to how we plan to apply imagery to the roles and processes of management.

PREVIOUS APPLICATIONS OF IMAGERY

Imagery has been applied in numerous disciplines and fields including six fields that seem to pertain most to management. These are briefly discussed below and in more depth in Chapter 2.

1. *Sports Performance.* Guided imagery, especially mental rehearsal,

has been widely applied to improving the performance of athletes. Athletes are taught to visualize themselves properly performing a specific action such as sinking a free-throw or jumping over a high-jump bar—and to mentally rehearse the series of actions involved. By "seeing" the right moves and practicing them in their minds, they can actually improve their performance even if they do not actually physically practice the task.

Sports performance relates closely to management in that managers also perform. This occurs many times in management—giving a speech, holding an interview, calming an angry employee, leading a meeting, arbitrating a conflict, and so on. We can learn much from the findings in sports performance.

2. *Career Development*. Imagery is applied to help people explore and develop careers. Managers have a dual responsibility here. They must be concerned about helping subordinates with their career paths, and they are also concerned with developing their own personal career paths. The process of visualizing the career search process and the sequence of steps involved in a career path or ladder will help managers to do a better job in this area.

3. *Counseling and Mental Health*. In this field, imagery has been used to help people solve problems and overcome behavioral dysfunctions in order to improve their mental health. Imagery helps people more clearly to picture their problems, thereby improving their understanding of what actions are needed to overcome them. Imagery can also help them "see" what they need to do in order to carry out new behaviors. For example, telling a high-strung, high-stressed individual to "slow" down is not enough. Imagery can actually help the troubled person see the specific actions required to "slow" down.

4. *Education and Learning*. Imagery has had a major impact in helping us to understand how people learn, especially through the processes of modeling and covert learning, and vicarious experience. Many of us practice certain management actions today because we have observed a good managerial role model in the past and have adopted those behaviors we think were effective. Additionally, the use of pictures and other forms of visual imagery have long played an important role in the learning process and in depicting various management processes.

5. *Personal Effectiveness and Development*. Imagery can help you to build a better self-image. You can increase your self-efficacy—or the ability to get things done—by helping you to see yourself in a positive light. Much of Peale's work, for example, on positive thinking rests on this premise.

6. *Medicine and Health*. Finally, imagery has actually been used to treat specific diseases such as cancer, depression, and other ailments. Patients have experienced reduction in cancers by actually visualizing the white blood cells attacking the evasive cancer cells. Imagery has also been used

to help create and maintain healthful lifestyles and to help individuals better manage their stress.

HOW IMAGERY CAN HELP MANAGERS TO IMPROVE PERFORMANCE

In Chapter 3, we describe the performance orientation to management. You perform when you carry out your interpersonal, informational, and decisional roles. When you plan, organize, staff, lead, and control you are also performing. You perform much like an athlete or actor. That is, you go through a desired set of actions necessary to achieve proficiency. And, like athletes, there are ways of carrying out activities that lead to achieving productivity better than other ways; and there are scripts that are better to use than other scripts because they lead to desired productivity goals.

In Chapter 3 you'll see how imagery can be used in the management process to enhance performance. Leading, interviewing, communicating, setting goals, rewarding, disciplining, coaching, negotiating, monitoring, resolving conflict and other management activities are more productive if the right behavior and scripts are patterned and utilized.

HOW CAN IMAGERY BE USED IN A CORPORATE MANAGEMENT EDUCATION AND DEVELOPMENT PROGRAM?

Imagery can be institutionalized within a corporate training and development program. In Chapter 4, we'll emphasize how imagery can be implemented as a developmental technique throughout the organization. It is a very useful technique for developing organizational resources and can complement many of the training and development techniques already used within organizations.

Later, we present a specific model called "The Imaginal Staging Model," that shows a step-by-step procedure in implementing an imagery program. We will also see how this model ties into the Organization Process Model for actually using imagery for specific training and developmental endeavors.

Finally, we'll suggest how credibility problems in using imagery can be overcome. As with any technique new to management, there will be some initial resistance to its use. There are various techniques that can reduce this resistance in order to overcome implementation barriers to the creative application of imagery technologies in organizations.

HOW IMAGERY CAN IMPROVE STRATEGIC PLANNING

Chapter 5 shows how imagery can be used to improve strategic planning. Imagery can help managers visualize their present environment better. It can also help to forecast potential environments by helping you "see" these futuristic environments better in the mind's eye.

Imagery can help you to set clear goals that have an inspiring effect on action. Crystallized goals provide symbols—images—that can rally and inspire performance much like the American Flag inspires performance in time of battle. By better developing a clear set of goals in the mind, you are better able to communicate this vision to others.

Imagery can help you to visualize scenarios better. Scenario building is a critical step in strategic planning. The clearer the scenarios, the better the plans that can be developed to deal with them. These alternative future states provide the groundwork for goal-setting and action.

There are many paths to a desired set of goals. The performance-oriented manager helps to articulate the best paths to subordinates so that they can clearly envision and comprehend, thus reducing misunderstandings on action required. Additionally, it helps them to visualize the specific steps that reduce wasted effort better and achieve the highest levels of performance.

Any strategic plan will encounter barriers to its implementation. Guided imagery helps managers better visualize such barriers or hurdles before roadblocks are actually encountered so that alternative plans and solutions can be prepared. The better anticipated a barrier, the easier it is to prepare for it. Clear images of potential barriers helps us to anticipate and prepare for contingencies that may evolve.

Finally, imagery helps to build a strategic plan that is futuristic in nature. A good strategic plan is built for the future rather than the present or past. It's success relies principally on this future orientation. This anticipatory management with a proactive approach can be enhanced by building clear images of the future and using those images as guides to choice and action.

HOW IMAGERY CAN IMPROVE PRODUCTIVITY IN LEADERSHIP AND PERSONAL RELATIONSHIPS

Good leaders have visions of the future that inspire performance. They are able to communicate their visions effectively to others while relating to others on an interpersonal level to ensure the achievement of their visions.

In Chapter 6, we explain how imagery can be used to improve linkages between bosses, subordinates, peer managers, and others with whom they must work. Clearly visualized linkage patterns are better than those that are fuzzy.

Imagery can also improve leadership by giving a clear picture of the actions and scripts effective leaders use to achieve desired performance. People are better leaders when they can actually imagine the desired role model of effective leadership they wish to practice.

All managers must achieve a certain degree of group cohesiveness if they expect teamwork and high group morale. High performance managers can use imagery techniques to build group cohesiveness by managing symbols and other imaginal tools to rally and coordinate group efforts.

Every group will experience conflict from time to time. Imagery techniques can help to prevent and reduce this conflict. These techniques can also help to channel conflict toward productive ends.

Finally, imagery can be used to reduce job stress among employees. Every job has its stress points and effective managers can help subordinates get through their stress points with a minimum of disruption. Relaxation techniques, rechanneling effort, and better perception of causes of employee stress all are enhanced through imagery.

HOW IMAGERY CAN IMPROVE PRODUCTIVITY IN COMMUNICATIONS AND INFORMATION MANAGEMENT

The communication process is rich with imagery. Words and other forms of communication are symbols that evoke images that represent relationships and promote understanding. Imagery techniques can help create and evoke the proper symbols to achieve maximum understanding and desired performance.

In Chapter 7 we identify how imagery helps you to visualize communication episodes better. We also indicate how imagery can help you take a better systems perspective in managing communication and information patterns. By better visualizing the entire system of communications, you are better able to manage it so as to achieve desired effects.

You must also monitor the performance of others. When you communicate, you send symbols or cues. When you monitor, you receive and observe symbols and cues. Imagery can help you show others how to send proper symbols better and how you can better monitor and interpret these symbols.

Finally, all managers are part of a total system of information management in the organization. You generate and receive information that makes the organization operate. By using imagery you can better see your role in the total information management process in the organization.

HOW IMAGERY CAN IMPROVE PRODUCTIVITY IN PROBLEM-SOLVING AND DECISION MAKING

In Chapter 8, we specify how imagery can be used to solve problems and make decisions. Envisioning a problem is a critical step in identifying a problem. Visualizing the dynamics and components of potential problems helps to prevent them.

Imagery can have a major impact on improving creativity through such techniques as brainstorming and other free-forms of thinking. Imagery can help to take off blinders and expand horizons to come up with new and creative solutions.

Imagery can also help better achieve employee participation and divergent thinking. Employees are a rich source of ideas for solving problems. By using imagery, this participation and divergent thinking can be channeled and tied to group-based creative solutions to problems.

Every manager must cope with uncertainty and an unstable environment when solving problems and making decisions. Imagery can assist in recognizing and reducing uncertainty and instability. In Chapter 8, we see how the techniques of framing and scoping uncertain environments can be used to make better decisions.

When decisions are made and problems solved, negotiation is often required to get the solution accepted and implemented. Imagery has a major part to play in the negotiating process in order to establish and bargain on positions, use power tactics, and reach mutually beneficial agreements often based on symbol and image.

Finally, the real test of any decision is whether it is implemented. By using imagery, managers can better achieve desired implementation whether they are dealing with short- or long-term effects of a decision.

HOW IMAGINAL TECHNOLOGIES CAN IMPROVE PERSONAL EFFECTIVENESS

Managers with great ideas are less effective than those with mediocre ideas if they do not have a style of management that enables them to get things done. In Chapter 9, we show how imagery can be used to enhance the personal effectiveness of your employees.

Imagery can help to build a sense of self-confidence—a "can do" attitude. Peale recognized this long ago in his best-seller *The Power of Positive Thinking*. Self-efficacy, the belief that you are indeed effective, helps you to be more effective. Imaginal techniques can build self-efficacy by helping you alter negative attitudes and establish positive behaviors.

Imagery can also help you to plan you career better. If you can clearly visualize a career path or ladder, you will be better able to achieve it.

You will have a clear sequence of events you wish to accomplish in order to reach our desired career goals.

Imagery can also help you to reduce the personal job stress you experience. As discussed later in Chapter 6, imagery can be used to reduce job stress between managers and subordinates. In Chapter 9, we show how imagery can be used to reduce personal job stress. By better seeing the causes of stress, you can better build clear routes to reduce anxiety and stress, thereby improving your effectiveness.

Today, we must all deal with change; it's a fact of life. Imagery can help you to deal better with change. Change is an abstract and ambiguous concept. Imagery helps to make it a concrete, clear panorama, which you can envision, and therefore understand and manage.

Finally, a very important key to personal effectiveness is time management. Imagery can help you to manage time better. If you can see how you now use your time compared to how you want to use it, you will be better able to manage it. Specific techniques needed to control time instead of letting others control it can be envisioned.

IMAGERY, PERFORMANCE, AND PRODUCTIVITY: A CREATIVE SYNTHESIS

Lastly, in Chapter 10, we show how the proper use of imagery can help to expand organizational brain power to achieve holistic management. By fully utilizing the untapped mind-power in most of today's organizations, productivity can be greatly improved. Enhancing creativity and problem-solving helps an organization to achieve a productivity and performance orientation. Rather than focusing on inputs and efforts, the organization focuses on outputs and results. Imagery helps the organization to achieve this high-output, results-oriented management style.

There's much in this book that is likely to be foreign to the thinking of many people in business and other organizations. However, by approaching this book with an open mind, you will find many innovative ideas, which can be tried to enhance performance. Don't be afraid to experiment with these ideas. You probably will make some mistakes, but learn from your failures and try again. You will eventually see some important results and come to realize how important your imagery is to your life and performance. You'll also see how you can be a catalyst to implement imagery techniques in your organization.

Throughout the book, we provide many specific exercises and examples affording you an opportunity to practice the techniques before you try them on the job or encourage others to try them. Pay particular attention to these and go over them several times. Also, note the many scripts presented that can be transferred directly to your work situation now or in the future.

In the next chapter, we see how imagery has been applied in other fields. We review this application for two reasons. First, we want to establish clearly the legitimacy of the technique; and, secondly, we want to point out the success imagery has had in areas closely related to management. By recognizing these previous applications, you can better understand the following chapters where imagery is applied to management.

2

PREVIOUS APPLICATIONS OF IMAGERY

Imagery, visualization, guided fantasy, and related techniques have been applied widely in many sports, education, and developmental settings. When a person imagines performing a specific behavior or encountering a specific scenario, a mental script is created that allows practice or performance of the desired sequence of activities.

In essence, imagery techniques allow rehearsal of a chosen path in advance of actual action. This helps you to reduce errors and increases the accuracy of performance under conditions of low risk and minimal cost. Imagery practice and rehearsal can save time, can promote self-confidence, and can lead directly to overall improved performance in work and lifestyle.

This chapter addresses some of the many applications of imagery techniques as well as areas in which this powerful tool can be applied in organizations.

Think back to the time you first learned to play golf or tennis. Do you remember how difficult it was to get the "feel" of the club or racket in your hand? Do you remember how difficult it was until you could actually see yourself going through the proper sequence of motions? Seeing ourselves doing the right thing in our mind's eye is critical for proficiency in sports. It is also critical for our proficiency in management.

Many actions in management are skill-specific just as in sports. We make talks, calm angry employees, or lead a meeting. We have much we can learn from how imagery has been applied to sports; but we can also learn from imagery applications to career planning, counseling and mental health, education and learning, personal effectiveness and development, and medicine and health. In this chapter we will see how imagery applications in these areas help us to understand how imagery can be applied to management.

HUMAN RESOURCE PROFESSIONALS AND COACHING

Most human resource professionals view their role in an organization as facilitative—they help to get things done. Since most human resource functions are supportive, human resource professionals have staff or advisory authority over line management. They do not have direct authority over line managers, rather they exist to help line managers in such areas as hiring, training, rewarding, counseling, and discipline.

In many ways the human resource professional acts as a coach of a sports team, especially those in training and development roles. Coaches do not carry out the actions of the team; rather they guide, instruct, and motivate others on how to perform. They encourage appropriate behavior and discourage inappropriate. They are catalysts that try to bring out the best in each of their players. They are facilitators of superior achievement.

Of course some coaches do this in an autocratic manner. But this breed is dying out. Today's coach tries to create a supportive atmosphere for the players and works hard at encouraging and building teamwork.

The modern human resource professional plays a similar role. Working with line managers, human resource professionals try to improve performance of both the managers and the entire organization. They do this by serving as instructors, helping line managers to instruct their subordinates, arranging for outside people to come in to the organization, and by sending people to workshops, seminars, and universities. They are just as concerned with the development of the organizational team as is a coach. The techniques of visualization and imagery are conducive for use in the facilitative role played by human resource professionals. As we see in the next section, one of the most successful applications of imagery has been in sports performance. Understanding how imagery has been used in sports and other areas, will provide guidance as to how it can be used in organizations.

SPORTS PERFORMANCE

In sports and recreational performance, imagery techniques have been used with many skill-specific activities. Jack Nicklaus has long asserted the power of visualization to rehearse golf shots prior to actually making them. Chris Evert Lloyd rehearses, imaginally, her entire tennis strategy before ever encountering her opponent. Olympic skiers, weightlifters, and gymnasts imaginally practice their routines before entering the competition arena and up until the moment of performance. Repeatedly, in popular sports literature, one notes how athletes use imagery to both stylize and enhance their performance.

Athletes realize how important it is to perfect their image of a performance so they can carry out the necessary movements to achieve both optimal performance and the competitive edge. It is likely that Mary Lou Retton had a perfect imagery sequence of her vaulting performance prior to hitting a perfect 10. In fact, Retton probably maintained a powerful image of herself standing on the victor's platform receiving both her gold medal and the accolades of the award. Dwight Stones, U.S. Olympic high jumper, uses imagery as he prepares for his jumps. Stones clearly sees and feels himself moving down the runway, counting the steps, launching himself above the bar, and falling into the pit.

Such champion athletes realize that mental performance of an athletic act precedes and greatly influences the eventual act. This applies to management performance as well.

It is important to emphasize that in athletics, imagery and visualization rehearsal is very skill-specific. Competitive athletes know the specific motor skills they must accomplish to produce coordinated action and optimal performance. In fact, imagery techniques have been most effectively used in part because the behaviors are well defined and easily replicable "in the mind's eye." Further, athletes who use imagery techniques have the needed abilities to perform at high levels, while also being committed to a training routine that reinforces actual and imaginal practice of their skills. They imagine not only the final goal they seek (a world record, a gold medal, or fame and endorsements), but also the process they will use as they move toward their goal. In other words, they envision both the process and the product of their performance efforts.

These points are important in applying imagery techniques to the various performance areas of management. Remember:

1. Visualize both the sequence of behaviors (process) and the specific acts performed (products) in practicing new behavior toward optimal performance. The clearer the image developed and maintained, the more efforts can be focused on achieving goals and perfecting actions.

2. Skills and abilities to carry out optimal performance are necessary. Imagery cannot be used to imagine accomplishing something that is either unrealistic or beyond one's capability. That's not imagery, its self-delusion. In other words, one can't dream one's self to success.

3. A high state of positive mental readiness is necessary through regular practice of imaginal scenarios and optimal performance. Practice time and effort is necessary because imagery skill is like any other skill—it only develops as it

is experienced, refined, and applied to important aspects of life. Imagery techniques are most effective when they become a part of one's regular mental repertoire.

Let's look at research on the use of imagery techniques in sports performance.

Research in Sports Performance

There are many anecdotal aspects of the effectiveness of imagery as a way to manage sports or motor skills performance. Some of these have already been noted. In distance running, we are all familiar with the image of "the wall"—that point in the marathon where bodily reserves of energy are exhausted and the runner faces collapse. What image could be more vivid than this appropriate metaphor? In this sense, a physical experience is transformed into an image that graphically bespeaks the experience.

During the 1984 Winter Olympics, the American luge team described how they imaginally negotiated the twists and turns of the course before embarking on a run. They prepared for each run through a mental transit of the course they were to challenge.

In archery, the use of imagination has played a crucial role in "seeing" the arrow leave the bow, enter its trajectory, and embed itself into the target. In fact, The Zen of Archery stresses the use of inner sight to improve the overall shield of the archer. Emphasis is on the archer becoming "one" with the act of archery through relaxation and imagery. As action comes to complement ideation, the archer becomes evermore adept.

The Inner Game of Tennis also asserts the need to rehearse and perform all shots mentally prior to going out actually on the court. The "inner game" precedes the outer game; in this sense, ideation precedes and prepares one for action.

Scientific research in psychology and education has investigated the role of imagery in skill acquisition and performance areas. Studies on mental practice of basketball foul shooting indicate that mental practice of performance exceeds no-practice control group's performance and significantly approaches the performance of groups who actually shoot free-throws. In these studies, the mental-practice-only group visualizes their performance the same number of times and for the same length of time as does the actual practice group. Similar results have been attained for bean bag tossing, dart throwing, and ring tossing. In numerous studies, the results are always the same—mental practice of the activity improves actual performance of the activity. Once again, ideation precedes effective action.

Given this brief overview of research on imagery and sports performance, it's important to understand how this data is translatable to applications in management. The next section of this chapter presents examples of this transfer.

APPLICATIONS IN MANAGEMENT

In general, managers must have technical, conceptual, and interpersonal skills, which they apply to the often turbulent job they face. How can we imagine or envision these skill areas?

Obviously, it is difficult to do so. However, if we reduce these global skill areas down to specific skills, we have specific behaviors that are amenable to imaginal practice. Once again, the more specific and defined the performance activity, the more imagery can be used to enhance performance. Let's look at a couple of examples:

Example 1: Making a formal presentation at a large meeting.

Depending upon previous experiences, successes, and setbacks with public speaking, a person will develop an anticipatory mental set about this experience. This mental set will include images of past experiences, feelings about good and bad performances, and some goals or desires related to the upcoming event. This mental set also serves as the foundation upon which a person would build an imaginal scenario of successful and effective performance.

In creating an imagery scenario for the speech, the individual will consider some of the following factors as the scenario is constructed:

—the self-image to be transmitted to the audience
—the nature, size, and general orientation of the audience
—the type of auditorium room or facility for the speech
—the key points that are to be transmitted to the group
—the jokes and attention-getters to be used to maintain the interest of the audience
—the supporting visual or auditory materials needed to reinforce key points
—the desired response to be elicited from the group.

With each of these factors, an image of what is expected or what is to occur during the presentation is created. Then these images are combined to establish an optimal scenario for the presentation. Next, this scenario should be rehearsed a number of times until the individual feels that what is imagined will actually occur when the presentation is made. Having established a vivid mental performance set for the presentation allows one to carry out the event as it was imaginally planned. From the feedback received, during the presentation mental adjustments can be made to the mental performance set so that the scenario can be fine-tuned as the presentation occurs.

Example 2: Managing a conflict situation.

Most managers deal periodically with the disgruntled or angry employee. For most of us, this activity is not a pleasant experience. In fact, dealing with the conflict created by an angry employee is often stressful for both parties. To apply an imagery strategy to this troubling event requires a review of how managers and employees handle conflict in your organization. In doing so, review managers' past interactions with employees, feelings about employees, tolerance of stressful situations, and willingness to be either proactive or reactive in conflict-laden and emotionally intense experiences. While it may be difficult to pinpoint one predominant conflict management style, it is useful to type or categorize the various styles used by different managers.

This audit is the basis of a new, productive imagined strategy for coping with not only the employee's concern, but also with the manager's anticipated reactions. Focusing on both the employee and the manager's patterns of reactions is necessary to effectively manage this and analogous future situations. Once you can describe past mental sets for dealing with conflict you can begin to create developmental approaches for helping managers deal with conflict by focusing on:

—the appropriate ways to handle employee's anger

—the best way to reduce the emotional level of the confrontations

—the optimal way to behave so that attention can be focused on the issues at hand and not on the emotions

—the ways to exhibit understanding of the situation to the employee

—the follow-up activity necessary by managers after the conflict event

—the eventual short-term and long-term consequences to be achieved by managers and employees in these situations

—the ways that this experience can be positively generalized to future events.

With each of these specific performance sets, specify definitive behaviors managers can mentally rehearse. For instance, you might ask managers to imagine themselves as remaining calm during the event by maintaining a relaxed body posture, by breathing deeply, by monitoring body tension, and by attentively, but selectively, listening for the "message" amid the madness.

This imaginal set is then combined with other behaviorally anchored imaginal sets so that an imaginal scenario script evolves. The more complete and comprehensive this script, the more likely managers will subsequently apply it to related encounters. As you mentally rehearse remaining "calm and in command" during emotional encounters, the managers will become able to implement the ideal script. As noted with sports performance, ideation precedes action. The same is true in difficult managerial performance situations.

These two examples indicate how you might help managers address concerns in their job environment through the use of explicit imaginal sets and scenarios. Remember the four important points:

1. Teach managers to review past experiences to establish their typical behavioral responses to specific events;

2. Ask them to imaginally identify behaviors or options that allow them to become more effective, proficient, or adaptive in their response repertoire;

3. Build imaginal sets for each of these new behaviors wherein they "see" themselves acting in a more effective manner; and

4. Create imaginal scenarios representing the full behavior script managers should apply in any given context. Then, help them to practice mentally these scenarios and transfer them to real-life activities.

Imagery and imaginal techniques can help fine-tune personal and managerial skills; however, such techniques cannot substitute for skills managers don't possess. While these processes and tools can help to enlarge and enrich a person's skill inventory, such techniques do not displace continuing personal development and education; rather, imagery techniques can be used as a personal development technique if continually practiced. Therefore, after a training session on using imagery to manage conflict, the participants need to be encouraged to practice mentally the imagery technique learned.

Obviously, imagery-based techniques are powerful personal and managerial enhancement tools. The evidence in sports performance shows the effectiveness of imagery as a viable practice format. In the following section, consideration will be given to ways that imagery applies to personal and employee career development.

PERSONAL CAREER DEVELOPMENT

During the past ten years, career development efforts have emerged as an important topic in organizations. The drive to find a "match" between the abilities and characteristics of the individual employee and the skill requirements of the organization has spawned this important field.

In your own career, you must monitor and manage your own development. A personal career development plan allows you to accomplish this goal. Imaginal techniques can be applied to your efforts in a variety of ways.

There are three important components of a personal career development plan: (1) self-assessment; (2) creating career aspirations; and (3) building realistic career scenarios. We will briefly review the self-assessment stages of this process and suggest how imagery is a tool you can use for self-exploration. Later, we will look at imagery applications for career development in more depth and how it can be used throughout your organization as a development tool.

During the self-assessment stage, you conduct a personal audit to determine: (1) your primary work values; (2) the strengths you possess; (3) the deficiencies you exhibit; (4) your primary interests; and (5) your short-term and long-term career goals. By reviewing and delineating each of these areas, you create an image profile of yourself and what you want from your career. This image profile represents your career self-concept and is the basis for determining what your evolving career actions are to be.

It may be that your image profile fits nicely with the career patterns of your current organization. In this case, adequate opportunities for personal growth and career advancement are available to you in-house. Thus, your career aspirations would relate to climbing the organizational ladder as far as possible.

However, you may instead find that you don't fit your present organization and you may have to look elsewhere for challenge and development. Imagery exploration of values, skills, and interests helps you to define the "match" between you and your organization and then to create an aggressive career action plan for yourself within or beyond your present job. Various imagery techniques, especially guided imagery/fantasy, have been used in career development programs to help adults clarify their interests and values, while affording insights into the ideal types of career experiences they desire. In this context, imaginal techniques help the individual to access creative resources and hidden aspiration/fantasies that are critical for optimal career development. Research indicates that career fantasies are often actually closely related to what people really want in a career. By articulating these fantasies in your inner experience, you begin to develop an understanding of career areas that may offer you the opportunity to perform at your highest potential. Further research has shown that effective, fast-track managers and entrepreneurs have the key ability to envision their own career movement and career goals.

Developing an image profile of yourself and an imaginal vision of your career evolution will improve your career-enhancement endeavors. Tapping your inner resources is crucial to utilizing other resources in pursuit of career challenges and satisfaction.

EMPLOYEE CAREER DEVELOPMENT

One of your primary tasks as a human resource professional is to develop your employees so they acquire new skills and attributes in their work roles. Generally, effective organizations have effective employees working for them because they actually help their employees to become effective.

As noted in the previous section, imagery techniques are used for career exploration efforts and in the development of action plans to help individuals reach their optimum career placement. You can use these techniques to help employees define their own career image profile and career goals. One application is to guide employees through an imaginal script that prompts them to visualize the different types of jobs available in your firm and to "feel" what it's like to hold the various positions. This technique helps employees to imaginally project themselves into new positions to determine and better understand the options that may be available to them.

Additionally, imagery techniques can help plateaued workers re-envision their roles in the organization so they discover new challenges and greater opportunities to contribute—even if the likelihood for upward advancement is limited. Likewise, imagery projection activities afford aggressive, "fast-track" employees the chance to enhance their own progress through a variety of jobs and skill areas in the organization. By "seeing" themselves in a progressive sequence of positions, those valued employees can then acquire additional training and development that will prepare them for the various positions they will hold.

Finally, guided imagery techniques can be used as an assessment center experience during the realistic job preview phase of recruitment and selection. You might develop scripts that outline the characteristic happenings on both typical and atypical days in your firm's operations. By imaginally placing the prospective employees in these scenarios, you transmit the psychological climate, the activity pulse, and the interaction patterns within your organization to them. This exercise may help applicants screen themselves from selection because of obvious mismatches between their personal styles and your organizational style and culture.

An example of specific imagery applications in career development follows; this one focuses on helping employees close to retirement.

Example 1: Helping the preretirement employee.

When you deal with individuals preparing to retire, you work with folks who have long work histories and uncertain, transitional phases to face in the immediate future. Imagery exercises and practice sessions can be used as supplementary tools to help these individuals cope with their transitions. Areas of application include:

1. Stress management and relaxation training to moderate the stressful aspects of transitioning. Through regular practice, employees can reduce their stress and increase their coping ability.

2. Work and life review imagery exercises to help individuals re-experience their important moments and to identify any "unfinished business" they may wish to complete before retirement.

3. Skill exploration and time planning exercises to help individuals inventory the resources they take into retirement and to use these resources for creative time management strategies and the development of new hobbies.

This concludes our current discussion of career development applications. We will return to imagery and career development in Chapter 9. The next section addresses applications of imagery technologies in counseling and mental health situations.

COUNSELING, MENTAL HEALTH, AND STRESS

Imagery techniques and applications have had their widest and most varied usage in counseling and mental health settings. A variety of imaginal techniques are used successfully to treat depression, phobias, stress, alcohol abuse, and other conditions that are common problems in today's hectic world.

Employee mental health is of increasing concern to organizations and employers. Employees who are troubled by excessive stress or other debilitating mental problems are unable to perform at an adequate level of effectiveness. The ultimate costs of such distress are huge in terms of productivity and loss of performance.

Imagery techniques allow you to help employees cope more efficiently with the various stresses that impact upon them in their work life and in other areas. While imagery can be used to teach stress management and relaxation programs, it is best that more serious mental health problems be referred to competent counselors.

In many of the mental health applications, clients are asked to envision themselves performing in more effective and adaptive ways. Research evidence clearly indicates that imaging performing an activity increases both the likelihood of performing it, and the likelihood that it will be performed effectively.

For instance, as people imagine themselves coping effectively with stress in a variety of settings, they reduce the chances that these stressful situations will arouse them as much as they once did. As imagined coping strategies are applied to new experiences, skill is reinforced and people become less open to aggravation during situational stress episodes. Further, imaginal techniques can be used to reduce tension during conflict situations, as we saw earlier. As you can see from Figure 2–1,

Figure 2-1
The Yerkes-Dodson Curve

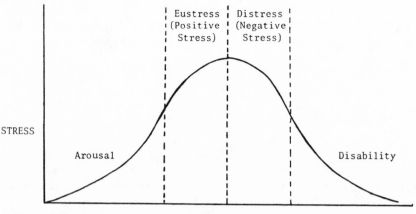

Source: R. M. Yerkes and J. D. Dodson "The Relation of Strength of Stimulus to Rapidity of Habit Formation," *Journal of Comparative Neurological Psychology* 18 (1908): 759–782.

as stress increases, performance also climbs—to a point. At this point of diminishing returns, performance declines rapidly until exhaustion sets in. You will be given practice examples on stress management you can use later in this book in Chapter 8.

Let's now turn to ways in which imaginal techniques apply to personal effectiveness and self-management.

PERSONAL EFFECTIVENESS AND SELF-MANAGEMENT

The effective individual is one who manages the challenges he/she encounters. In our view, this occurs as a result of sound personal planning and the ability to organize one's self. Additionally, the effective individual holds him/herself responsible for both the successes and setbacks that he/she experiences. In psychology, this self-responsible perspective is known as internal locus of control.

The internally locused individual doesn't blame others, situations, or fate for his/her success or failure. Rather, he/she realizes that 90 percent of all events result from his/her action or inaction. When one takes such a perspective, one begins to develop a sense of self-efficacy. That is, you believe you can get the job done.

In many research settings, internal locus of control has been related to a positive self-concept, better problem-solving, good personal mental health, sound physical health, and enhanced job satisfaction. Through the use of imagery techniques, the self-image can be modified so that

Figure 2-2
The Self Triangle

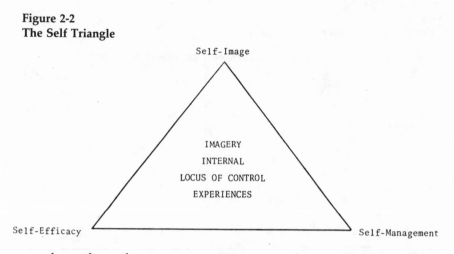

people see themselves as more positive, more adept, and more in control of their personal affairs. The following diagram illustrates the relationships between self-image, self-management, and self-efficacy.

1. Self-image: is that internal view or vision one holds of ones self. It is the cumulation of all experiences capsulized into a mental image of who you are, what you look like, what your strengths and weaknesses are, what you say to yourself (self-talk), and how effectively you perform your various responsibilities. Your self-image also includes emotions related to how you feel about yourself.

The self-image is the basis of efforts for self-management and self-efficacy. If the self-image is tainted or negative, this internal state of disequilibrium is projected onto all affairs and interactions. A negative self-image undermines efforts to become more effective in both personal life and work. The reverse is also true. As self-image becomes more positive, it makes for a more effective and self-responsible individual.

2. Self-management: the second characteristic of the Self Triangle relates motivation, abilities, and efforts to efficiently manage time, relationships, health, goals, and stress. In short, self-management expresses overall intention and action to gain and maintain organized control of the roles and responsibilities in life. It is enhanced and strengthened by a positive self-image and a feeling of self-efficacy.

3. Self-efficacy: is the expectancies of positive performance and outcome that are carried in the mind. When one has a sense or feeling of self-efficacy, one expects to do well and experience accomplishments in most, if not all, of the primary life areas. Self-efficacy expectancies influence style of work, motivation to achieve, self-confidence, and the competency image that is projected to others. Low self-efficacy can be equated with passivity, timidness, and withdrawal from challenge. High self-efficacy correlates well with dynamism, assertiveness, creativity,

and willingness to take risks. Self-efficacy influences and is influenced by self-image and self-management performance.

Note that these key factors impact upon the Self Triangle:

1. the ability to recognize, appreciate, and manipulate imagery and inner experiences, including self-talk;

2. ability to acquire and maintain an internal locus of control;

3. willingness to encounter new experiences, take risks, and to discover new talents.

Later in this book, we'll describe an Imaginal Inventory that can be used to investigate the status of self-image, self-management style, and feelings of self-efficacy.

The next section of this chapter briefly reviews some of the applications of imagery in the medical field.

MEDICINE AND HEALTH

As noted, imagery techniques are often used in conjunction with other stress reduction activities. As medicine has found that many chronic illnesses are caused by mental states or psychosomatic agents, the connective interaction of mind and body has become more appreciated. What occurs in mental experiences, including ongoing imagery, influences the wellness of the body. Likewise, the health and equilibrium of the body influence the clarity, consistency, and balance of mental experiences. One cannot forsake either arena without jeopardizing one's overall health.

In medicine, imagery has been used to combat cancer by having patients envision their immune systems as armies fighting against the invasive enemy—unrestricted cell growth. Results from a series of studies indicate that regular imagery practice of this type enhances one's ability to resist and repress the cancerous condition. Elsewhere, imagery has been used in conjunction with biofeedback to reduce chronic pain, to manage various phobic conditions, to curb chronic ear-ringing, and to increase circulation to hands and feet with diabetic individuals.

Since wellness (mental and physical health) impacts directly on energy level, attitude set, and performance, regular imagery practice can bring about a personal state of balance that contributes to effectiveness, self-image, and sense of well-being.

Lastly, we shall look into the applications of imagery in education and learning environments.

EDUCATION AND LEARNING

Imagery techniques are readily applied in learning contexts with both adults and children.

Vicarious learning or learning by observing involves observing a model and then replicating the model's prescribed behavior in one's mind. Such a technique forms the basis for much of our early and ongoing learning. We watch what others do, see the consequences of their behavior, and then integrate the new behavior set into our own action repertoire.

Covert or imaginal processes facilitate this learning and are even used as the focus of attention when a model is unavailable. In this case, people imagine themselves carrying out a behavior set and experiencing the consequences of the behavior. An example can be of a job interview. To covertly rehearse this event, one would imagine one's self well-dressed and confident, exuding an image of competence and confidence, and being relaxed as one provides all the appropriate answers to the interviewer's questions. As you'll note, this is the same technique that would apply in mental practice of a sports skill. Obviously, covert rehearsal can be used to seek to develop new skills as well.

Imagery is also being used to enhance memory and recall of information. One such technique involves pairing an information set with a mental image associated with the set. For instance, if you've been told to recall your best friend's face, you automatically associate his/her name with an image of his/her face. This can be applied to many learning events.

Research indicates that imagery is a key process as we encode and recall new information and knowledge. Often, we can't integrate or remember total bodies of knowledge; instead, we imaginally create symbols that represent the body of knowledge we integrate. This symbolic processing function of imagery complements and enriches our verbal/semantic processing functions based on language. For instance, imagine the layout of your office—you should experience both a descriptive, language-based inventory of the furniture, and a spatial-schematic "picture" of the office arrangement. This dual processing ability allows for flexible learning and recall of complex information.

It is apparent that imagery processes, including rehearsal, symbolic coding, and covert learning can have wide use for personal skill development and or organizational training and development. When you teach new skills by activating both the verbal and imaginal abilities, you enhance the rapidity and effectiveness of educational or performance programs. Classroom training, on-the-job training, or skill-specific development all should take this holistic approach.

Information as to how the right and left hemispheres of the brain affect learning and creativity specifies that mental imagery is a resource we can no longer ignore in learning endeavors within organizations.

SUMMARY

This chapter has specified some of the relevant areas where you can use imagery to improve your own performance or that of your employees. Many of these areas will be revisited in later chapters as we provide specific techniques and activities that you can learn and use. A crucial thing to recall is that imagery is not a panacea for all problems. It is, however, a very powerful resource that we frequently overlook or discount in our search for personal and managerial excellence.

The wise individual and the effective manager use all the techniques available to improve their knowledge and skills. We challenge you to resist the temptation to judge the value of your imaginal resource before you practice it on the job. Afterall, you have nothing to lose and much to gain. Try the following exercise.

Skill Practice Exercise

Find a relaxing quiet place to sit back and stretch out. Then run this scenario through your mind.

Imagine yourself reading this book with interest and enthusiasm. See yourself realizing that you've always had a hunch that your imagery was an important personal resource. See yourself taking notes as you read—taking notes as to where and how you can apply imagery in your life and in your work. Imagine yourself having an open mind as you encounter new ideas in this book and as you develop your own creative ideas about imagery. Imagine yourself talking with others about these ideas and helping them understand these techniques. Imagine yourself talking to your fellow managers about using these techniques at work. Imagine yourself benefiting from opening yourself to your imaginal experiences and to their use in your life. Imagine your self-image improving as you become more effective. Feel your sense of self-efficacy grow as you feel the power of your abilities and of your positive self-image. Imagine yourself having the confidence to risk the task of creative learning. Relax now and think of the positive consequences you'll experience as a more productive individual.

Now try to jot down some answers to these questions:

1. how has imagery affected you today;
2. where have you intentionally used imagery in your life;
3. how creative do you consider yourself; specify the creative acts you've completed in the past week;

4. what is your attitude toward what you have read in this book to this point; try to establish why you feel the way you do.

5. where can you apply an imagery technique or activity in your work tomorrow?

Let's now move to a discussion on how imagery can help with goal-setting and strategic planning, a key performance area for managers.

3

HOW IMAGERY CAN HELP MANAGERS TO IMPROVE PERFORMANCE

Performance . . . that is *the* key word in management. All managers in your organization are ultimately judged on this factor. It means getting the right things done in the right ways. This means doing what is supposed to be done and doing it in the most efficient (least cost) way. Proper use of imagery can help managers improve performance.

A PERFORMANCE ORIENTATION

Unfortunately, too many managers do not have a strong performance orientation: they busy themselves with the mundane, routine aspects of their job; they are indecisive; they wait for others to make decisions and take action; they, in the words of Peters and Waterman, lack a "bias for action."

They seldom anticipate possible problems in hope of avoiding them. Instead, they manage by reaction, and it is a slow reaction at that. They can be paralyzed by a problem. In fact, they often suffer from "analysis paralysis." They do not move quickly from accurately pinpointing a problem to designing and implementing a realistic course of action that works.

Imagery can help managers move off of dead center so that they can have a performance orientation. Clearly visualizing success helps to achieve it. Through vivid imagery and visualization, the way to top performance can be clearly depicted.

Recent developments in imagery indicate that the clearer a person can visualize the process involved in reaching a desired level of performance, the greater the chances the performance level will occur. For example, if you want to sell your boss on a new idea, the clearer you can actually visualize in your mind the process involved in presenting the idea, including the actual words involved in the conversation, the greater the chances are that you will be successful in getting your idea accepted. By practicing the event in considerable detail through vivid mental imagery, you can increase the likelihood that your boss will accept the idea.

Differs from Positive Thinking

We have been admonished for years by Peale and others to think positively about something we want to accomplish. We have also been told to plan an event carefully before we undertake it and to have confidence that we can successfully complete it. But imagery goes beyond these admonishments. It involves anticipating conversations, non-verbal behavior, feelings, and possible problems, and rehearsing them *prior* to the behavior. Thus, imagery involves these steps with respect to high performance:

1. vivid mental pictures and scenarios of the successful attributes of the situation;
2. rehearsal of the scenario including conversation and the desired behavior of each person involved;
3. an attempt to actually feel the emotions that will be involved;
4. anticipation of possible problems that may come up;
5. rehearsal of ways to prevent and respond to problems as they come up.

For example, suppose you plan to have a performance appraisal session with a subordinate who is performing at a marginal level. Using vivid imagery and scenario rehearsal you would do the following.

1. Prepare for the interview by reviewing the subordinate's record. (This should be done even if you do not use the imagery technique.)
2. Imagine the setting for the meeting you plan to have, including who will be sitting where and the room where it will be held.
3. Imagine the conversation you want to have, including the specific things you want to say and the specific responses each of your comments will likely elicit from the subordinate, including emotional as well as verbal responses.
4. Imagine the problems that may come up in the conversation and how you plan to deal with each including the *specific* words you will use or things you will do. For example, what will you say and do if the subordinate becomes angry and raises his voice? Or, what will you say if he says he is already working as hard as he can?

5. Imagine the successful close of the interview, and the specific behaviors you
   hope to see in the employee in the future, as a result of the interview.

Performance-oriented managers are not satisfied with marginal performance of subordinates; but many managers are not comfortable talking with their subordinates in order to improve performance, so, after
a conversation or two, they let things slide, hoping somehow they will
get better. But imagery gives us a tool to deal with the root of the
problem. It helps us to prepare properly for a thorough appraisal and
corrective action interview in order to correct the problem.

You probably use imagery to some extent in situations such as that
described above, but few managers actually rehearse the event in as
much detail as is required under vivid imagery; nor do we go through
the vivid mental rehearsal of possible scenarios and attendant problems
that systematic use of imagery requires. Let's now examine how imagery
can help us to achieve a performance orientation in management.

THE MANAGEMENT PROCESS, PERFORMANCE, AND IMAGERY

Managers who have a strong performance orientation know how to
get the best out of themselves, their subordinates, their boss, and their
organization as shown later in Figure 3–1. They realize that they exist
within a team and think of themselves as a catalyst or spark that en-
ergizes the team. Of course your role as a human resource development
specialist is to help managers light that spark.

Performance-oriented managers are also strongly goal directed. Fur-

Figure 3-1
Performance-Oriented Managers Get the Most Out of Themselves, Boss, Subordinates, and Organization

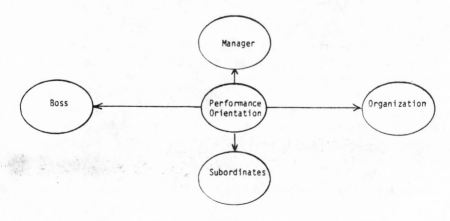

thermore, they tend to see their goals in quite clear and explicit terms. They have a vision of the goals they want to achieve and they can clearly see the paths or steps that need to be followed in order to reach the goals.

The Management Process

Recall that we said earlier the essence of management is decision making and influence in order to reach goals. That is, managers make the right decisions and use influence to get the decisions implemented. In making decisions, managers decide how to plan, organize, staff, lead, and control resources in order for the goals to be achieved. The final desired output of the entire management process is goal achievement. In a word it is performance.

The key to high level management performance, then, is to make the right decisions, those that best use the resources available so that the desired goals can be achieved. How can this be done?

High performance managers know that they depend on many people in the organization for their success. When making decisions to best utilize resources they know that their bosses, subordinates, organization, and themselves each will have a role to play. Furthermore, these managers can inspire others for high performance in their respective role. So, high performing managers:

1. are goal oriented;

2. know what decisions can best reach the goals;

3. know how to use resources to achieve goals;

4. can clearly define each person's role in reaching goals;

5. can inspire performance in carrying out the role.

Now, for many managers it is difficult to make this rather abstract process work. This is where imagery can help. Imagery can make the process more concrete and, thus, more realistic. Let's look at an example.

Suppose a manager in your organization decides that the best way to improve the operations of her unit is by reorganizing the jobs and functions of the people working for her. She comes to you for advice as to the best way to go about this. She wants to achieve this reorganization and, at the same time, provide opportunities for professional growth for the people in her unit. Through a proper reorganization, she concludes that she will be able to achieve the following goals:

1. Increase unit productivity by 10 percent.
2. Achieve more flexibility in job assignment. People can work on critical tasks as they come up.
3. Achieve a smoother transition for growth.

In order to achieve these three goals, she realizes that she must initiate the action and that many people will be involved. You help her to make the following decisions:

1. To reorganize as quickly as possible.
2. To keep everyone informed so as to minimize rumor.
3. To reduce the specialization of each job role.
4. To give employees the right to transfer if they do not want to stay in the newly defined jobs.

You then define with her the role that each party will need to play in the process as follows:

1. Subordinates: stay informed of decision; be willing to experiment with and accept reorganization; provide feedback on progress.
2. Boss: understand and approve of reorganization; be supportive.
3. Personnel Department of Organization: change policy and job descriptions to permit reorganization.
4. The manager: initiate change; sell people on accepting it; monitor and continue to implement change; solve problems that come up; make adjustments as necessary.

You both believe if each person carries out their role as you define it, the change will be successful. How does she get them to do it? How should she inspire performance so that they carry out their role as she desires?

The first thing you can help her do, using imagery, is to visualize each person carrying out his/her role. Let's see how this works for each party.

Her Subordinates

In order for subordinates to carry out their role, she would see them doing the following:

1. listening to her while she explained the reorganization;
2. asking questions about the reorganization;
3. listening to her answers;
4. raising possible problems;

5. talking among themselves as to how the reorganization is likely to affect each of them;
6. learning the new job roles;
7. providing both negative and positive feedback to her and one another on the new job;
8. becoming proficient in the new jobs and increasing output;
9. liking and accepting the new job reorganization.

You help her see this sequence of events happening and to anticipate various problems. Sally will likely accept it easier than Fred, for example. Therefore, she may need to do a little more arm twisting with Fred. Jim may be very unhappy and transfer. Mary is close to retirement and may need some encouragement. Hank will really be enthusiastic about the change and she can ask him to help sell the others, and so on. The point is by using guided imagery, you help her to visualize the role that each subordinate will play before she makes the change. She decides how she can best get them to carry out the desired change before she makes the change. You help her to visualize in her mind the desired scenario as she wishes it to happen and she prepares for any problems that may come up.

Her Boss

In order for her boss to carry out his role in the reorganization, she would see him doing the following:

1. listening to her while she explained the need for the reorganization;
2. reviewing data/figures she has to support the change;
3. asking her questions about the data/figures and the need;
4. listening while she responded to the questions;
5. telling her he likes the idea and giving her a preliminary go-ahead, subject to personnel's approval;
6. congratulating and praising her for being innovative and taking initiative;
7. checking with her a few weeks after the change is made, and praising her because things are going so well.

This is what she should see as the desirable sequence of events. If she does not see this happening, then she should do some more work before she approaches her boss. For example, suppose she sees these steps in place of 5, 6, 7, and 8 above.

5. asking for additional data/information that she does not have;
6. asking her to get additional data/information, and telling her he wants a few days to think it over;

7. telling her he wants her to check with a few people on problems that might come up;

8. implying that she hasn't done her homework by saying the idea sounds half-baked.

Now if she envisions steps 5 through 8 above instead of the original scenario, she should prepare in advance by getting the data/information her boss is likely to ask for and by checking with the people. By using this imagery scenario, you will help her to avoid a potentially embarrassing situation.

Personnel Department

Let's assume that you are located in the personnel department. In order for the department to carry out its role, you would see the personnel director doing the following:

1. reading the written request with attached new job descriptions;
2. listening to the discussion of the request;
3. asking questions of justification;
4. asking if approval of the department head's boss has been obtained;
5. listening to responses of the department head;
6. giving approval of the reorganization;
7. praising the department head for taking the initiative and telling her that she wished more managers in the company would try innovative reorganization proposals.

Again, this is the desired scenario. Anything that you would see different from the above should raise a red flag and cause a rethinking of the plan.

The Department Head

In order for her to carry out her role, you and she see herself doing the following:

1. gathering data/information supporting the desired change;
2. preparing a written report;
3. preparing the oral report for:
   a. boss,
   b. subordinates,
   c. personnel director;
4. presenting the oral and written reports to each;
5. answering questions from each;

6. monitoring subordinates;
7. getting feedback from subordinates;
8. praising subordinates;
9. providing feedback to boss and personnel department;
10. acknowledging praise graciously.

Again, this is a desirable scenario you would visualize for her. If you see something less desirable, you would need to advise her to prevent it from actually occurring.

This example shows that performance-oriented managers can clearly see the roles that people will need to play in order for them to carry out desired decisions. The more clearly they can see their roles and anticipate the problems that are likely to arise, the more successful they are likely to be in having their decisions implemented properly. As a human resource professional, your role in a situation such as this is to use imagery as a way to coach the principal party involved in order to bring about a successful reorganization request.

PERSONAL IMAGERY AND PERFORMANCE

How can people create imagery scenarios, such as those above, which lead to desirable levels of performance? There are two ways. First, people can originate mental scripts within their own mind based upon personal experiences and cues observed around them. This is called *personal imagery*. Second, people can respond to someone trained in imagery, such as a professional trainer, who puts them through an imagery experience. We discuss both of these types of imagery in this chapter and elsewhere in this book. First, however, let's look at personal imagery.

The key factor for personal imagery is to have positive scripts. Positive scripts come from a strong sense of self-confidence and a "can-do" attitude. It is a belief that we can make things happen. This belief leads to *positive self-talk*—phrases such as "I know I can do it," "Things will turn out okay," "I'll just do my best," or "I've done it before, I can do it again." This is not mere wishful thinking or being in a dream world; rather, it is an honest assessment of one's ability to complete a given task based upon knowledge and prior experience.

Developing positive self-talk based upon an optimistic attitude helps us to develop personal imagery scripts. These scripts are not unrealistic, rosy pictures of the world. While they reflect a positive sense of self-accomplishment, they also explicitly acknowledge possible barriers or negative outcomes; however, the scripts provide for ways to prevent or overcome possible problems.

For example, suppose you decide to ask a subordinate to take on a rather distasteful task that needs to be done but which will require long hours of hard work. Let's call the subordinate Bob and let's assume you plan to ask him to help streamline the paperwork flow in your office. Bob has knowledge of office equipment and has worked similar projects in the past. He's the most logical choice of your people to do the project. However, you know Bob dislikes this type of work and that he already has been assigned work that will require him to work a full forty-hour week for the next several weeks. This work cannot be transferred to someone else. Your task, then, is to convince Bob to accept this extra assignment. How can you use personal imagery to accomplish this goal?

The first step is to formulate in your mind a clear image of the scenario required of Bob to complete the special project. What, exactly, will Bob have to do? Can you see him actually accomplishing these steps successfully by the deadline? If you cannot form this image or if you do not see Bob completing the project successfully, you should find out a bit more as to what is required in the project or you should find someone else to do it.

Second, you need to formulate a mental script of your conversation with Bob asking him to accept the project. Once this script is formulated you need to rehearse it. The script could go something like this:

You: Bob, I'm glad you have a couple of minutes, because I want to discuss a very important project with you. As you know, our office seems to be drowning in a sea of paperwork. With today's automated equipment, this is really unnecessary. There should be a way for us to eliminate much of this paperwork. I've thought a lot about a way for us to approach this. Of all the people we have here, you are the only one with knowledge and experience in office automation. Now I know you are very busy, but this is such an important job that it must have a high priority. We need to get it done in three to four weeks. Will you do it?

Bob: Gee, I don't know. I am *really* busy. Can't it wait?

You: Not really. Actually, if we get this analysis done and get this office automated with the latest equipment, it will really help all of our efforts. You'll really be doing us all a big favor, Bob. How about it?

Bob: Well, I suppose I could put in a couple of extra hours each day.

You: Great! I knew we could count on you. Of course, I'll be available to help you as much as I can. Let me know. Thank you very much. I really appreciate it.

In this scenario, you visualize a positive outcome: Bob accepts the assignment. What if he is reluctant? Here is a mental script you might formulate and practice if you think he will be reluctant to accept the assignment:

You: (same as before)

Bob: Gee, I'm just so busy. I don't see how I can do it. Plus, you know I hate doing that kind of work. Can't you get someone else?

You: Not really. You're the logical choice. I know you are very busy but we need it done as soon as possible. It will really help us all out. You'll be doing the whole office a big favor.

Bob: But, I'm already up to my neck. I just don't see how I can do it.

You: Well, maybe we can work something out once you're done. You know, maybe an extra day of leave or vacation. Come on, what do you say? We're depending on you!

Bob: Okay, I guess so. But I really am busy.

You: Good. I knew we could count on you. Thanks a lot.

You might also rehearse another scenario where Bob becomes quite adamant about refusing. In this case, you might give him a few days to think things over.

Only as a last resort would you rehearse a scenario where you couldn't convince Bob to take the job or at least to think about it. This "worst case" scenario would be a negative script. If you thought this was likely, then you should first decide whether it was even worth it to raise the issue with Bob to begin with. If chances are he won't take it and you won't be successful in convincing him, then why approach him? What do you have to gain by it?

Success Breeds Success

There's nothing like success to give us confidence for the future. This is one of the best ways to develop positive imagery scripts. Start with relatively minor situations where you are confident you'll accomplish something without experiencing many problems. Practice scenario scripts for these situations. Then experience them and the feelings of success that go along with satisfactory accomplishment; then, gradually, take on more challenging tasks. As you experience success with these, you'll gradually build your self-confidence and positive self-talk. This will better enable you to create success-filled scenarios of future situations.

Remember though that success-oriented scenarios do not ignore possible problems. Rather, they are realistic in that they anticipate them— even the worst case scenario—and they prepare for them. The difference is the possibility of a potential problem does not paralyze action. Rather, it is dealt with ahead of time through mental scenario rehearsal. Once proper scripts have been formulated to deal with the problem should it arise, you should feel confident to proceed with action because you are prepared for any eventuality. You've practiced in your mind what you will do or say.

Avoid No-Win Situations

In building positive personal imagery scripts, try to avoid situations loaded with failure. If you experience significant failure situations it will become difficult to prepare positive imagery scripts. You'll see everything through a negative bias. This may create a sour, give-up attitude, which will paralyze action and lower your performance level.

For example, if you are given the chance for a promotion to a new job, but you honestly don't believe you are really prepared for it, refuse it. This is better than taking the job and failing miserably. Make it clear that you appreciate the offer but that you don't believe you are quite ready. Also make it clear that you are preparing yourself so that you will be ready the next time an opening comes up. Turning down a promotion is very risky, but it is better than taking a job in which you're certain that you will clearly fail.

There are other times to avoid no-win situations. Don't push for an idea that you know is doomed. Don't try to win an argument where you know you are clearly wrong. Don't try to hide or overlook an obvious mistake on your part. These plus other failure-prone situations will affect your ability to develop positive scenario scripts.

Learn from Good Models

We can also develop positive self-scripts by learning from models who do what we want to do. "If Bob can do it, I can surely do it." We need to find models we can identify with who are not so different from us but who can teach us. We need to observe how they perform particularly difficult tasks, such as running an effective staff meeting, and then we can develop mental scripts to use when we have to conduct the staff meeting.

GUIDED IMAGERY AND PERFORMANCE

From time to time, you may have the opportunity both to experience and provide guided imagery for managers in your organization. This is imagery generated by one person, either orally or in writing for other people. For example, by reading this book you experience guided imagery as we review examples. There are other books that discuss imagery; many of these are listed in our bibliography. You might also have the opportunity to experience guided imagery under the direction of a group facilitator or a trainer experienced in the technique; eventually, you can become experienced enough to lead imagery sessions. In fact, that is one of the purposes of this book.

In general, a guided imagery experience follows the following eight steps, although specific guided imagery techniques may vary:

1. Tonesetting and Centering

Here the guided imagery facilitator explains the process to be used in the imagery sessions while requesting the participants to focus their attention on the present.

Example: Today, ladies and gentlemen, we will use a new technique called guided imagery to help you solve on-the-job problems. Please be open to this technique and be willing to go along with me and practice it. It can do wonders for you.

2. Relaxation Induction

The facilitator uses a brief three-minute relaxation exercise to induce a state of calm attentiveness in the participants.

Example: Close your eyes. [Pause.] Now relax. Feel your worries escape from the top of your head. Relax your feet. [Pause.] Relax your legs. Take a deep breath and exhale. [Pause.] Relax your arms and shoulders. [Pause.] Your hands and fingers are limp. Relax your facial muscles. [Pause.] You are now completely relaxed. You float as light as a feather. See a feather lightly float in front of you. Your problems are gone.

3. Imagery Script Presentation

After relaxation is achieved, the facilitator presents the guided imagery script in a clear, well-modulated manner. Participants are asked to imagine the script vividly and to involve themselves in the imagery scenario.

Example: Sitting before you on the table is an artichoke. The artichoke represents one of the most important problems in your job. You will eat this luscious dull green vegetable. As you peel off each leaf to eat it, you see a symptom of the problem. Take the first leaf. Feel it. Taste it. Look where you pulled it from the vegetable. See the problem symptom you uncovered. (This is repeated several times until the heart of the artichoke is reached. The heart represents the core and thus the cause of the problem.)

4. Free Imagery Practice I

The facilitator asks the participants to focus on their experience and realizations during script presentation and to spend a few minutes reflecting or expanding on these experiences.

Example: Think about that artichoke you just ate. How easy was it to see it? How easy was it to peel the leaves to expose symptoms? How many problem symptoms did you see? How clear were they? Did you clearly see the heart of the artichoke and thus the core of the problem? What does this tell you?

5. Retrieval and Recentering

Upon completion of the imagery practice session, the facilitator instructs the participants to refocus attention on the present in preparation for continued training.

Example: Okay. Now you are back in this room. Everything is normal. Open your eyes. Look around you. Look at me. We will now continue our session.

6. Presentation of Informational Materials

After recentering is complete, the facilitator provides participants with informational material relevant to the purpose of the sessions.

Example: Here is an outline of the problem solving process that we will discuss. Also attached is a short article on creative problem solving methods, which you can read at your leisure.

7. Free Imagery Practice II

After presentation of the above information, the facilitator once again induces the participants into a state of relaxation, during which they combine the "soft" data generated during the previous guided imagery session with the "hard" information from the materials just presented.

Example (after once again achieving relaxation): Let's now think about that artichoke. We know there are several ways to solve problems. Using the problem solving materials we have just discussed, do you see another way to approach peeling the artichoke to get at the heart? Do you see the symptoms differently? Does the heart look different than it did before? What does this tell you about the problem you are trying to solve?

8. Processing and Debriefing

At the conclusion of the second free imagery session, the facilitator recenters the participants and leads a discussion of the various experiences and outcomes of the guided imagery process.

Example: How did the guided imagery process work for you? Could you use the artichoke to represent the problem you face? Did it help you to see and solve your problems better? Will you be able to solve the problem once you get back to work? If not, what else must you do?

While it might not be possible for you to lead a guided imagery session at this point, by the time you complete this book you should be able to act as an imagery facilitator for groups of employees. It will require practice and more study to improve your skill. Throughout the book are practice exercises and the bibliography at the end of the book contains many additional sources for further study.

Probably the best way to practice imagery is to use a combination of personally generated imagery and guided imagery. One form will enhance the other. As you become more familiar with the technique, its use will become almost second nature to you. You will not need to devote so much time and effort to making it work as you need initially.

GUIDED IMAGERY AND MANAGERIAL ROLES

Recall that we discussed that managers play three key roles that can classified as either interpersonal, informational, or decisional. Under each of these classifications are the specific roles as follows:

Interpersonal Roles:
   Figurehead
   Leader
   Liaison
Informational Roles:
   Monitor
   Dissemination
   Spokesperson
Decisional Roles:
   Entrepreneur
   Distribution handler
   Resource allocator
   Negotiator

Let's see how imagery can help managers to carry out each of these roles better to enhance performance.

Interpersonal Roles

These roles feature the manager as a pivotal point in carrying out interpersonal interaction with others. The roles of figurehead, leader, and liaison require managers to be visible to others with whom they work. Imagery can enhance this visibility by helping to project the proper sense of self to others, which will enhance effectiveness.

For example, suppose you wish to enhance managerial effectiveness in conducting staff meetings. By using imagery you can help managers project a stronger image of self to their staff. Try this imagery exercise yourself:

> Go to a quiet room. Shut your eyes. Relax completely, let your mind wander. Next, think of yourself at your typical staff meeting. See

the room. See the people in their seats. Everyone is looking at you. You smile and talk easily. Your efforts at humor bring quiet laughter and smiles. People are interested in what you say. They respond enthusiastically to your questions. You respond to theirs. You anticipate their questions and have the required information in your head or at your fingertips.

You end the meeting on an upbeat note. The staff leave recharged feeling the meeting was worthwhile. They tell you "Good meeting" on the way out. You leave feeling good about the meeting. You are pleased it went so smoothly. You're happy you had so thoroughly prepared. You had rehearsed the words to get across the ideas you wanted to communicate. You anticipated their questions. You generated a list of questions you wanted to ask them and you anticipated their answers. You were thoroughly familiar with the information to be discussed.

Practicing this exercise by reading the above script and thinking about each sentence before your next meeting will help you to improve your interpersonal roles with your staff by improving your ability to conduct a staff meeting. Let's look at how you might improve your ability to coordinate with other units with whom you work (liaison role). Try this imagery exercise:

Go to a quiet room and relax. Develop a picture of a spoked wooden wagon wheel in your mind. You are at the center of the wheel. Each wooden spoke represents a contact with another group in or outside of your organization with whom you must deal. The length and diameter of the spoke represents the importance and distance of the contact: the greater the diameter of each contact, the more important; the longer each spoke, the greater the distance from you to the contact.

Now draw a picture of your wheel that reflects the length and diameter of each spoke. Label each spoke. What does the wheel look like? Are there important liaison contacts you must maintain that are far away from you? [Long, fat spokes.] Do you actually see some spokes not hooking securely to you in the center? Are there gaps in your wheel where you cannot visualize spokes but where spokes are needed for symmetry and balance? How would you like your wheel to look? What can you do to make your wheel more like the shape you want?

Informational Roles

Managers communicate. The three informational roles of monitor, disseminator, and spokesperson, require managers to be adept at managing information flows. They must monitor and gather information, must pass on or disseminate this information, and must act as spokesperson for their unit and, sometimes, their organization. To carry out these roles effectively requires several skills: listening, speaking, memory, and monitoring. Let's see how imagery can enhance these skills. Try this exercise to enhance monitoring skills.

> Relax. Feel yourself becoming very light. So light that you actually begin to rise off your chair. You slowly float out the window to your place of work. You are slowly floating over your office. The roof of your building is removed. You can see your office and the offices of those with whom you work. They cannot see you. As you float over their offices, you hear their conversations. To whom are they talking? What are they saying? About their work? About other people with whom they work? About the organization? About you?
>
> Now, take a few minutes and jot down your imagined conversations. When back at your office, be more aware of conversations and see how actual conversations are either similar to or different from your imagined ones.

This exercise can help listening skills:

> Imagine that your ears have a radar-like locking device. When you hear a voice, your ears immediately lock in on the source of the voice. It is as if they shoot out a line to the source that actually ties you to it. Your head and eyes are focused on the source because your ears are actually tied to it. You cannot get away. Your entire attention is focused on the voice. Your ears act as big funnels capturing every sound heard and channeling it to your brain.
>
> Finally, the voice stops. You are now free to move, respond, or walk away.

The next time someone is speaking to you, try to visualize the above situation. It will improve your listening ability by improving your attention.

Practicing the following imagery scenario can improve your ability as a spokesperson:

> Go to a quiet room and relax. Shut your eyes. You will be giving a speech to fifty people in the next few days about the progress of an important project on which your unit is working. You picture the room where you will be speaking—the chairs, the floors, the ceiling, the walls. You see people sitting in the chairs and looking at you. You see how they are dressed and their facial expressions. You see yourself at the front of the room. You feel comfortable. You have an outline and notes in front of you. You have a slide projector (which works!) and well-prepared slides. The screen is in place. The lectures and mike are functional.

You begin by making some opening remarks to relax the group. You welcome them and make them feel relaxed. You thank them for attending. They you discuss the progress of the project using the slides as appropriate. You are well prepared because you have rehearsed what you plan to say.

You summarize and conclude and open up the discussion for questions. You correctly hear and answer all questions. You have anticipated the questions and have prepared appropriate information.

You conclude the meeting by thanking the audience again for attending and for their attention. As they leave they congratulate you on a fine presentation.

Decisional Roles

Effective managers make good decisions. Four kinds of decisional roles are carried out.

Entrepreneurial decisions start action. They are innovative and risk-taking. They capitalize on opportunities. Examples of entrepreneurial decisions are a radical reorganization of the unit, the introduction of a new product, the creation of a new promotional campaign, or a redesign of an assembly line. *Disturbance handler decisions* involve resolving conflict between two or more people or organizational units. *Resource allocator decisions* involve allocating money, space, equipment, and other resources to people or units. Finally, *negotiator decisions* involve helping parties to reach common ground and agreement through processes of bargaining and give and take. Let's see how imagery can help in each of these roles.

Entrepreneurial decisions require managers to be willing to create, experiment, innovate, and try something new without a strong fear of failure. They ask people to be risk-takers. Here is an exercise to improve these types of decisions.

Relax. Close your eyes. You have been experiencing problems with the way your unit is organized. You see in your mind's eye a diagram of the present organization chart of your unit. You see names and faces in each box. You see lines connecting boxes that show reporting relationships.

Now, imagine that you can move the boxes around at will to create an entirely new organization design. There are no organization policies, existing job descriptions, rules, or regulations to prohibit you from moving the boxes around at will. Create your perfect organizational unit! Show the new reporting relationships. Create new positions. Change old positions. Redistribute authority. Do anything you want. See the names, faces, and job titles in your new organization chart.

Now write your chart down on a sheet of paper. Make three lists below it. Show on the first list why it is a good chart. On the second list, show the reasons why you can*not* create this ideal chart today. On the third list, indicate the things you can do to remove the barriers on the second list. Also indicate the things others will need to do to remove the barriers.

Disturbance handler decisions require managers to smooth over differences among subordinates or with other units. Managers need to remain calm during an emotional storm. Here is an imagery exercise to help with these decisions.

Relax. Imagine that you are sailing a very sturdy sailboat during a thunderstorm. You are a competent sailor. Your boat is well built and in excellent condition. It is a large boat of thirty-four feet—built to withstand a thunderstorm. You are well protected with rain gear. The waves are breaking over the bow. The wind is howling. The rain is coming down in sheets. You have lowered the sails and feel confident in your abilities to handle the storm. You study the wind. You are familiar with the area where you are sailing. You know the bottom and the currents. You feel a bit anxious but also calm and collected under the circumstances.

Now imagine that you have the power to stop the storm if you put your mind to it. You can command the wind to stop blowing. You can stop the rain. You can make the waves subside. To do this, you must concentrate very hard on the wind, rain, and waves, and understand them. Then you must use your mind to tell them to subside. While you do this, you must remain calm, cool, collected, and have full confidence in your abilities.

As you practice this, you actually see the rain beginning to slack. You feel the wind dying down. The waves begin to subside. Off in the distance, the sky begins to brighten. Soon the sun is shining brightly. You raise the sails and enjoy the pleasant wind blowing across the deck.

This imagery scenario helps to prepare a person to remain calm under violent, unpredictable circumstances. The mind's eye is used to help see and know the disturbance so it can be better managed. This is critical if managers are to carry out their disturbance handler roles properly.

As a resource allocator, managers must parcel out scarce resources to many deserving people. There are never enough dollars, space, positions, and other resources to go around. Nevertheless, managers must efficiently allocate their resources to achieve the highest levels of performance possible. This requires that they know what people need, what resources are available, how people will react if they do not receive what they expect, and how resources lead to results. This imagery scenario can help to refine the resource allocator role.

> Relax. Imagine that you are a bird. Imagine that you are a mother robin with five baby birds in the nest. The babies are always hungry. They constantly have their mouths open pointed skyward. You continually fly from the nest looking for worms and insects to feed the babies. Of course, you must eat also. You know that the longer you search, the more food you will find, but the more calories you will burn, thereby increasing your need for food.
>
> During daylight hours you continually fly to and from the nest with food, but the chicks are never satisfied. Toward the end of the day, you become tired but you continue to search for and bring back food. You do the best you can to feed the babies hoping that they will take and digest the food to grow into healthy birds, eventually leaving the nest. You know they are not ever completely satisfied, and you know you can never find enough food to satisfy them and keep yourself alive. You do the best you can. You are conscientious about meeting their needs, but if you die from starvation because you search too long, so will they. You are confident you can keep them alive and help them to grow, even if they continually beg for more.

This is the plight of the resource allocator—trying to help the units by getting more resources. This takes time and energy. It can become all consuming to try to satisfy all the needs of each employee. This reduces overall effectiveness by keeping one from performing other duties. So a balance is struck. You learn to live with mouths open to the sky, and you do your best to fill them without burning yourself out.

The final decisional role is that of negotiator. How can negotiation skills be improved? How can bargaining and the necessary give-and-take of negotiation be fine-tuned? How can an equilibrium be reached that leaves everyone reasonably satisfied? Here is an imagery exercise to help:

> Imagine that you are sitting in your office reviewing performance data on one of your marginal subordinates who is performing just up to minimum standards but no higher. You are convinced that the person is placed in a job he cannot handle and believe if you move him to another job his performance will become satisfactory.
>
> You have discussed this with him but he flatly refuses to change jobs. While the job you wish to transfer him to pays the same as his present job, it is viewed by those in your work unit as significantly below the status of the job he currently holds. (You agree the job connotes lower status.)
>
> Furthermore, this subordinate is very well liked by his fellow

employees. He is a long-time employee, who is looked up to and respected by other employees in your unit who consider him an informal leader. You do not want to do anything to alienate him toward you or the organization, or to have your other subordinates lose respect and admiration for you. You also consider him a personal friend.

You decide to negotiate the job transfer. Your approach is to upgrade the duties of the new job, modify its title, and raise the salary by 5 percent. You realize that this will not erase the low status stigma attached to the job, nor will the newly defined job have the same level of responsibility of his present job. But you believe he can handle the new job. You decide to make him this offer and to tell him that if he does not accept it, he will be asked to resign.

At this point, you must compute the zone within which you will be willing to negotiate with him. If he listens to your offer and suggests a 10 percent pay raise in the new job instead of 5 percent will you accept it? If he asks for an even loftier title, will you grant that? Just how much will you allow before you ask him for his resignation? How much will you be willing to give up to get him to take the new job? Visualize each item that you give up as a piece of your body that you lose. You may be willing to lose a piece of your fingernail but are unwilling to lose an arm or a leg. What pieces in your negotiation represent the fingernail and which represent the arms and legs?

This exercise helps to determine the value of the items negotiated and the degree to which a person is indifferent as to whether they are kept or not. It helps to weigh the value of these items relative to what is obtained in return—in this case the support, and friendship of other subordinates. In most negotiation decisions, these types of judgments must be made as bargaining occurs toward a settlement.

SUMMARY

We've seen several ways imagery can help managers achieve a performance orientation. The positive, can-do attitudes of high performing managers can be enhanced by positive scripts and by practicing imagery scenarios. Both personal imagery and guided imagery are useful here and both should be used.

In the next chapter, we see how imagery can help managers improve strategic planning, an extremely important management function.

4

HOW IMAGERY CAN BE USED IN A CORPORATE MANAGEMENT EDUCATION AND DEVELOPMENT PROGRAM

Compare the following paragraphs.

Management involves five essential functions as follows: planning, organizing, staffing, directing, and controlling. A manager makes decisions in each of these functional areas on using resources to achieve organizational objectives. There are five essential resources: people, money, physical resources, information, and time. Organizational objectives include profitability, customer satisfaction, employee satisfaction, and proper quantity/quality levels of products and services. Making good decisions in order to set and reach objectives is the primary function of a manager.

The essence of management is decision making. A manager is like the leader of a Boy Scout troop who's job is to lead his pack through a large, thick forest in the dead of winter. Using a compass, he must guide them through the woods to the other side. He's got to plan and organize the trek, insure that they have enough food, water, clothing, and other items essential for survival. He must organize the effort and determine the most efficient way of reaching the objective. He must be sure the boys are properly trained and that they perform their duties as assigned. He must lead, coach, and instruct. While doing so, hundreds of decisions will need to be made as emergencies arise, weather changes, and landmarks become confusing.

Wording similar to the first paragraph can be found in most management textbooks and in reading material often used in corporate management training and development programs. The second paragraph uses imagery to convey the same ideas as those found in the first paragraph. Notice how the second paragraph creates a vivid picture in the mind—a large woods, a sunny day, a scout troop preparing to hike through the woods, etc. The development of instructional material and development programs using the approach shown in the second paragraph is the theme of this chapter, which reviews the role of the training and development specialist in integrating imagery into an organization's training and development programs.

HUMAN RESOURCE PROFESSIONALS IN TRAINING AND DEVELOPMENT

The responsibilities for creating and implementing a training and development program in an organization vary along a continuum as shown in Figure 4–1. At the far right end are training and development specialists who have no supervisory responsibility and conduct programs, primarily of an orientation nature, for semi-skilled to skilled employees. At the far left-hand side are training and development professionals who supervise a large staff in a department responsible for all training and development efforts for all levels, including top management, in the firm. This type of responsibility is also likely to have a strong organizational development flavor to it.

In the middle is probably where most training and development professionals operate. They have some supervisory responsibility for a small staff and are concerned with developing and conducting training and development programs for supervisors, clerical, and skilled staff. They may also implement selected programs for middle managers.

The extent to which you can implement imagery techniques in your organization will depend on where you see yourself on the continuum. If you lie to the right, you will be able to use imagery in the actual programs you conduct. If you lie to the far left, you can actually build imagery into all of your organization's development efforts as appropriate from top management on down. In the middle, you will have an opportunity to build the technique only into programs for appropriate groups with which you deal.

Regardless of where you lie on the responsibility continuum, you'll be able to use imagery. The only difference is if you lie to the right you'll only be able to use it in your own programs rather than influence the organization to use it throughout all training and development programs.

IMPLEMENTING IMAGERY THROUGHOUT THE ORGANIZATION

Imagery is a generic technique that has wide applicability to a variety of training and development programs throughout the organization. The

Figure 4-1
Responsibility Continuum for Training and Development

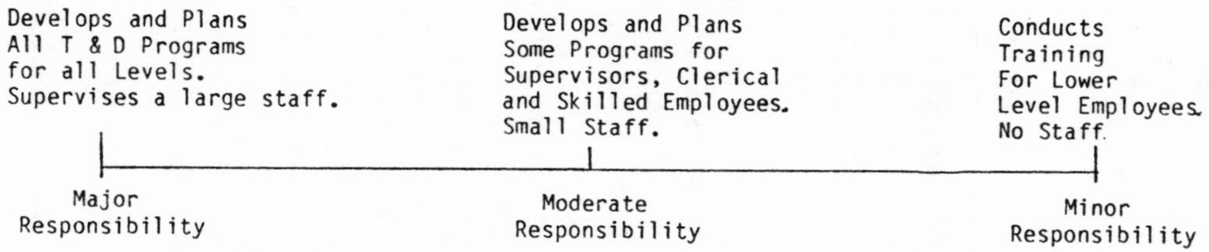

Develops and Plans
All T & D Programs
for all Levels.
Supervises a large staff.

Develops and Plans
Some Programs for
Supervisors, Clerical
and Skilled Employees.
Small Staff.

Conducts
Training
For Lower
Level Employees.
No Staff.

Major
Responsibility

Moderate
Responsibility

Minor
Responsibility

focus of this book is to implement imagery in management development programs, from supervisory to top management development, with emphasis on imagery experiences conducted in a classroom or seminar-like setting. We show how imagery can be used to improve strategic planning, leadership, interpersonal relationships, communications, problem-solving and decision making, personal effectiveness, and overall managerial performance. Through guided imagery, a facilitator can apply imagery to improve managerial skills in each of these areas.

Guided imagery can also be used in any performance-oriented type of training, such as in teaching the specific craft skills of carpentry, electrician, tool and die making, and so on. Wherever a performance skill needs to be taught, having participants visualize ideal performance opens the door to using imagery. The better they envision carrying out skill dynamics and the consequences of skill acquisition, the more likely they will be able to actually learn the given skill. Research has shown that if an individual can imagine himself completing an action successfully, the probability of actually succeeding at the behavior is enhanced. This process of covert rehearsal is a powerful imagery technique that can be used in almost any training format.

Personal imagery, that is the use of imagery by an individual without the aid of a facilitator, is another area covered in the book. By reading scripts and practicing various imagery techniques, an individual can experience the benefits of imagery to better see a problem, mentally rehearse a speech or interview, or prepare to confront a difficult employee, among other activities.

Imagery has applications in both on- and off-the-job types of training both in individual and group settings. We will explain a method that can be used to implement the technique throughout the organization in both types of training settings. The Organizational Staging model actually describes how to implement imagery in the organization. The Guided Imagery Process Model actually shows how to present a guided imagery experience in a classroom or one-on-one setting. Both models are summarized in Figure 4–2 and are discussed below.

ORGANIZATIONAL STAGING MODEL

There are six steps in this process which we have developed and experimentally implemented with various financial, retail, manufacturing, non-profit organizations, and independent consulting efforts. Since imagery practice will be new to many members of your organization, thorough understanding and careful implementation of the process is essential.

Figure 4-2
Organization Staging Model

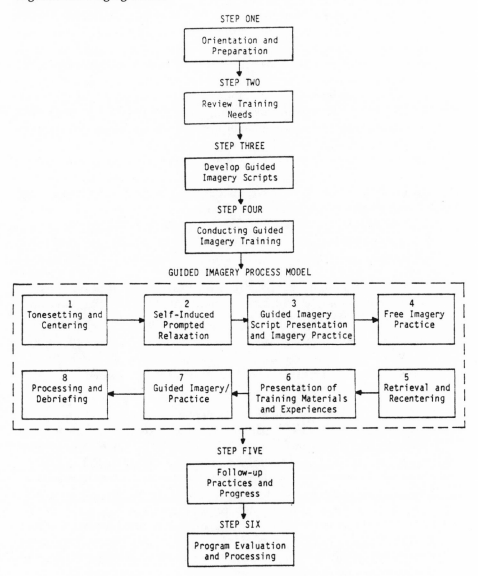

STEP ONE

Orientation and
Preparation

STEP TWO

Review Training
Needs

STEP THREE

Develop Guided
Imagery Scripts

STEP FOUR

Conducting Guided
Imagery Training

GUIDED IMAGERY PROCESS MODEL

| 1 Tonesetting and Centering | 2 Self-Induced Prompted Relaxation | 3 Guided Imagery Script Presentation and Imagery Practice | 4 Free Imagery Practice |

| 8 Processing and Debriefing | 7 Guided Imagery/ Practice | 6 Presentation of Training Materials and Experiences | 5 Retrieval and Recentering |

STEP FIVE

Follow-up
Practices and
Progress

STEP SIX

Program Evaluation
and Processing

Step 1: Orientation and Preparation

There will be some initial resistance to imagery techniques. Some folks will call it flaky—a throwback to the sixties; others will view it as simply wishful thinking. Therefore, in this stage it is critical to acquaint organizational members with the basic concepts, uses, and specific types of imagery. Stressing its frequent use and high success rate in sports, education, counseling, and medicine will help to make your personnel receptive to trying out the techniques. Citing specific examples where imagery is used to teach tennis, golf, skiing, free-throw shooting, etc., shows it is an effective technique for enhancing performance. Tying it to management by reviewing management performance episodes such as making a presentation, interviewing, negotiating, and making decisions will demonstrate how imagery practice can be used by your personnel to pay personal and professional dividends.

Providing mini-workshops and seminars to staff will acquaint people with the rationale and purposes of imagery. Supplementing this introductory phase with books such as Singer and Switzer's *Mindplay* (1980); Samuels and Samuels' *Seeing with the Mind's Eye* (1981); and Van Grundy's *Training Your Creative Mind* (1982); as well as this book should help your potential trainees to reduce resistance they may have toward these techniques.

Initial orientation and preparation should be targeted to a specific segment of the organization, such as the sales force or office supervisors, so experimental implementation can occur here first. In this way problems or difficulties can be worked out prior to introducing the concepts to the entire organization.

Step 2: Review Training Needs/Programs Where Guided Imagery Might Apply

This step involves an initial assessment of where guided imagery is likely to have its greatest impact in the organization. Since our focus is on management education and development, it is probable that guided imagery would be found useful for programs in managerial communication, problem-solving, strategic planning, leadership, or supervision. Integrating imagery techniques into an already existing program will be easier than creating an entirely new program around imagery. However, if certain programs do not exist in an area, then building imagery into the development of a new program is quite feasible. This book explains how imagery can be either built into an existing program or used in designing a new program.

It is important in this step to preview the specific skills to be covered and the specific behaviors involved in performing these skills in a sequential fashion. The imagery trainers must focus on the skills to be practiced.

Step 3: Develop Guided Imagery Scripts Relevant to Training

Here appropriate scripts are either obtained or developed for the learning experience. Scripts in this book may serve as models for scripts or as guides to development of your own script. There are seven important ideas to keep in mind in script selection and development:

1. A script must be relevant to the participants' work or personal experience. It is difficult to create an image of an apple if none of the participants has ever seen one. Scripts must address factors that are recognizable and important to trainees.

2. Scripts should promote positive outcome expectancies related to the goals of the program by creating a can do attitude and by encouraging self-confidence. For example, a mental rehearsal script of a presentation would include statements such as: "See yourself successfully answering questions because you are well-prepared"; "See the audience looking at you intently with high interest."

3. Scripts should address all appropriate senses involved: images, smell, feelings, and so on. Notice the script for the beach scene at the beginning of Chapter 1 where all senses were called into play as part of the imaginal depiction.

4. Scripts should use clear, vivid unambiguous language. Avoid words people will not understand and those with double meaning such as "ball" (a dance, a fun time, or a round plaything).

5. Scripts should promote transferring learning to the job environment; in other words, the participants should clearly see how the script relates to the management skill being taught as it is to be practiced. This can be done by having trainees envision themselves using new skills in the work environment.

6. Scripts should be kept *short*. Generally, five to seven minutes is a good length for an individual script. Scripts longer than this may lull people to sleep or may lose their impact because of being overly complex.

7. Finally, every script should be *pretested* by reading it aloud to a small group to ensure it has the intended effect prior to using it in a session. Feedback from your trial group can help you to articulate your script and its learning intent better.

Sample scripts are provided throughout this book.

Step 4: Conduct the Training. The Guided Imagery Process Model

This step involves conducting a guided imagery session and has eight substeps.

A. *Tonesetting and Centering*: The facilitator orients participants to the overall training/program and identifies the key learning objectives of the program; these outcomes are clearly presented at the outset. Then, guided imagery scripts that are to be used during the program reinforce these outcomes. The facilitator may seek participant feedback regarding the basic program or may solicit questions related to any concerns that still may be present. Tonesetting allows trainees to acclimate themselves to the training environment. Once such matters are resolved, the facilitator asks the participants to settle down, stretch out, close their eyes, and center their attention in the present.

B. *Self-Induced/Prompted Relaxation*: At this point, the facilitator suggests or leads participants in relaxation practice both to induce concentration and calmness as well as restful attentiveness to the upcoming imagery scripts. A three-to-five-minute period of relaxation will be sufficient to arrive at this point. Dimmed lighting and a quietly paced set of relaxation prompts can enhance the depth of the relaxed state for the participants. Throughout this book there are many examples of relaxation scripts. The key points are to read or recite them slowly, calmly, and clearly and to give people a chance to relax before you move to the next step. Research shows that relaxation promotes the emergence of more graphic imagery.

C. *Guided Imagery Script Presentation and Guided Imagery Practice*: Upon completion of the relaxation sequence, the facilitator presents the selected imagery scenario script. Participants should remain relaxed as they are guided and coached to visualize vividly and comprehensively the details, thoughts, feelings, and sensations described in the script. The trainer guides the participants so that they place themselves fully in the imagined scenario. The guided imagery scenario script details the specific objectives and outcomes of the given training experience and the paths required to acquire or experience these objectives and outcomes. Upon completion of script presentation, the trainer directs the participants into the fourth step of the process model in a natural transitional manner.

D. *Free Imagery Practice*: The trainer initiates a period of free or open imagery, during which participants personalize, elaborate upon, or simply follow the pattern of imagery created by the just-read scenario script. This exercise allows participants to translate script imagery into personally meaningful experiences and expectancies of positive skill acquisition, self-efficacy, or favorable behavioral consequences, which facilitates the transfer of training to the work life of the participants. Cues such as "Imagine yourself doing the task successfully," or "Think about what this means to you personally and to your organization" give people the opportunity to think about the process. In this stage, you may give trainees the opportunity to jot down thoughts or notes on a sheet of paper. No discussion, however, should be permitted at this time.

E. *Retrieval and Recentering*: After completion of the free imagery exercise, the facilitator instructs the participants to refocus their awareness and attention to the present and the training environment. Relaxation and imagery practice create considerable internal focus, and it is important for participants to reacclimate to the program agenda. Once this is accomplished, the facilitator can move the group into the instructional phase of training, when materials and lessons are presented.

F. *Presentation of Training Materials and Experiences*: After recentering, the facilitator distributes and presents the designated training materials. Use of graphics, visual materials, and displays may reinforce imagery that evolved during the guided imagery sequence. Additionally, training materials should contain elaborated examples of the objectives and outcomes considered important for the participants. Time should be allocated for group discussion of the materials and the objectives of the program. This part of the program is much like any other training program where materials are presented and discussed on the topic at hand.

G. *Imagery Practice*: After completion of the instructional phase of training, a second imagery session is used to reinforce learnings and awarenesses developed during the initial imagery practice and during the presentation of training materials. Combining a short relaxation period with an imagery script helps participants use new perceptions and learning during this imagery practice. The objective is to use the ideas presented in the previous step where specific content knowledge was presented.

During this experience, participants visualize how acquisitions of the outcomes or objectives of training will impact on their work and on the context of their job environment. An opportunity for group discussion of the experience should be provided. Additionally, the facilitator may ask for either demonstrations or role-plays by participants, so that they can practice what they have learned from guided imagery and from the presentation of materials.

H. *Processing and Debriefing*: At this point, the facilitator gives the participants the opportunity to review and discuss the following topics: (1) the overall effectiveness and relevancy of the training experience; (2) reactions to the use of both guided and free imagery; (3) suggestions for facilitating future training programs; (4) review of the pros and cons of the experience; (5) summations of the learning that the participants acquired; and (6) ideas on how to transfer the learning outcomes to the job environment successfully.

This step concludes the guided imagery process model for conducting an individual guided imagery session. Now let's move back to the overall model for use in introducing imagery in an organization.

Step 5: Follow-up Practice

Additional practice of the imagery material by the participants allows them to internalize the concepts/skills the imagery technique focuses on. This practice can vary in length depending upon the background and experience of the participants and the subject matter of the training. It can be done by the individual at the office or at home or in guided imagery sessions conducted by a facilitator. Consequently, participants should be allowed to have scripts used in the session and to develop their own scripts.

Step 6: Evaluation of the Program and the Progress of the Participants

The facilitator should encourage and solicit critical feedback from the training participants in order to evolve more imagery programs. A variety of techniques from casual discussions to written questionnaires may be used to gather this necessary data. Such information can be used to improve both the presentation of materials and the use of imagery in subsequent programs. Participants should be informed of the outcomes of the data collection and evaluation efforts. It will take time to refine the process. There is still much to be learned about applying imagery to management training and development. Facilitators should be very willing to change scripts, methods, and approaches in view of critical comments made by participants and others in the organization.

The above model has been found useful; however, we do not intend that this should be the only way to implement imagery in an organization. Certainly variations of the process will occur and may very well be appropriate. For example, in a smaller organization, the first imagery program might start with all top managers of the organization with little experimental implementation.

LINKING IMAGERY TO OTHER FORMS OF TRAINING AND DEVELOPMENT

Does imagery work in all forms of training and development? Does imagery work with all forms of management training and development? While we believe imagery has wide applications in organizations, it may not be applicable to certain forms of training and development. However, we have found, and this is supported by research, that the technique seems to work best in both skill-specific and conceptual planning and problem-solving types of situations. It may have applicability beyond these situations, but so far our experience and those of other researchers do not support this idea.

Consequently, when looking for places to apply imagery, look first for skill-specific areas where a person must practice to master a specific skill. As indicated, there are many facets of management that are skill-specific, some being easier to visualize than others (making a speech vs. solving a problem). Breaking down the performance of the skill into a series of sequential steps is extremely important for using the imagery technique. A person has to see him/herself actually going through the motions successfully. This involves being able to depict specific behaviors clearly and the specific consequences of these actions. For this reason videotapes and role playing practices are natural techniques to use with imagery.

Let's look at an example of how an imagery technique can be applied in a training situation. In this example, we will apply the organizational staging model and the guided imagery process model, which we just discussed, to tie imagery to a key management skill—conducting a performance appraisal interview.

Step 1: Orientation and Preparation

Here managers who are possible participants for the program are given a brief (approximately one-half hour) introduction to imagery: what it is; where it has been used; how it is used; etc. Supplemental reading material could also be provided in advance of the trainee program to promote familiarity. Specific reasons for using imagery to improve performance appraisal interviewing is explained and questions are fielded. One technique we have found especially effective is to encourage trainees to describe other times when they have used imagery.

Step 2: Review of Training Needs Where Imagery Might Apply

Careful consideration is given to the performance appraisal interview to ensure that imagery has application to this management skill. The process is reviewed in step-by-step fashion and the specific behaviors and language to be used are identified. Let's assume that we have developed the following objectives and step-by-step skill and language breakdown that characterizes a performance appraisal interview:

Objectives:

1. To create a good dialogue with the subordinate;
2. To clearly review the subordinate's performance;
3. To praise good performance and to identify problem areas;
4. To develop a plan to correct or improve performance;
5. To build a collaborative overall development plan for the employee that serves as a guide for performance.

Skill	Language
1. Greet pleasantly when subordinate enters office.	"Hi Chris. Come on in. Glad you could come. Have a seat."
2. Relax subordinate.	"How was your weekend?"
3. Establish eye contact and proper open body language.	Continue above conversation.
4. Initiate dialogue on performance.	"What do you believe to be your significant accomplishments over the past year?"
5. Praise accomplishments.	"We are all proud of you for what you've done."
6. Diagnose problem areas.	"Which areas in your job seem to be giving you the most difficulty?"
7. Develop a method to improve: Corrective action.	"What can we do to improve these areas?"
8. Convey your evaluation.	"I believe you have done a good job in etc., etc., etc., but we will need to do the following to improve, etc., etc., etc."
9. Tie to a development plan.	"As I see it, you are progressing nicely. We need to be sure you have the following learning experiences, etc., etc., etc."
10. Be prepared for worst case.	"Why are you reluctant to discuss your problem areas?"
11. Close on an upbeat note.	"Thank you for coming, I'm sure next year will be even better. I'm here to help."

The above does not list all the skills that one may need in performance appraisal; rather, it illustrates the detail needed when enhancing certain key skill areas. There may be others. For example, if the employee becomes angry and very defensive, calming skills will be required. If the employee becomes emotional and cries, empathetic skills are needed. Prior to the interview, observational and evaluative skills will need to be used to formulate a judgment as to how well the subordinate has done during the review period. Your scripts should include all elements you see as important.

Step 3: Development of Performance Appraisal Script

Now we are ready to write an imagery script to be read to the participants for mental imagery practice and scenario rehearsal. Many scripts and variations can be developed depending on the group, problems encountered with performance appraisal interviews in the organization, and desires of the facilitator. The script below is meant only to be illustrative.

Performance Appraisal Script

Close your eyes and relax. Take a few nice deep breaths. Let your tensions fall away. Imagine a calm restful scene, be it at the beach, the mountains, or your own backyard. Let the tension flow out of your body. Relax your feet. [Pause.] Relax your legs. [Pause.] Relax your arms. [Pause.] Relax your shoulders. Feel your neck relax. Your face is totally relaxed. Where there was tension, there is now warmth and relaxation. Imagine that you are about to have a performance evaluation interview with one of your average subordinates. Pick one of your average subordinates and form a mental image of hm or her in your mind. See his or her face. Re-envision some of the encounters you've had with this individual. What do you think of him/her? How do you feel about him/her as an employee?

Now think about this person's performance over the past year. Note the good areas and areas in need of performance improvement. Now picture your office. See the subordinate sitting in a chair. See yourself sitting in your favorite chair. You are relaxed, calm, and ready for the interview. Note the carpeting, walls, windows, desks, and other furniture. Smell the room. In your mind, build a clear and vivid picture of you and your subordinate preparing for a frank and adult discussion.

Now begin the interview. Welcome and relax the subordinate. [Pause.] Ask the subordinate how the job has gone? Ask about significant accomplishments. See yourself projecting a calm, confident air that puts your subordinate at ease. Hear the responses he or she will say. [Pause.] Ask about problem areas. [Pause.] Hear the responses he or she will make. [Pause.] Ask what he or she can do to improve problem areas. [Pause.] Anticipate his or her response. Convey your evaluation. What will you say? [Pause.] What will be his/her response? [Pause.] What will you say in reaction to the response? [Pause.] Now tie to a development plan. Imagine the two of you brainstorming goals for the coming year. What will you say to encourage further career development by the employee? [Pause.] What will be the response? [Pause.] How will you handle the response? [Pause.] Imagine that you are collaborating in a positive way to build better performance for the employee.

Be prepared for any unplanned events. Do you see the employee becoming angry? [Pause.] How will you handle that? [Pause.] Do you see the employee crying? [Pause.] What will you do ? [Pause.] Do you see the employee being reluctant to talk? [Pause.] What will you do if this happens?

Now close the interview on a positive note. See the employee's face. What will you say to encourage the employee? [Pause.] What will the employee say? [Pause.]

Now see the employee leaving the room. [Pause.] How do you feel? [Pause.] How do you think the employee feels? Was it a good interview? Why or why not? What can you do or say to make it better? [Pause.] What other problems do you think might come up in the interview? Will you be interrupted by phone calls or office walk-ins? Will you have enough time for the interview? Will you be prepared with facts and documentation?

You may wish to make a few notes on your observations.

The script you develop should be tested by reading aloud to one or two people before using it in the session. This will help to establish clarity, intended meaning, and length of time. Script variations could also be developed and tested if necessary.

Step 4: Conduct the Guided Imagery Session

A. *Tonesetting and Centering*: Now that you have your script and have tested it, you are ready to conduct the session. Here are the steps you will go through in conducting the session [read this]:

> Today, we are going to discuss ways to improve our performance appraisal interviews. As most of you know, we are trying to make these more meaningful communication sessions for both boss and subordinate. We will be using a technique called guided imagery as part of this session. Guided imagery requires you to use your imagination to visualize yourself doing something. Most of us use our imagination everyday, but few of us use it in a constructive way. You'll have that opportunity today.
>
> Don't worry. I won't hypnotize you. This is not some Far Eastern religion. This technique is used everyday in sports coaching, counseling, medicine, and education. It's fun and enjoyable.

B. *Self-Induced Relaxation*: Here the relaxation portion of the script is read.

C. *Guided Imagery Script Presentation*: Here the previous performance appraisal interview script is read.

D. *Free Imagery Practice*: Here the subordinates elaborate on the script experience. A short cue: "Now review to yourself how you'll handle this performance appraisal" will help trainees build personally related scenarios. They might jot down notes. You might make additional prompts such as: "Imagine a successful interview." Imagine one that goes haywire." "Think about what this interview process means to you, the employee and your organization."

E. *Retrieval and Recentering*: Here you bring trainees back to the present and to full wakeful attention.

> Okay, now that you have experienced the imagery portion of this session, we are ready to move on.

(Note: a brief discussion of the imagery experience is appropriate in this step to help trainees process what they have experienced.)

F. *Presentation of Training Materials*: Here the training materials on performance appraisal interviewing are presented and discussed. These should include at a minimum the following:

1. the objectives of the interview;
2. why it is important;
3. how it should be conducted;
4. common errors made;
5. how to make it a true communication session.

This portion of the program can contain some role-play experiences, if desired.

G. *Imagery Practice*: Now that the participants have heard the training materials on conducting performance appraisal interviews, another imagery experience is appropriate. This experience will differ from the previous one in that it will stress the concepts and issues covered during the presentation of the training materials. Here is an *example script*:

> Relax. [Go through relaxation exercise.] Form a picture in your mind of a subordinate of average performance. You may use the same one as before if you want. See the subordinate and yourself in your office about ready to conduct the performance appraisal interview. How will you both be seated to maximize communication? [Pause.] What will you say to relax the subordinate? [Pause.] What questions will you ask to get the subordinate to talk about his or her performance? [Pause.] What points do you wish to make? [Pause.] What will you say to make these points? [Long pause.] What will be the likely

employee response? [Pause.] What could the employee do that would really surprise you? [Pause.] What will you do in response if this happens? [Pause.]

How will your desk table look during the interview? [Pause.] How will you handle a telephone or walk-in interruption? [Pause]

What will you say to tie the performance to a development plan? [Pause.] How will you close the interview on a positive note? [Pause.] This script emphasizes questions to get the participants to recall and use material covered in the knowledge presentation session.

H. *Processing and Debriefing*: Here, much group discussion will take place. Participants should be asked at least the following questions with sufficient time for discussion of each allowed:

1. What was your reaction to both the first and second imagery experiences?
2. What was your reaction to the content/knowledge presentation?
3. What are the key points that you learned today?
4. What suggestions do you have for future training in performance appraisal?
5. Do you see other areas of management performance where the imagery experience could work?
6. How can you successfully transfer what you learned today to your job?
7. What is your overall evaluation of this total training experience? This step concludes the imagery session. We continue with the remaining steps.

Step 5: Follow-up Practice

Participants should be encouraged to practice imagery on their own prior to meeting with each subordinate for the performance appraisal interview. Since each subordinate is an individual, the dialogues will be different for each; as with other performance skills, the more practice that is given to the skill, the quicker and more powerful the skill acquisitions are gained for each. Reading the scripts used in the training session for each different employee will help them to use the concepts of effective interviewing and to be prepared for the interview better. This practice should involve the development of vast case scenarios and what the manager will do to handle each.

ACHIEVING CREDIBILITY FOR THE IMAGERY PROCESS

Implementing imagery in an organization will require that you explain and sell the process to both superiors and subordinates. As we point out in this chapter and elsewhere in this book, imagery is commonly misunderstood. Probably the biggest misunderstanding, and one that is seen as the most damning, is that it is an undisciplined process. This is not so; using imagery properly is simply not dreaming. It requires discipline and practice. A person must concentrate and project him- or herself into an imagined scene or situation. This requires total concentration. While imagery utilizes the right brain function, it combines this side with the analytical-logical left side. An imagery experience is logical as well as intuitive. This requires discipline.

Others may object to imagery simply on the basis of efficacy: does it work? Applications in such diverse fields as counseling, medicine, sports, and education show it does work. It is a very powerful tool. However, people do vary in their ability to use imagery. Some individuals have a high imagery quotient and easily go through an imagery experience. Others have a more difficult time getting into the experience. Practice can help all people, especially those who have trouble using the imagery technique.

Some may believe imagery substitutes for other forms of learning such as physical practice; it does not. Rather, it can provide a mental template for physical practice. It supplements other forms of learning, it does not replace them. For example, in many situations, combining imagery with role-playing is an excellent technique.

There will be some joking and ridicule when you first introduce the concept. You may even be called a flower child. Accept this good-naturedly. Be sure to point out how widely used imagery is in sports, counseling, and medicine. Point out that IBM and General Electric use an art teacher, Betty Edwards, to help managers draw on the right side of the brain. As various managerial groups use imagery in your organization and become accustomed to it, they will see how powerful a technique it is and how well it can work when properly applied. They will tell others, and word will spread about the effectiveness of the approach.

Finally, pay very close attention to script development. Good scripts are essential to effective imagery. We have many good scripts in this book, which you are free to use, but do not be afraid to develop your own scripts using the guidelines we suggest, which are in the appendix at the end of this chapter. Other scripts appear in the sources cited in the bibliography.

We're now ready to look at specific areas of management where imagery can be applied. The first area we examine is strategic planning. In the next chapter we see how imagery can improve a manager's ability to understand and forecast the outside environment as well as visualize strategic goals and ways of reaching them.

APPENDIX: CREATING EFFECTIVE IMAGERY SCRIPTS

To build effective scripts, it is important to be thoughtful and creative during script development. Care must be taken to write and present scripts that are provocative, yet inoffensive to trainees or program participants. This section identifies basic guides for creating and presenting scripts.

WRITING SCRIPTS AND SCENARIOS

To build good imaginal scripts and scenarios, you must project yourself into the script or scenario you wish to build. The more vividly you can use and manipulate your own mental imagery, the better scripts you'll create. Hence, it is critical that you just sit back and envision what you wish to accomplish through imagery and transmit through your training. Rather than starting your efforts on paper, let your mind wander around the topic and build up your imaginal reservoir of ideas. Then take time to jot down your ideas. Finally, build your script as you would any good piece of writing. Here are specific ways to improve your scripts.

1. *Use a multimodel approach.* Imagery is active and can be activated in all the primary sensory categories. Use visual, auditory, kinesthetic, and tactile imagery in your scripts and scenarios to build the power and vividness of the experience. The more complex the imaginal environment you build, the more likelihood trainees will involve themselves in the script depictions and gain the learnings you wish them to achieve.

2. *Use gender-free terms.* It is necessary to make your scripts free of gender bias or double entendres that can distract trainees into tangible imagery tracts. Further, use simple language that requires minimal cognitive processing while generating the intended meaning. Keep your sentences and prompts short and direct.

3. *Be sensitive to trainees' values.* One way to render a script useless is to offend the sensibilities of your trainees. It is preferable to focus on objective statements related to training goals than to add opinions, humor, or your own perspectives to a script. If you turn someone off, they will react to or resist your scripting efforts and will be skeptical of future imaginal applications.

4. *Use of reflective pauses.* Your scripts and scenarios should be liberally dosed with brief pauses that give trainees time to envision the imaginal depictions and prompts you offer. Pauses of five to fifteen seconds have worked well within our training programs. While scripts are designed to guide trainees' imagery, there must be room for the individual to personalize his/her experience of the script.

5. *Tighten the focus.* Your scripts should clearly depict the skills, actions, and consequences of action that a trainee must integrate. Use of redundancy and repetition helps strengthen covert rehearsal of desired outcomes. Especially in skill-specific training, it is important to graphically denote what a trainee should and shouldn't do within a skill area. Reduce ambiguous cues and go for clarity in your prompts.

6. *Use real world environments.* Your scripts should focus on the real-world environment of work that your trainees experience. It is difficult for all of us

to imagine unfamiliar environments. Therefore, you should craft your scripts to replicate the organizational environment your trainees regularly experience. If you aren't familiar with this environment, do homework so that scripted cues and prompts project trainees into their work. This effort increases the immediate relevance of the learning and promotes greater transfer of training to work environments.

7. *Reinforce mental note-taking.* Within your script protocol, develop and reinforce mental note-taking. This cues trainees to activate memory structures for integration of ideas and for recall of these ideas after imaginal sessions.

PRESENTING YOUR SCRIPTS

Here are several guidelines that will help you present your scripts so they have the greatest impact.

1. *Practice your scripts beforehand.* Take considerable time to practice your script presentation before training. You must be fluent in your presentation and prior practice definitely enhances fluency. You may wish to tape record yourself presenting the script. Listen to the tape to determine where rough spots can be improved. Over time script presentation will become more natural and you can begin using more extemporaneous approaches.

2. *Pace yourself.* Present your script evenly and articulately. Don't hurry or muddle through. Remember that it takes some time for trainees to process a suggestive prompt and bring it to mind. Rushing through a script will convolute or backlog trainees' images and undermine success. If you hurry with a script, you have too much information in the script. Re-edit or break it into several shorter scripts.

3. *Script timeframes.* Invariably, we have found that scripts that run twenty minutes or longer lose their effectiveness. Remember, pairing relaxation and imagery practice induces quietude in trainees. Scripts that are too lengthy will put participants to sleep as will any lengthy presentation. We suggest an ideal presentation with an experienced group should include four minutes of relaxation induction and twelve minutes of imaginal scripting. Again, if you can't accommodate that timeframe you probably are writing busy scripts that need reduction and more direct articulation.

4. *The physical environment.* All imaginal exercises should be presented in an area free from noise, distraction, or physical discomfort. Outside distractions (rumbling trucks, muffled conversations, whirring machines) will inevitably reduce attentiveness to the script and will therefore decrease learning or skill acquisition. A poor physical environment (uncomfortable seats, extreme temperatures, or crowding) will also restrict trainee readiness for learning. These considerations are particularly important with groups that have little previous imaginal experience. If a poor training environment combines with natural trainee reluctance to do imaginal work, you may find that the groups' resistance to imaginal applications is increased and generalized to all other imaginal episodes. Refrains of "I knew that wouldn't work" or "what a waste

of time" indicate poor planning for imaginal scripts or presentation environments.

5. *Always use "you."* In both scripting and presentation, you should always use
   the pronoun, you, or an indefinite open statement, such as "imagine the
   layout at work." Few of us can imagine "we" or "they" as consistently as
   we can imagine ourselves in a given environment. Feedback from our trainees
   indicates that the use of "we" or "they" is confusing because people never
   know exactly who should be included or excluded from the designation. Use
   of "you" automatically prompts an individual to self-reference and to manipulate images of self-in-situation.

6. *Be conversational.* Scripts and scenarios can be quite powerful when well
   crafted. However, restrict inclinations to be either pedantic or dramatic in
   your presentation style. This will distract trainees' attention from the meaning
   of the script to your style and that will undermine effectiveness. Its best to
   present the script in a normal, conversational manner. Mystical pedant or
   vacilating sermonic tones break the continuity of an otherwise objective learning session.

7. *Play some music.* In a number of training contexts, we have found that gentle,
   background music facilitates relaxation and withdrawal of attention from
   outside distraction. Music is processed in the sight-brain, which is also the
   primary seat of imaginal experience. While it would seem that music could
   distract from attention, debriefings with many trainees indicate that they
   either lost awareness of the music during script presentation or didn't realize
   that music was being played. Obviously, you'll want to select classical themes
   that don't override the verbal script presentation.

Writing and presenting scripts becomes increasingly easier over time.
When we started our work five years ago, we were nervous and hesitant
in our scripting. Most of these guidelines have arisen from our own
mistakes in training environments. Today, we feel confident in taking
almost any topic and building scripting protocols for training purposes.
While some people will continue to resist the use of their rich, imaginal
resources, we feel that properly crafted scripts are powerful tools for
employee development and organizational effectiveness.

5

HOW IMAGERY CAN IMPROVE STRATEGIC PLANNING

Remember the last time you made plans for your vacation? You may have decided to go to the mountains or to the beach. You probably wondered what the climate and water conditions might be like at the beach. Would it be crowded this time of year or would it be quiet and peaceful? If you went to the mountains, would you be able to find a good campsite? Would the insects be as bad as they had been on prior trips? How should you pack for the weather conditions? Would it be hot or cold? Rain or shine? Finally you may have said in frustration "If only I had a crystal ball to gaze into the future so that I could make the right decision!"

We are not suggesting that utilizing the mind's eye is going to provide a view of the future that will allow the right decisions to be made time and time again. What we are suggesting is that imagery helps to combine past experiences with best current expectations in order to prepare better plans. Carefully thought-out plans developed by envisioning many different scenarios of what might happen are effective in adequately preparing for future events. The old adage of haste makes waste is particularly true when it comes to preparing plans for the future.

Imagery does not substitute for logical analysis based on facts when planning. In fact, proper use of imagery relies on a foundation of knowledge and skill. Imagery does not replace logic; it supplements it. Proper use of imagery also requires discipline and practice.

As we have all experienced all too often, finding the time to adequately plan is a real task in and of itself. But making the time to plan now and using the benefits from guided imagery will provide more time in the future. The same is true for strategic planning. More time invested now in planning will pay dividends in the future via better managerial performance. Our purpose in this chapter is to demonstrate how guided imagery techniques can be used to improve strategic planning in your organization.

WHAT IS STRATEGIC PLANNING?

Earlier we defined what guided imagery is and how it works. Now let's discuss strategic planning and how it works. To begin with, the ultimate criterion of an effective organization is survival. In order to survive, an organization must adequately acquire information about its environment and form and adapt its strategies accordingly. This process of acquiring and analyzing information about the outside environment to facilitate policy making is called strategic planning. It is a process that deals with uncertainty by creating futuristic scenes, i.e., scenarios, of the way that our political, economic, technological, and social systems will appear in the years to come.

The term strategy was employed in the Old Testament having a military and often political connotation. This is not at all surprising when one considers that the early Greek civilizations commonly used terms such as "strategus" meaning to "plan the destruction of one's enemies through the effective utilization of resources" and "strategos" meaning "the art of the general." This often macho connotation ensued through subsequent generations.

Shortly after World War II, the use of strategy became a very common term in the business language. This was due mostly to its use in business gaming by the German mathematicians John Von Neumann and Oskar Morgenstern. As the business world became more dynamic and competitive, the use of the term strategy became more popular. But by now it had lost much of its military connotation and had been sublimated to mean the skillful process by which organizations respond to the environment in the pursuit of long-term goals.

The term "planning," however, does not have near so romantic a history. Planning has been defined as the charting of courses to obtain some future goal. For business applications, we define planning as the process of setting objectives, assessing the future, and developing courses of action to accomplish these objectives.

Buidling upon all of the above, we define strategic planning as a process of determining what an organization's identity is now and three to five years in the future, envisioning what the environment will prob-

Figure 5-1
Strategic Planning Model

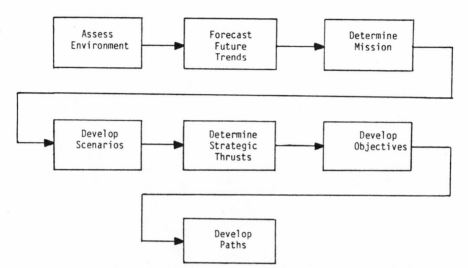

ably look like then, and setting the goals that will have to be achieved by then in order to survive and prosper.

To make our concept of strategic planning more viable, we use the strategic planning model that appears in Figure 5–1. The major elements of this model that have particular application to imagery are the development of trends in the organization's external environment, the combination of these trends into scenarios, and the setting of goals to be accomplished in these scenarios. Let's look at each of these major elements beginning with the trends in the external environment.

VISUALIZING THE ENVIRONMENT

As we mentioned earlier, an organization must adequately acquire information about its environment and form and adapt its strategies accordingly if it is to survive and prosper. An organization out of touch with its environment would soon use up all of its resources, rely on dated information for decision making, and lose contact with consumer wants and needs. Consequently, in the long run such an organization would eventually die.

As an example of this we can reflect upon this country's once powerful passenger railroad industry. At one time our railroad industry was king and was marveled by the rest of the young and industrializing nations. But this proud industry failed to keep in touch with its environment. It refused to accept the fact that the market place was demanding faster, cleaner, more convenient transportation and kept right on "railroading."

Figure 5-2
Organizational Environments

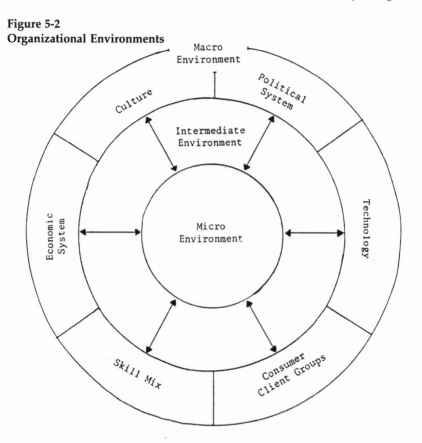

Source: B. J. Hodge and W. P. Anthony, *Organization Theory*, 2nd ed. (Boston: Allyn and Bacon, Inc.), 1984.

Consequently, railway passenger service lost out to the airplane and the automobile in the United States (this has not happened in Japan and Western Europe where high speed, convenient railway service is provided). Today, this industry is only a shadow of what it used to be in the United States. States like Florida, for example, which are looking toward efficient high-speed rail systems to alleviate congestion problems, are seeking technological assistance from abroad rather than from our own domestic industry.

When we envision the environment, it is helpful if we arrange it in some schema in order to make it more manageable. We use the schema as shown in Figure 5–2. This schema divides the external environment into six subcompacts: culture, political/legal system, technology, consumer/client groups, skill mix, and economic system. A brief discussion of each of these schema is presented next.

Culture

Over time every society develops its own culture. This culture, which consists of societal values, norms, and accepted behavior patterns, determines to a large extent how the members of society will interact with one another. Organizations must operate on a certain set of assumptions about how society will behave. Using the mind's eye to imagine what changes will impact culture becomes a very important aspect of strategic planning.

Political/Legal System

The government and political processes, which make up the political/legal system, affect virtually every aspect of an organization's activity by providing the laws and regulations that govern these activities. Managers need to be familiar with applicable laws because most of their operations are affected by legal considerations. In addition, the major philosophies of our two major political parties will impact the external environment affecting the way we do business.

Technology

The techniques and science of production and distribution comprise the technology force existing in the external environment. To be able to compete successfully, organizations must have access to modern technology. It is simply not feasible for an organization to compete unless an adequate level of technology is available to it, and the organization adjusts to and employs technological innovations. The Xerox Corporation announced a few years ago that it envisioned a time in the relatively near future when technological advances in electronic mail would greatly reduce the need for multiple copies. Because of this, they intended to enter the electronic communications market with their "Ethernet" system. This type of example of managerial behavior demonstrates the obligation of today's management to maintain a spirit of creativity and ingenuity among its members, so that continued progress on the technological front can be made.

Consumer/Client Groups

Organizations process various resources (input) into some goods and services (output). In order to survive over the long term, they must be successful in their efforts at satisfying the wants and needs of their consumer/client group(s). The prudent manager will insist on adequate information about potential consumer tastes and desires prior to opening a business or introducing a new product, or eliminating an old one, for that matter. Only time will tell the prudency of the change in the Coca-Cola formula. Although the world will probably never know for sure, it would be interesting to know what type of visions the company's management had before making this change in an American institution. A classic example of not properly envisioning the needs of its consumer client groups is that of our automobile industry just a few short years ago. Detroit saw, or wanted to see, nothing but demand for large size passenger cars. This apparent lack of vision resulted, in part, to a dramatic loss in market share to foreign competition during a period of rapid increases in energy prices. Therefore, it is imperative that today's management try to explore the future needs of their consumer client groups, no matter how radical these needs may seem at the time.

Skill Mix

Another facet of the external environment that deserves attention is the skill mix that is available to the organization and the changing composition of this skill mix. Today, labor is more female, more educated, and primarily service-oriented. Because of these changes, radical notions that were out of the question years ago such as paternity leaves, flextime, job-sharing, paid child care, and cafeteria-style benefit programs are now in vogue. The use of quality circles and the concept of comparable worth add challenge to the management of the work force.

The Economic System

Organizations exist within some form of economic system that exerts a tremendous influence on how they behave. One major influence is the "invisible hand," the law of supply and demand. This is of course influenced by interest rates, among other factors. Who would have ever imagined a 21 percent prime rate under the Carter administration? Inflation and real Gross National Product, as well as productivity increases and import/export balances, are items to be reckoned with. Thus, because of the important role the economy plays in the daily life of their organizations, managers have an obligation to familiarize themselves both with how it operates and affects their organization specifically.

Taken together, culture, political systems, the economic system, technology, skill mixes, and consumer/client groups make up an organization's external environment. It impacts the organization by serving as a source of input and a receiver of output. It is not static, to say the least, but is quite dynamic and very volatile. In order for your organization to survive and prosper you must stay in tune with the development of trends in your external environment. Your organization must insist that its managers engage in strategic planning that generates the creativity and imagination necessary to cope with these trends. How are these trends incorporated into future scenarios for your organization? Let's look at how imagery can help with scenario building.

BUILDING SCENARIOS

Organizational scenarios are written narratives that attempt to describe future hypothetical situations that might develop in the organization's external environment. Anticipation of these contingent future possibilities is essential to the survival of organizations. Characteristics of good scenarios are:

1. identification of key variables existing in the economic, social, political, cultural, skill mix, or technological environments;
2. development of a plausible chain of events; future events are logically linked to past events;
3. some elements of surprise; not merely a pure extrapolation of the past;
4. use of a timeframe not fewer than three years and not greater than five years;
5. understood by those who are to develop means to cope with them.

In developing good scenarios we should incorporate the above concepts. First of all, the heart of any scenario is to identify the key variables involved. We have discussed the importance of the external environment on the strategic planning process, but we need to elaborate this a little more. No matter which of the six major components of the external environment you are working with, you must identify key variables and then develop the "what if and so what" for each sector. For example, if the process begins with the economic environment and the key variable selected is the prime interest rate, decisions must be made about what will result from possible changes in the prime rate and what impact these changes will have upon your organization. It is not enough to ascertain just certain changes in key variables; all of the subsequent ramifications and their impact upon your business must also be determined.

The future scenario should be plausible in that there is some logical sequence of events leading to these future states. While we encourage creativity and imagination, we must still be practical about these futures. While the visitation of some aliens from a faraway planet or a complete nuclear holocaust could be a consideration, how realistic could it be to consider such events as a future scenario for the plan?

While there is considerable difference of opinion on a timeframe for scenarios, we recommend three to five years, although this could vary by type of industry. The goods and services that will be provided for the next couple of years have already been determined by existing orders for capital goods; there is little that can be done at the present to alter this process. Besides, any major product innovation developed would probably take a couple of years to reach the market place. Given the rapid changes taking place in technology, most considerations beyond five years would likely be highly speculative. However, there are groups, such as General Electric's long-range planning group, that do deal with forecasts as far as ten to twenty years in the future. So even though we recommend a three- to five-year planning horizon, it may suit your organization's needs to plan for a longer period.

Even though scenarios should be plausible, this is not to imply that they could not contain some element of surprise. For example these questions need to be addressed: Could our product be obsolete in five years? Could our production technology be completely outdated? Should we explore alternative products? Remember, managers at Xerox believe that paper copies may eventually be replaced with electronic mail.

And, finally, scenarios for planning purposes should be understandable by the people in your organization who will work with them. The relationships should be clear and the impact well-defined. Remember that these scenarios represent the premises upon which the future planning for your organization will be based, so they need to be communicated well.

Examples of alternative scenarios that meet the above criteria could be:

Scenario 1: The return of a Republican administration to the White House in 1992 will result in a continuation of the status quo. Inflation will continue at a modest level with real Gross National Product growing at a slow but steady pace. Unemployment will continue at existing levels.

Scenario 2: An unchecked national debt will push the economy into a major depression. High interest rates and a large import deficit will suppress domestic production. Increasing unemployment will place more pressure on government for greater social program expenditures.

Scenario 3: A major military action in the Mideast will drastically reduce oil availability. Energy prices rise astronomically pushing inflation to record high levels. Fixed-income recipients demand government relief from soaring energy costs, while more energy-efficient imported automobiles dominate car sales.

Scenario 4: High technology advances contribute to a strong, growing Gross National Product. Unemployment is virtually non-existent, affording lower government deficits. Low interest rates are allowing for a major reinvestment in capital equipment in the domestic economy.

CRYSTALLIZING THE PATH

Let's look at how we can crystallize the path from the present into the future through the utilization of guided imagery. Using what we have examined in our discussion on the development of viable scenarios and goals, we can apply imagery techniques to design clear paths and reach goals.

Take the relaxation techniques that we discussed earlier in the book. It is important to relax as completely as possible when using imagery. If you or those you work with are a little uncomfortable at first, then practice relaxation. In moments of reverie, ideas and answers to your problems will often pop into your head almost like magic. To truly realize all the benefits of imagery, people have to take a few moments to snuff out daily fires that arise from their minds. Encourage people to relax by doing what usually works for them; it may be going to a quiet room, taking a long peaceful walk, jogging, taking a long bath, or listening to classical music. In a guided imagery session, it involves reading a relaxing script such as those found throughout this book.

When the relaxation technique has been mastered, people can let their mind's eye see things that can help improve the planning process. To assist you, we have prepared the forthcoming script on scenario building, which can either be read aloud during an imagery session or serve as an example to guide your own personal imagery experiences. We suggest the following sequence to really activate your imagery experience. First read the script's passages very slowly, allowing your mind to daydream and to wander. Second, close your eyes and carefully and slowly try to remember the script in sequence. Again, do not try to be exact and concentrate too hard. Allow plenty of time for daydreaming and for trying to actually picture in your mind what the script suggests. Finally, have someone else read the script to you while you recline and reflect upon the passages. Remember that while the individual is reading slowly, your mind can process information at a much greater pace, thereby allowing it a vast amount of time to drift and to evoke images of what you hear.

Another final thought on the imagery process: practice makes perfect. Repeat these exercises over and over again and begin to notice how much clearer your images become. As you place yourself in the scenes, notice what you are wearing. Look around and see what pictures may be hanging on the walls. Note how clear you can see the faces of the other people in the scene with you. As you practice your imagery technique, you will be amazed as to what you see. For a lot of reasons, most of us have not been adequately trained to fully utilize the full capacity of our imagination, and, in learning to do so, it will seem new to us. As you read the script to others, encourage them to relax and practice it in the future.

What follows is the script for scenario building.

Guided Imagery Script for Scenario Building

Imagine yourself resting against a large oak tree beside a large beautiful meadow. The sky above is a brilliant blue with small marshmallow clouds lazily gliding their way along. The meadow has a very sweet fragrance and in the distance you hear the gentle sound of small children as they play. Ever so slowly, you become a part of nature very much at peace with yourself. [Pause.]

At this time I want you to keep your attention on the sound of my voice and on what I say. We are going to experience a guided imagery script that will enhance your ability to create better plans in your job. [Pause.]

I am going to give you suggestions and instructions. As much as possible, visualize what you hear in a clear, vivid, and detailed way. Try to put yourself within the scene that is described as completely as you are able. [Pause.]

Imagine yourself in the future. You are the general manager of a very successful automobile company. [Pause.]

You are in a planning meeting with your staff. Things have been good for your company for the past several years and are expected to remain good for at least the next few years. However, you know you cannot just relax and rest on your past accomplishments. In order to begin preparing plans for your firm, you and your staff must first determine what the future might have in store for your company. [Pause.]

Your sales manager says he sees a change in your customers. They will be demanding different colors. The products must be more efficient, they must last longer, and use less energy. He also sees more safety requirements demanded by the government. You ask him about foreign competition. Will there be products that will make yours obsolete? [Pause.]

Your manager of manufacturing sees a whole new technology in the way your firm will make the products—higher speeds, fewer workers, and a much more educated work force with much more sophisticated demands. [Pause.]

Personnel informs you that employees want to work to an older age, and she says there are going to be increasing demands for more company paid education, day care, and protection from layoff. [Pause.]

The manager of finance has great concerns about the economy. He sees higher interest rates, more government control, local increases in community taxes. All will affect both your firm's borrowing power and the borrowing power of your customers. Stockholders will demand greater returns. [Pause.]

Your quality manager sees greater quality requirements in your products and greater participation in your employee quality circles. Pollution controls will be much tighter. [Pause.]

You and your staff all discuss major changes in foreign countries, major government changes, society changes, and even the weather. As your meeting is about to adjourn, you ponder the opportunities and problems the future has in store for you. You also reflect upon how important it is to anticipate and prepare for the future if your business is to survive and to grow. [Pause.]

At the conclusion of the meeting you write down a list of the major opportunities and challenges (threats) that appear to surface. What would be on your list?

This is just an example of what a guided imagery script to elicit an environmental scan for strategic planning could look like. Let's look at how you can design scripts for your own scenarios.

As always, the first thing you do is relax. Sit back, put your feet up, and let your mind journey to some peaceful setting, be it a lake, a meadow, or perhaps the seashore. Whatever works for you is fine. Next, let your mind see a key variable. Let's use the prime interest rate as an example. Visualize television reports of the prime rate coming down. See more people buying houses and cars. You see the unemployment rate coming down. Experience the exciting feeling of good times all around. Notice that certain feeling within you and how exhilarated you feel. Now, experience what this particular occurrence could mean to your business. You can now get that new loan to expand your production facilities. Your orders are up as people are buying more. Now where do you take your business? Do you begin to expand your sales force as you have always dreamed? Is this the time to think of adding to your product line? How about that notion of making your own TV commercial? What impact does all of this success have on your family?

After you have experienced your script in your mind, continue to relax for a few moments in order to allow yourself to reflect on your imagery experience. In addition, you will find your imagery experiences becoming a very relaxed event, so a few moments to readjust to the world is a good idea. The next time, develop for yourself a scenario that sees the prime rate going up, instead of down in order that you will be able to entertain how to best deal with this trend. And then later on use different key variables and see how they impact your business.

As you gain confidence in your imagery ability, writing your own scripts and scripts for others will become very easy and very rewarding. Just remember that there is more than ample evidence existing that tells us the attributes of creativity and imagination can be enhanced through training and practice. Remember a good script is about a half a page long, very vivid, related to your group's experience, allows for relaxation, and uses ambiguous words. Now let's see how imagery can be used to help us set better goals.

Seeing Clear Goals

Organization goals are those specific desired objectives to be achieved in a specific timeframe. Obtainment of these goals is essential to the survival of organizations. Good goals characteristically are:

1. concrete and specific, with the ability to lead and motivate;
2. attainable, requiring a little aggressiveness, imagination, and hard work;
3. understood by those who are to develop means to achieve them;
4. conforming to ethical and social codes accepted by society as well as to basic corporate policy;
5. mutually supportive to all other goals.

In developing good goals it is imperative that we observe these characteristics. Goals that are concrete and specific tend to motivate better because people know exactly what is expected of them. How many more units must I sell in order to improve sales? How many more units should be produced in order to enhance productivity? People like to know exactly what is expected of them.

Goals must be attainable. Although a little stretch is desirable to motivate individuals to higher levels of performance, the achievement of the goals is necessary for self-esteem. If the goals are set too high, then frustration will be experienced and individuals will just quit trying to accomplish the impossible.

Since overall goal-setting is normally a function of upper management, the accomplishment of these goals is delegated downward to the rank and file. Care must be exercised to ensure that the wording of the goals is understood by those involved in their achievement and that these people see how they will individually benefit if the goal is achieved. The relationship of achieving these goals to the overall betterment of the entire organization should also be pointed out.

While one would think that it goes without saying that goals should conform to ethical and social codes accepted by society, it is necessary to reflect upon this aspect of goal-setting. In the increasing competitive business environment in which organizations must carry out their activities, it is always a temptation to short-cut affirmative action plans, OSHA requirements, pollution standards, and so on. Our feeling is that the ends do not justify the means. Setting goals that are socially acceptable is just good business practice.

Finally, goals must be mutually supportive. Goal-setting is like hitching horses up to a wagon. To get anywhere, the horses must all be pulling in the same direction. It is of little use to set a goal to increase sales by 20 percent and then, to reduce cost, set another to cut your sales force by 30 percent. Essential to strategic planning is a goal system whereby the entire organization works together in the same direction to achieve company goals. Examples of goals that would meet this criterion could be:

1. to attain a 10 percent return on sales;
2. to maintain a 30 percent share of the total market;
3. to have at least two suppliers for all major raw materials;
4. to introduce one new product a year;
5. to keep absenteeism below 5 percent.

What follows is a script for goal-setting, from a general manager's perspective.

Guided Imagery Script for Goal-Setting: General Manager

Imagine yourself lying on the beach. You feel the sun shining on your body. A cool breeze is gently blowing all of your cares away. The sound of the surf lapping against the sand lulls you into a deep, relaxed state. As you stretch out you haven't a care in the world. [Pause.]

Now you are going to receive suggestions and instructions. As much as possible, visualize what you hear in a clear, vivid, and detailed way. Try to put yourself within the scene that is described as completely as you are able. [Pause.]

Imagine yourself in the future. You are the general manager of a very successful business. [Pause.]

You are in a staff meeting with your managers discussing next year's objectives for your firm. [Pause.]

Your sales manager tells you that although sales are good, there is a need to add some additional product lines if you are to expand market share. In addition, something must be done to speed up deliveries. [Pause.]

You are pleased to hear that the new high speed equipment is working well, offering a good productivity gain, but your manager of manufacturing is concerned about some labor problems that might arise because of it. [Pause.]

Zero defects has always been your firm's goal, but your manager of quality control has some reservations about the quality of the raw materials that have been received lately. You ask if maybe a change in vendor is necessary or if there are substitute materials that your firm could use. [Pause.]

There have been large improvements in lost time accidents says the personnel manager, however, she informs you that absenteeism is becoming a problem. There is general discussion on what levels these items are acceptable for good business practices. [Pause.]

Your manager of finance tells you that earnings are up over budget, funds flow are better than expected, and that the return on assets is at a new all-time-high level. There is some concern about the levels of inventory and accounts receivable, particularly when interest rates seem so volatile. You then lead a discussion on increasing the dividend payment. [Pause.]

As you conclude this initial meeting, you thank everyone for all of the hard work in achieving last year's goals. You encourage them to work with you in setting new goals for next year in order to keep your company strong and growing. You then jot down a list of key goals for review at the next planning meeeting, and you ask others to do the same. [Pause.]

The above script on goal-setting was quite general by design. It is intended to facilitate wide-reaching images that allow individuals to see the big picture of the firm. Later on managers might want to concentrate on more specific parts of the organization in greater detail. To do this requires scripts that involve individual departments and that concentrate on the goals that have been set for each department.

For example, let's use the financial department. The general manager would see himself in a meeting with your comptroller. He would discuss all of the important financial ratios and what they mean to the firm. He would then visualize what must be done in terms of financial performance to meet the long-range growth goals of your firm. With the comptroller's help, he would see himself setting the necessary financial goals to realize this growth potential. He would actually see before his eyes the financial statements and how they would look when these new goals were accomplished.

Next time the general manager would use another department. He would concentrate more on specifics and see as much detail as possible in terms of faces and reports and so on. The first step in attaining good goals is to set good goals. And this begins with visualizing them clearly.

Let's now discuss how to anticipate and remove obstacles that prevent us from planning effectively.

ANTICIPATING AND REMOVING PLANNING BARRIERS

There are factors that can hinder the effective implementation of strategic planning. These factors need to be explicitly recognized at the outset if the planning process is to lead to final implementation. Let's discuss some of these factors.

1. No time to plan: Participants are so caught up in their routine that they believe they do not have any time to do planning.
2. Too many crises and changing priorities: Here people feel that there is no sense in planning, since priorities change so quickly that the plan soon becomes meaningless.
3. Information overload: Since strategic planning requires a great deal of information, people feel overwhelmed.
4. Too much paperwork: This is closely related to the above. People feel that all they do on their job is to fill out strategic planning forms.
5. Too much politics: Planning is a rational and logical process and the operation is believed to be too political for it to work. This complaint is common in government organizations, but one also hears it in some large companies.

Not only can the utilization of guided imagery enhance the level of creativity and imagination in strategic planning, but it can also be used to anticipate and remove these barriers to effective planning. Let us see how.

Using the above as examples of barriers, guided imagery scripts can be written that will enable your organization to deal with them better. Use these scripts to determine what information is absolutely necessary and to find ways to employ the computer to help manage information. Ask yourself what can be done to keep forms to an absolute minimum, and put into your script cues to imagine better ways to use the computer to store and report planning information. Envision ways to recognize the politics, not ignore them, and build them into your planning scripts. Design scripts that incorporate your plans into your decision making process. Further, imagine how you can tie your plans to your management performance appraisal process and to evaluation and control. Let's look at some examples on how to do this.

Consider that big job that you must complete in the next couple of months. Assume that you have already experienced considerable concern wondering if you will be able to finish it on time. Using the imagery techniques that we have been discussing will enable you to reduce your anxiety level and probably allow you to complete this task ahead of schedule. First of all, stop worrying and relax. Put your feet up on your desk and visualize a clear picture of all that is involved in getting this job done on time. Think of the tasks that must be completed, step by step. What information do you need and from whom? How much of this is already available to you? How much of this job can be done on the computer and how much can be delegated to members of your staff? What parts of this job can be done while you are waiting for the input from others? Now imagine what can go wrong and determine what courses of action will be available to you if this happens. Finally imagine the positive feelings you will have when the job is completed on time.

This image will serve as inspiration and afford you a much more positive mental set.

Now let's consider the common problems of insufficient time to plan and too many changing priorities. These two barriers are not really barriers to effective planning, but are the results of not planning effectively in the first place. As we have mentioned before, the time invested in planning will be returned many times over in fewer problems, fewer crises, and even more time to do a better job of planning the next time around. This is a vicious cycle that we would all like to have. Can you imagine that? You and the managers in your organization can! Put into scripts cues that will allow your imagination to show you how to provide time to prepare plans better.

How could this work? Have your managers visualize their typical work week. In this scenario, ask them to see how much of their time is really gainfully spent in work activity and how much time is really spent doing other things. Ask them to be honest with themselves. None of us likes to think that we waste time at work, but let's examine how we might more efficiently use time. Ask: Do you have a short list of goals to accomplish each day or do you work on what is hot at the time? Do you have a clear vision as to how these daily goals are tied into more long-term goals? Do you spend precious time going through all of that junk mail or do you read only what is truly necessary? What about your open door policy? Walk-ins appreciate it, but it can be quite disruptive. What if you had specific open hours and spent the rest of your day working without interruption? Are you delegating efficiently? Do you spend a lot of time trying to find information? Are you using the telephone efficiently? Are your meetings run efficiently?

By periodically going through this mental exercise you will find yourself working with fewer wasted motions. With this extra time, you will be able to engage in imagery practice enabling yourself to improve your planning and job performance greatly.

FUTURISTICS

As you begin to develop different scripts to enhance strategic planning activity, keep in mind the futuristic orientation of strategic planning. The underlying theme of strategic planning is that it is future oriented behavior concerned with the dynamic and complex relationship of the organization with its environment. In order to cope with the future, we must be able to envision it to design a solution that will enable us to deal with it. Remember:

1. The present is determined by the future, as well as the past;
2. Planning has little relevance to organizations seeking only to project their present performance into the future.

The plans that are prepared should address "radical" and "searching" ideas. When planning becomes a methodical and programmable activity, its usefulness should be questioned. Unfortunately, some organizations continue to develop their strategic plans based on a virtually surprise-free future. Managers in these organizations are unwilling to consider radical departures of future events. In their planning they are making certain safe assumptions and hypotheses about the future. Strategic planning, for many organizations, is a matter of extrapolating the present. However, time and time again, history tells us the blunders that are made by those who thought that in order to predict the future, all that they had to do was to project the status quo.

To be more effective, strategic planning must generate more radical scenarios of future events in the external environment. Strategic planning should be concerned with the betterment of not only the organization in the future, but also the betterment of the entire industry in the future. There is a need to create images of the future. It is simply not enough to talk about the future, but energy must be expended to make clear pictures of how we want that future to be. That is the major thrust for utilizing guided imagery in our strategic planning; it provides us with a means of creating images and clear pictures of how we would like that future to be, in order that we might take action today to better prepare for it.

What follows is a script that you can use to help managers anticipate the future.

Crystal Ball Gazing—Strategic Planning

At this time, close your eyes, take a few deep breaths, and imagine that your tension is flowing down your body, down your legs, and out of your toes. Allow all of your tension to flow from your body. Good, relax. Allow yourself to sink gently into a state of complete relaxation. [Pause.]

You are now relaxed, and quiet, and open to seeing the future.[Pause.]

Now, use your imagination to picture yourself in a quiet room. You see a chair and a table in the center of the room. You approach the chair and sit down. You notice a hazy, crystal ball in the center of the table. You may use this crystal ball to look into the future—take a moment to become comfortable gazing into the foggy mists of the crystal ball in front of you. [Pause.]

Now it is time to use this crystal ball to gaze into the future. For our purposes today, you will use the crystal ball to estimate what the future may be like for the organization in (one year/five years/ ten years). [Pause.]

Look deeply into the ball and imagine the mists parting so you

notice and record future scenes relevant to your organization. Try
to visualize newspaper headlines concerning your company and
your industry in the future. Allow your creative imagination to flow
as you envision the future. Do not edit your thoughts or insights.
Imagine yourself as a witness of the future and identify future factors
that are relevant to your organization. Gaze deeply into your crystal
ball. Let your creative imagination go and imagine relevant newspaper headlines important to your company. [Pause.]

Take about twenty seconds to think about significant outside
events and think about possible headlines. [Pause.]

What do you see?

What are your impressions of:

1. the nature and identity of your competition [Pause.];

2. the general economic conditions such as, inflation, GNP, unemployment, interest rates, and economic growth that influence
your organization [Pause.]

3. the political environment and laws that you must deal with
[Pause.]

4. new technological developments that will affect your company
[Pause.]

5. changing social conditions and demographic factors you will
need to deal with [Pause.]

6. changing customer wants and desires.

Now that we have made a detailed crystal ball excursion into the
future, let us return to the here and now. Recenter your thoughts
and attention to the present. When you are comfortably recentered,
you may wish to take a moment to jot down your experiences, your
insights, and your views of the future. [Pause.]

After each person completes this exercise, then each may read from his
list and a summary list prepared. This list will serve as an excellent basis
for preparing an environmental scan and analysis for planning.

ORGANIZATIONAL AUDIT

From the above it is quite apparent that strategic planning is very
much a futuristic activity. We prepare scenarios that depict the ways
things might be in the future. We set goals that we wish to obtain in
order that we might be able to survive and prosper in the future. However, before all of this can be accomplished, we must know where we
are now in order that we can plan for the future.

This process of finding out where we are now is called an organizational audit or situation audit. The organizational audit consists of analyzing in detail the current status of your organization and its immediate
environment. It identifies the strengths and weaknesses of your firm.

In what areas is your organization formidable and in what areas is it vulnerable?

Next, examine the organization's immediate environment. What opportunities are there that it could capitalize upon? Finally, what threats do you see to your firm's safety and well-being? Do you see possible hazards that could lead to some very rough times?

This organizational audit is designed to allow planners and managers to see where the organization currently is in order to plan better where the organization should be going. Here is a script that will better enable people to perform the organizational audit.

Organizational Audit Tour

Today, you are going to take an imaginary tour of your organization. You will use your creative insights and imagination to place yourself within the physical and psychological structure of your organization.

Once you have accomplished this, you will imaginally tour and assess the conditions of your firm as it now exists in a number of crucial areas. [Pause.]

During your excursions to the various departments and functional realms, let your imagination fill in both obvious and subtle details. Do not constrict or evaluate your impressions. Let your impressions and evaluations flow freely from your powerful, intuitive mind. You will use these rich impressions to paint a picture of your organization. [Pause.]

In each situation, envision the positive factors and the negative factors that influence the performance of and behavior in each unit. Be sure to include all factors that are important to building a complete picture of the unit. Include the positive and negative aspects of *personnel,* of *operations,* of *supervisory style, communication patterns.* In your mind, visualize and elaborate upon the optimal and suboptimal levels of performance in each area. What do you see people doing? Be relaxed as you float through the organization, taking in details you may not have previously noticed. [Pause.]

We shall now begin our tour.

Imagine yourself standing outside your facility. What do you see? What are your impressions? [Pause.]

Next, imagine yourself entering the front reception area of your organization. What do you see? What are your impressions? [Pause.]

Now, walk to your office. What do you see on the way to your office? [Pause.]

Now, walk to the offices around yours. What do you see? [Pause.]

Now, walk to your boss's office. What do you see? [Pause.]

Walk to your mail room; now to your subordinates' offices. What do you see? Try to think about what you see in vivid detail. What are the people doing? What conversations are they having? How are they sitting or standing? [Pause.]

Now that we have completed our tour, take a moment to recollect your insights and impressions. You have completed an imaginal tour of your firm. Trust your impressions. At this time, recenter your thoughts and attention in the present moment. Imagine yourself leaving your visit and returning to this room. Take a moment to recollect and review your impressions. You may wish to jot these impressions down for discussion and future reference. [Pause.]

After the individual lists are compiled, they should be discussed and a master list developed. This list will probably point out areas where additional information is needed, no study groups may be established to obtain this information.

THE LACK OF CREATIVITY AND IMAGINATION IN STRATEGIC PLANNING

Sometimes, managers and planners are promoted into planning positions based upon their skills as operational thinkers. The impact of this situation can reduce the necessary creative and imaginary skills that are so important for these positions. The end result of all of this can be the formulation of strategic plans that are limited in creativity. This dilemma has prompted programs to be developed that are designed to train and educate managers and planners to think creatively and explicitly about the future. To a large extent that is our purpose in writing this text. The utilization of guided imagery techniques will enable organizations to train and educate their managers and planners to think more explicitly about the future and to deal with it in a more creative way.

History has witnessed many incidents of creative greatness that have been attributed to the use of imagery. An image of himself riding on a ray of light enabled Albert Einstein to posit the theory of relativity. Mozart and Tchaikovsky often reflected upon imaginary experiences prior to composing their great works. Samuel Taylor Coleridge wrote "Kubla Khan" from a dream he had experienced. The molecular structure of benzene was discovered by the German chemist Friedrich August Kekule von Stradonitz from imagining a snake swallowing its tail, while Poincaré, a French mathematician, solved complex mathematical problems in moments of visual reverie.

In addition to creativity, philosophers and psychologists have long attributed the importance of imagery to the other cognitive processes of individuals. John Locke, an English philosopher, believed that thought consisted of images derived from perceptions of the outer world, while Aristotle believed that thought was composed of images that have power to stimulate a person's emotions and to motivate him to effort. Sigmund Freud, in his early work in psychotherapy, believed that the use of spontaneous images would improve the mental state of his patients. Carl Jung felt that visualization would enable his patients to get in touch with their unconscious through a process he called "active imagination."

Currently it is felt by many in the psychology community that imagination is a "vital human capacity" and is a "precursor of creativity" that when combined with the functions of knowledge and judgment forms the "essence of the creative process." Based upon these notions it is our intention to demonstrate how planners can utilize guided imagery to instill the much needed qualities of imagination and creativity into the strategic planning process thereby enhancing the effectiveness of the process. This exercise can be used to help enhance the creativity in goal-setting among your firm's managers and planners.

Creativity in Goal-Setting

Imagine the serenity that exists after a spring shower. Take a deep breath and sense the clean, cool air. Feel a gentle breeze on your face. Smell the damp ground. Feel the warm sun return to your face. Envision a rainbow that is very vivid and high in the sky. [Pause.]

See yourself climbing on the rainbow. You climb from the deep, velvet purple down through the rich, soft blue. The dazzling green that you come upon gives way to a pale yellow bordered by a brilliant orange. Finally you see yourself slowly gliding down the most magnificent red aura you have ever seen. It overwhelms you with a sense of invincible power. [Pause.]

As you gaze out from this sea of brilliant hues you see your organization below at the end of the rainbow. From your lofty position in the rainbow, high in the sky, you are able to envision things in a manner that you have never been able to do before. New ideas and ways of doing things appear before you almost as if it were serendipity. [Pause.]

You see your product being made in a totally new fashion. You watch as the product comes off the production line. You are amazed at this new process and wonder why you never thought of this before. [Pause.]

New types of products are being packaged. Different colors from before. Different shapes from before. [Pause.]

You gaze around and see new customers buying your product. They represent a totally different market segment for you. They are quite happy with your product. See them smile. What do you hear them saying? What do they look like? [Pause.]

Now you see people using your product in a totally unique way. You have never thought that this could be an alternative use for your products. Why didn't you think of this before? [Pause.]

Slowly the vividness of your rainbow begins to dissipate. And just as slowly you begin to readjust to normal. However, there are many new ideas that you never before dreamed possible buzzing around in your mind. You may want to jot these down. [Pause.]

After each person has jotted down their individual ideas, they are discussed and a master list prepared. This list is then discussed and possible strategic goals are developed depending upon what people saw in their mind. The goals are then refined and studied at a later meeting to determine their feasibility.

Achieving creativity in strategic planning in forecasting is challenging for managers and planners. Imagery can help people to become more creative by allowing them to use their imaginations in a structured and disciplined way to see future superior and desirable goals. In the next chapters, we see how imagery can improve leadership and interpersonal relations in organizations.

6

HOW IMAGERY CAN IMPROVE PRODUCTIVITY IN LEADERSHIP AND PERSONAL RELATIONSHIPS

Imagine for a minute that you are experiencing the great American dream. You are your own boss in your very own business. You see in your dream the product that you have originated. You remember how your critics told you that your idea would never fly—that nobody would buy it—that you were crazy for even suggesting such a notion. But you knew you were right on target. You can see the smiling faces of customers who now wonder how they ever got along in the past without your product. How much better it has made their lives. Why hadn't anyone thought of this product before you?

You see your place of business that you practically built single-handedly. You see your name proudly displayed high over the entrance foyer for everyone who enters to see. That's right! It's your name! Feel how proud it makes you to see your name up there. This is your business!

In your vision you see yourself directing the activity of your subordinates. What a great group of people! You observe yourself making decisions that affects their behavior in a forceful but very caring style. Everyone in your organization admires you and respects you. The amazing accomplishments that you have made are truly unbelievable. But here you are. You can see what your company is today and what it is going to be in the future. When asked if years ago had you ever, in your wildest dreams, thought that you would be where you are today, you reply, "I could see it all the time!"

Does the above version of the American dream seem more like a fairy tale? Do you detect hints of Don Quixote and Walter Mitty as you read it? Well, by now you have gained a very positive appreciation for the power and the "magic" of fully using your imagination. The above script could just as easily as not have been experienced by one of the greatest entrepreneurs of this century—Thomas Watson, Jr. Many scholars attribute the success story of the rise of the International Business Machines company to the energies of this great leader. One time, when IBM was a much smaller company, Watson was asked if he ever thought that it would grow into the commercial giant it is today. His reply was, just like in our script above, "I could see it all the time!"

You too, as a human resource professional, can enhance your own leadership skills and the effective management of your organization's personnel by recognizing and developing your innate imaginal capacities.

THE QUEST FOR EFFECTIVE LEADERSHIP

Effective leadership is the ability to influence others to work together in the pursuit of organizational success. Effective leadership is envisioning what the organization must do in order to be successful. It is the mannerisms and managerial style that enables an individual to be accepted by others. However, an inadequate supply of effective leaders has prevailed through the ages. In fact, many notable commentators feel that we suffer from a leadership crisis in our political and economic systems. To deal with this dilemma, many different approaches have been employed in the search for the variables that comprise effective leadership.

One of the first attempts was the search for the "great man." The idea here was that perhaps there existed certain key traits that were more reflective of effective leaders. There would include such things as intelligence, ability, self-confidence, and enthusiasm. Individuals who possessed the majority of these traits were believed to have a natural tendency to be leaders. There was, however, an obvious problem with this . . . too many exceptions to the rule. No sooner was a list of effective leadership traits identified than an effective leader emerged who did not fit the list. We may sit back and laugh at this practice today but the obsession with the "great man" search can be exemplified by the actions of Nazi Germany and their crusade for the great race.

Giving up on the trait approach, researchers turned their attention to observing what effective leaders did. Rather than concentrating on who the leader was, efforts were now directed toward understanding what the leader did. Many initial studies focused on a two-dimensional behavior scheme involving concern for the job and concern for people. It became apparent that some combination of these two variables held the key to effective leadership. However, when defining complex behaviors in terms of continua, one has problems with the extremes. If too much emphasis is placed on getting the job done, human motivation will suffer. If all of the emphasis is placed on human satisfaction, then productivity will suffer. While the dual-factor behavior approach still serves as a basis for leadership research, it did not capture the composite image of leadership.

What evolved from the difficulties experienced with these two-dimensional models was an "it depends" explanation for effective leadership. There are times when the situation calls for a lot of concern for the subordinates, for example, in developing methods to implement major change. However, if the office building is on fire the effective leader will become extremely task-oriented in getting the workers "the hell out of the building!"

It is a currently held belief that the key to effective leadership exists not within the leader or in what the leader does per se, but within the situation. The situation dictates what an effective leader should do. Therefore, the effective leader is an individual who can accurately assess the demands contingent in the situation and act accordingly by creating images of potential actions and results that fit the demands of a critical situation.

As the human resource professional responsible for the training and development at your organization, it is important that you consider different situations when you design leadership workshops. You should develop many different scenarios that will allow trainees to experience a multitude of varied leadership behaviors. Consider the following scripts which will illustrate two diametrically opposed leadership styles.

Implementation of a New MIS System

Assume you have been asked to help update your organization's master information system. In particular, your organization wants to ensure adequate attention to the human resource aspects of the intended changes. You are aware that many technological advances have been made since your system was installed several years ago. Your main competitors are already in the process of upgrading their inhouse information processing capability. Enhancing your system at this time would also allow you to serve your clientele better.

Since you realize that making the decision to update the system and actually doing it are two different things, you begin to envision how you might go about the process. You see yourself helping to prepare a memorandum detailing the decision and the need for it. You will need to help advise managers of the need and benefits to be derived from the new system and the possible impacts on the use of human resources. You see yourself answering the many objections to making a major change, especially from those employees most directly affected.

You envision the informative meetings that you plan to conduct so that everyone involved has a chance to voice their ideas on the project. Painstakingly you and the MIS manager review many details, exploring all available scenarios, trying to prepare a plan that should ensure a successful implementation of the new system.

Since you are very sensitive to the natural resistance to change and the high level of uncertainty and fear that many employees will exhibit regarding a move of this magnitude, you then envision yourself conducting training sessions to alleviate these anxieties. In these workshops you see yourself explaining how it will enable employees to be better able to perform their jobs. You assure them that in no time they will be performing like real pros.

Now let's look at another leadership situation.

Dealing with a Toxic Waste Spill

Imagine that you are the human resource manager of a major chemical processing facility. Your firm is extremely careful and cautious about every aspect of its chemical processing operation, but still the fear of a possible accident is always present in the back of your mind. Although you and your staff have very detailed plans of what would be done in case of an emergency, you are aware that there could always be complications. To anticipate possible complications, you play over in your mind what steps you would take should disaster strike.

You see yourself at work in your office going over normal production reports. The phone rings. It is the foreman at line seven. A spillover valve on a toxic waste tank has blown and a deadly cloud of gaseous waste product is rapidly dissipating into the air. You see yourself quickly determining whether or not there are any injuries to employees. Next, you order the emergency maintenance crew to cut off pressure to the tank and seal it off immediately.

Without wasting a breath you see yourself calling the local police and fire departments for assistance. You direct the safety coordinator to contact local schools for evacuation. You issue an immediate statement to the local radio and television stations with instructions for local residents. Having alerted all concerned you then rush to line seven. Fortunately, all of the training and disaster rehearsal has paid off. The damage was quickly repaired with a minimal amount of leakage. A major disaster has been averted.

In both of the above situations, you envisioned yourself as an effective leader; however, in each case the behavior was drastically different. In upgrading a management information system, a very participative leadership style is the key to success. You need to hear from everyone involved. You need to make your personnel feel that they are a very vital part of the decision making process. You need to do everything in your power to overcome resistance to change gently. A little time slippage up front in assuring everyone is on board with you will more than be made up for with a smooth start up of the new system.

However, in the case of the toxic waste spillage, time is of the essence. Rather than asking for inputs and opinions, it is necessary to bark orders and pull rank. A lot of the expected behavior has already been rehearsed; therefore, simple but direct commands, in autocratic fashion to elicit behavior, can be the difference in saving lives.

From these examples it is quite evident that the situation dictates what is required if a leader is to be effective. The traits of the leader can be different and the leader's behavior is obviously different. What makes the difference is the leader's ability to perceive accurately and make an assessment of the important variables that exist in the situation at the time. Once this assessment has been made then the effective leader takes the appropriate action in the appropriate manner.

IMPROVING LEADERSHIP—THE ENVISIONARY LEADER MODEL

"There are none so blind as those who will not see."

Down through history the determining factor between leaders who were effective and leaders who were not has been the acuity of perception. Those leaders who chose to utilize their imagination and creativity have gone forward while those who relied on their power and dominance have not. As we have mentioned above, the effective leader analyzes the key variables in the situation and then adopts a leadership style that is appropriate for the situation. To better illustrate this notion, we have developed the Envisionary Leader Model shown in Figure 6–1.

The focal point of the model is the imagination and creative talents of the leader. The effective leader utilizes these talents to envision many different scenarios that may exist in an environment that contains both opportunities and threats for the organization. Next, it is important for the leader to see what the organization is, and based upon his or her perceptions of the future environment, what the organization is to be. With these images focused in mind, the leader then looks to his or her subordinates and reflects upon their needs, expertise, abilities, and expectations. Then the leader mentally examines the complexity and de-

Figure 6-1
The Envisionary Leader Model

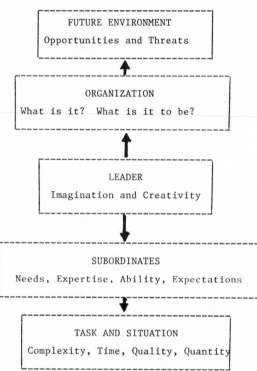

Source: Adapted from W. P. Anthony and E. A. Nicholson, *Management of Human Resources* (Columbus, Ohio: Grid Inc., 1977).

sirability of the tasks to be accomplished in order to move the organization forward, ever mindful of time constraints existing in the situation. Lastly, the leader looks deep within his- or herself, perceiving his or her strengths and weaknesses and finally selects a leadership style that would be appropriate, given all of the above key variables.

We will now examine the major elements of the Envisionary Leader Model in detail.

Future Environment

To be an effective leader, one must have an idea of where one wants to go and where one wants to be. To do this, an effective leader must anticipate the future in order that his or her organization may play a role in that future, rather than being totally subject to it. When envisioning the future, one should attempt to see what new opportunities will be there that will allow their organization to prosper and to grow.

To illustrate this point, we suggest this simple exercise. Make a mental list of all the products and services that are currently available and are an accepted part of our current lifestyles. This list will include such items as microwave ovens, personal computers, satellite television transmission, artificial hearts, pocket size calculators, and computer dating. The longer you sit and fantasize about this, the longer your list will become. But you can bet that the majority of these new products and services began with an entrepreneurial leader who dared to make his or her dream a reality.

However, the future also contains some threats that could harm the future prosperity of our organizations. If we can envision these threats well in advance, we will be able to avoid them, or at least minimize their negative impact upon our well-being. There are many experts today why attribute the major loss of United States automobile market share to the industry's failure to see it coming. The need for more fuel-efficient, smaller, and higher quality cars should have been recognized in ample time for Detroit to deal with it more successfully. Some industry analysts even argue that the possibility of the OPEC embargo should have been expected and anticipated and dealt with in a much more prepared fashion. Although we do not find it a comfortable exercise to dwell on unpleasant events, the future survival of our organizations and society, itself, mandates that we try to anticipate worst-case scenarios and develop creative methods to manage them.

Organization

Once the effective leader has visions of what could happen in the future, then it becomes imperative that he or she envision what their organization is and what it is to become. The once almost invincible Pennsylvania Railroad Company saw itself only as a railroad, and not as a transportation service. This lack of understanding of what the organization really was, a transportation service, eventually led to the deterioration of one of the greatest companies in history.

It is important to realize that the nature of organizations changes over time. What a firm may have been at its inception may not be what it is today. Providing an economical means of transportation via large passenger buses was the initial service offered by the Greyhound Bus Company. Today, the original organization named Greyhound no longer is in the people transporting business having sold its bus line to Buslease Inc. of Dallas, Texas. (However, a new company name of Greyhound Lines, Inc. is used.) Thus actions taken by this firm's leadership in the past would not currently be effective because of the different businesses that the firm finds itself in today. Different strategies are required because the nature of the business is different.

While it is very important to understand what the organization is today, it is equally important to envision what the organization is to become. Most major tobacco manufacturers have evolved into large organizations producing tobacco products, but they have a much different vision of who they want to be tomorrow. With the image of a smoke-free society being a possibility, these firms have undertaken massive diversification tactics, which would allow them to have a future should the smoke-free society become a reality.

Thus, effective leaders have one eye on today and one eye on tomorrow. To guide their organization successfully, they must know where they are today and where they are headed in the future.

Subordinates

An effective leader thoroughly perceives who his or her subordinates are and can accurately envision their needs, expertise, abilities, and expectations. The important word here is accurately. All too often ineffective leaders think they know who their subordinates are and how they will behave, when, in fact, they really don't know. A good communication network with one's subordinates will allow a leader to know his or her subordinates. Using his or her imagination will allow for better understanding of how they will behave.

An effective leader will expend large amounts of energy trying to picture in his or her mind what the needs and expectations of his or her subordinates are. These mental images will provide an understanding of how to motivate them better. Time spent in reflecting on their expertise and abilities will allow for more success in assigning tasks to be accomplished.

To illustrate this point we offer the following script.

> Imagine that your firm designs and builds custom packaging equipment. Your company's president has been approached by another organization that has a major problem in packaging a new product item. Your firm has tried unsuccessfully to obtain this account for a number of years and now you have an excellent opportunity to acquire a large share of their business, if you are successful in solving their problem. Your firm's president has asked you to become involved.
>
> As you begin searching to find which one of the design engineers should be recommended for this task, many images begin to appear. The most innovative senior design engineer is already immersed in a major job, and, as soon as she is finished with it, is expecting to spend some well-deserved vacation time with her family. The only other design engineer available has a lot of enthusiasm but not enough experience to manage such a difficult assignment.

You have positive visions of the engineer successfully completing the task and your firm enjoying a major new customer. However, you also see some very negative outcomes when you ask her to give up her well-deserved vacation time by assigning her more work. You see your junior engineer energetically tackling this important assignment and possibly failing to get it done thereby losing this major account for your firm and demoralizing his young ego.

Finally, you see a possible solution. You see yourself asking the senior engineer to make the initial contact and to suggest some possible solutions. Next you invite the junior engineer to follow through on this very important project. In your imagination you see the value of the senior's expertise in solving this problem without jeopardizing her expectations of her well-earned vacation, while you enlist the energy of the junior engineer to successfully debug and implement the new design. Your customer is happy. The engineers are satisfied. And your imagination has served you well again.

Task and Situation

The effective leader will perceive the complexity of the task to be performed as well as the quantity of the task needed to satisfy the given situation. In addition, the effective leader will envision the level of quality needed as well as how familiar the subordinates are with the task that is to be completed. With all of these images in mind, the effective leader will then imagine what leadership style will be the most successful in influencing his subordinates to complete the task in the time allowed.

In reflecting upon the scripts we presented above involving the implementation of a new MIS system and dealing with a toxic waste spill, different leadership styles were required depending upon the task and the situation. In the script involving the implementation of the new MIS system, time was a factor but was not the major factor. Subordinate inputs were solicited and considered in order to overcome resistance to change. A very participative leadership style was employed in completing a rather novel task. In dealing with the toxic waste spill, the leadership was quite autocratic. Actions had been rehearsed just in case this crisis did arise. One-way communications and directions were essential in order to save lives.

In both cases the effective leadership style was dictated by the task to be accomplished, its complexity, and the time allowed to get the job done.

IMPROVING LINKAGES

In order for an effective leader fully to utilize his or her imaginative and creative talents to envision differing scenarios, it is important that

Figure 6-2
The Effective Leader's Information Linkage Network

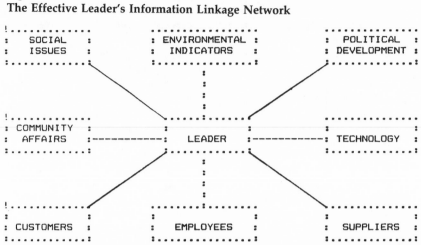

as much information as possible is accessible. One cannot be creative in a vacuum. Thus, it is imperative for a leader to develop a network of sensors that detect information from every pertinent source existing in the environment that impacts the leader's organization. As a human resource professional, you are in the ideal position to provide information to your organization's managers to help them become more effective leaders.

This network of information gathering sensors is referred to as a linking system. The linking system provides information from the environment to the organization. It is the communication channel between the environment sensors and the decision-authority center, which is, in this case, the leader. This system of linkages serves as the organization's lifelines with its environment. Without this lifeline to valuable information, the leader cannot effectively utilize his or her imagination and creativity and, therefore, will have a difficult time surviving.

An example of an information linking system is shown in Figure 6–2. In this figure we have displayed some of the more important sources of information vital to any organization. The sources are by no means all inclusive but do provide a good working example of the type of information linking network to which a leader must subscribe.

The effective leader will have access to major environmental indicators, such as projected interest rates, employment figures, and capital expenditures to give him or her an idea of future economic conditions. There are many services today that provide a more than adequate menu of these various economic indicators.

Political developments inform the leader of how government directives could possibly affect the leader's organization. Here again there are services that provide current status reports on major political developments. Some firms have gone so far as to establish their own Political Action Committees (PACs), to try to shape political developments to their benefit.

Social issues and trends determine the opening of new markets and the closing of existing ones. Failure to maintain an effective information link to this dominant force in one's environment can only have detrimental consequences to the organization.

On a more local level, the leader has a vested interest in the area's community affairs. Involvement in local civic groups offers timely information about such activities.

Keeping abreast of technological innovations can mean the difference between a profitable business and a non-profitable business. Reading professional journals and attending trade conventions will provide state-of-the-art knowledge in this vital area.

Keeping in touch with suppliers not only provides valuable knowledge about the well-being of your suppliers, but will also provide information about new materials and equipment that could be of benefit to your organization.

The life support of any organization is its customers. An effective leader can never know too much about them. Regular contact with them through the sales force, customer surveys, and personal visits helps to maintain a healthy communication network with them.

Last, but most certainly not least, is the organization's employees. The effective leader will maintain a truly open door policy, not one in name only. Suggestion incentive programs and regular informative meetings provide a very efficient information generation link to the organization's vital assets.

As a human resource professional, one of the most effective workshops you can utilize to enable your organization's managers to be more sensitive to the needs and wants of their employees centers around role reversal. In these workshops, have them envision themselves in the roles of their employees. Here is a sample script you can use for this purpose.

> Imagine that you are one of your key employees. You awake one morning with your manager's latest directive still on your mind; you are still not really sure how you feel about it. Sure, your boss thinks it's a great idea, but then he doesn't have to carry it out. A lot of benefits could accrue to the company if you are able to accomplish this task successfully, but what if you fail?
>
> Your wife notices that you are unusually tense at breakfast and asks if there is anything wrong. You reply only some extra problems at work. As you ride to work you ask the other guys in the car pool

what they think about this situation. You earnestly listen to their comments.

At work you sit at your desk trying to decide how all of this work will get done. Not only do you have your normal duties that take up almost all of your time, but now you must find a way to accomplish this new assignment. How will you ever get it all done?

IMPROVING THE LEADER'S PERSONAL RELATIONSHIPS

Throughout this chapter we have defined leadership as the ability to influence others to generate efforts toward the accomplishment of organizational goals successfully. This definition strongly suggests the importance of maintaining good working relationships with other individuals. It is this obtainment of full, cooperative effort of all of the individuals involved that yields the synergy necessary to obtain the successful attainment of organizational goals.

An effective leader accomplishes this by actively improving group cohesiveness, by positively managing group conflict, and by providing an environment that minimizes job stress among his or her employees.

Improving Group Cohesiveness

Years ago it was a common belief that group formation was the root of many problems, therefore it was an accepted practice to do whatever was necessary to break up these groups. Today we realize that group formation is a very natural phenomenon, and that effective leadership techniques dictate that we actually encourage subordinates to work in groups. The synergistic effect often manifests itself in very cohesive groups affording greater productivity.

The leader is often referred to as the glue that holds the productive work group together. The tighter the group is held together, the more productive the group should be. To improve the cohesiveness of the work group there are many things the effective leader should do.

To begin with, each work group should have an identity. Whether the identity comes from the workplace such as "A shift" or "Department 6," or comes from local sports teams such as "The Buckeyes," this identity legitimizes the group in the eyes of others and provides a focal point around which the members form an allegiance. When goals and objectives are met, praise and rewards should be presented to the group as a whole. This action will further solidify the group increasing its *esprit de corps*. When there is more than one group involved in the work environment, it is often of value to create some friendly competition. Creating a game-like atmosphere among your sales teams, for example, with differing rewards for those who exceed quotas, not only pulls the group members closer together, but quite often results in a greater generation of sales volume.

Size is also a very important factor for the leader to consider. The group must be of adequate size to be able to effectively accomplish its mission, but at the same time must not be allowed to grow so large that subgroups begin to develop.

One final factor that the leader should be cognizant of is the need for agreement among the group members concerning the group's goals. The effective leader will consistently influence the group's behavior in order to ensure that there is common agreement on the purpose of the group and its goals.

Managing Group Conflict

Just like group formation, group conflict, earlier on, was also believed to be of no benefit whatsoever to an organization and was to be prevented at any cost. However, we now realize that group conflict is also inevitable and on some occasions can actually be beneficial to the greater well-being of the organization. While it is still a good course of action to prevent conflict, when it does arise the effective leader needs to understand the nature and the causes of the conflict and then choose an appropriate action to deal with it.

Group conflict often arises over differences in perception; one individual analyzes a situation from one point of view or set of values, which gives rise to conflict when another individual sees the same situation from a totally different point of view or set of values. The effective leader can minimize the occurrence of these types of conflicts by using imagery to open up the communication channels and airing these differences. Often this opportunity to "clear the air" will be sufficient to allow both sides to understand each other better and thereby reduce the conflict.

Scarce resources are also a primary source of conflict. Limited equipment to complete the necessary tasks, insufficient budget funding for major appropriations, or not enough human resources available to accomplish the work often are the culprits that give rise to group conflict. To be effective in these situations, the effective leader must use all of his or her envisionary skills to see ways of obtaining more resources or better ways to utilize existing ones.

Group conflict can also arise when there exists job interdependence among a group of individuals. One party cannot complete higher tasks until they receive some tasks from another party. For example in an accounts payable office the disbursement clerk cannot process checks for payment until the receiving clerk has verified receipt of product. This often results in friction because the prior tasks may be tardy or not completed satisfactorily. Here the leader needs to intervene and either change existing procedures to preclude the conflict, or develop common goals for the parties involved that will encourage them to work together.

To utilize imagery in managing conflict we suggest the following approach:

Step 1. Assemble one or more of the parties involved who share the same opinion. Have them envision the conflict situation. What role do they see themselves playing in the conflict? What are the sources of the conflict?

Step 2. Next, have them envision what steps they would take to resolve the conflict.

Step 3. Now have them do a role reversal and assume the position of the party with whom they are experiencing the conflict. Have them envision what they feel they are doing to cause the other party to be in conflict with them.

Step 4. Summarize the findings from these sessions.

Step 5. Conduct the same sessions with the opposing parties.

Step 6. Hold a summit session with all of the parties involved and discuss the findings. Select a course of action in which they will mutually strive to resolve the conflict.

Step 7. Have follow-up sessions where the groups envision where they are making progress. Have them also envision areas where they need to work harder, and take appropriate action.

We strongly feel you will find the use of imagery to be a very powerful tool with which to manage conflict. However, there are times when the best of efforts cannot prevent conflict and, in these cases, probably for the best interest of the organization, conflict should not be prevented. There will be occasions when the individual dynamics are such that a confrontation is the only answer. In this case the leader must channel all of this confrontation energy into positive outcomes. Either the individuals involved are then able to see the causes of their conflict and are willing to correct them, or one of the parties involved decides to leave the organization. This was apparently the situation at the Ford Motor Company that resulted in the departure of Lee Iacocca to join Chrysler.

Reducing Job Stress Among Employees

One of the by-products of our fast-paced, zealous, modernized organizational society is commonly called stress. Although it comes in many varieties and is caused by any number of events or circumstances, it is normally thought of as any form of negative tension arising from an unpleasant situation existing in the work environment.

Stress is normally the first discomfort felt by individuals when the above-mentioned causes of conflict begin to become apparent. In addition, stress can be linked to job frustration resultant from lack of proper training, job boredom, or job overload. It can be caused by insensitive coworkers or time constraints. Stress is also caused by not really understanding what it is that is really expected from a particular position, i.e., role ambiguity.

Whatever the causes, the symptoms are quite negative on the individual and co-workers. The symptoms begin with the individual becoming difficult to work with and irritable. Productivity begins to suffer as the individual becomes lackadaisical about his or her duties. The individual then becomes habitually tardy and incurs a much higher than normal level of absenteeism. Eventually the stress can push a person into a situation of alcohol or drug abuse.

Obviously the effective leader must do everything possible in his or her power to eliminate the sources of stress that prevail in the work environment. All of the efforts mentioned above that encourage group cohesiveness and minimize group conflict will have a positive effect in reducing stress. In addition, seeing that people are properly trained and that they understand their job responsibilities is also a very important stress reduction technique. Probably the most effective means of encouraging a healthful work environment is to maintain an open communication channel that people are invited to utilize knowing that they can find a sensitive ear to their problems.

To allow you some practice on using mental imagery to enhance your interpersonal relations leadership skills, we offer the following script.

You have finally received that big promotion you always dreamed of and are now the new vice president of human resources of your organization. Having said goodbye to all of your old acquaintances, you have moved to a brand new home in a brand new city. You see yourself arriving at work for your first day on the new job. As you settle down in your new office you realize how important it is for you to succeed in this new position. You are aware that you received this promotion due to your success in your old job and that upper management is expecting big things from you. If you are to live up to their expectations you will need the help of your entire staff and their full cooperation. How will you pull this off?

The major reason for your past success was your open communication policy and your ability to get people to work together as a team. You see yourself having an informative meeting with employees. You emphasize your open door policy and encourage them to use it. You inform them that you would like to have some formal meetings for brainstorming and troubleshooting purposes and some informal meetings just as an excuse to get together.

You see yourself walking through the organization and introducing yourself to everyone. You make mental notes of who sits where and what kinds of interactions seem to be taking place—who seems to work together more closely and who seems to be distant. You see yourself often visiting them informally during their breaks. You do more listening than talking and see yourself being welcome at these gatherings.

You then see yourself building work teams among logical work units trying to include those folks that have a common attraction. You set mutually accepted goals for these teams and try to build in some form of friendly competition. The teams adopt their favorite sports logo as their team logo. You hear people stating that this is going to be fun!

Finally, you see yourself acting as a coach while maintaining a watchful vigil. You stay involved by helping and offering suggestions while watchful of potential problems. You suggest better ways of working smarter.

This script can help you better understand your role as facilitator and coach in helping to achieve teamwork.

EFFECTIVE LEADERS ARE NOT AFRAID TO DREAM

Although we have mentioned many ways in which an individual can improve his or her leadership effectiveness by utilizing their imaginative and creative talents, the one most important thing that characterizes all great leaders is their desire to dream! *Effective leaders are not afraid to dream.* Everyone can remember those immortal words of Martin Luther King, Jr., the leader of this country's civil rights movement, who proclaimed to the world "I have a dream."

Just like King, all great leaders openly admit that they do have a dream. No matter what arena they happen to be in—whether it be in politics, business, religion, or the military—great leaders are not afraid to dream. The dreams of Thomas Jefferson and Karl Marx have directed the destinies of nations. Henry Ford's dream of the common man owning his own car gave birth to a middle class of society. John F. Kennedy's dream of putting a man on the moon breathed new life into a space program that had fallen behind the Soviet Union.

Ray Kroc's dream of clean and efficient hamburger shops was to be the beginning of the now famous McDonald's. Thomas Alva Edison's proclivities for dreaming gave birth to many inventions. The company that would manufacture his products would one day become the General Electric Corporation. At the time of this book's publication, GE's chief executive officer, Jack Welch, still leads this corporate giant with dreams of being number one or two in every business in which GE engages.

As we mentioned earlier, good leaders have visions of the future that inspire performance. They are able to see bigger and better ways of doing things. Good leaders are able to effectively communicate their visions to others while relating to others on an interpersonal level to ensure the achievement of their visions. Nothing is impossible for the leader who is not afraid to dream!

7

HOW IMAGERY CAN IMPROVE PRODUCTIVITY IN COMMUNICATIONS AND INFORMATION MANAGEMENT

We mentioned in Chapter 6 that successful leaders have visions of what needs to be done as well as the ability to effectively communicate their visions to others. This implies quite emphatically that the successful leader be an effective communicator as well as an individual with keen imaginative and creative skills. Consider the following script.

You are in your office quite exhausted from a very trying morning. You receive a call from a key union leader requesting immediate action on your part. He is threatening to shut down a critical manufacturing line very soon unless you take action to resolve what he deemed to be a major job assignment crisis, which had been brewing for some time. The shut down could very easily cause a missed delivery date resulting in the loss of a major contract. He desperately needs your intervention. You inform him that you will do whatever you can.

You summon your staff together to determine a course of action to meet this emergency situation. You see yourself giving very precise directions on what needs to be done and how it can be accomplished. Shifting job assignments and allowing inventory quantities to fall below accepted levels for a temporary period would generate the necessary output even if the line were shut down while you were trying to work things out. Other plans were established. Everyone seemed clear as to what they were to do. All bases seemed to be covered. Everything seemed to be in order.

However, before meeting with the union leader you receive an-

other very unpleasant telephone call from the foreman of the line
stating it had been shut down by an unauthorized employee action.
Extremely embarrassed you frankly admit that you have no idea of
what had gone wrong because you had told everyone involved exactly what to do and how to do it and believed that you had everything worked out. Now this comes up.

You have spent the last hour talking with people trying to understand what went wrong. Everywhere you turn the answer is the
same—communication problems. When you said "this" someone
else heard "that." How could you have possibly said things any
clearer?

Unfortunately, this particular script is re-enacted all too often. Every
one of us can see ourselves in this script at one time or another. We
think we tell people exactly what to do and how to do it. We wonder
how we could have been any clearer? Yet we are constantly encountering
examples of ineffective communication. Perhaps the major factor contributing to organizational problems is ineffective communication.

The results of ineffective communication range from minor embarrassment to critical problems. Minor embarrassment occurs when we
show up at a friend's house for a party on the wrong night; a critical
problem occurs as in the case of the IranScam of the Reagan administration. As a human resource professional, one of your responsibilities
is to enhance the communication process in your organization. In this
chapter we explain how imagery can enhance the communication process.

IMAGERY AND COMMUNICATIONS

To improve the communication process it is imperative that one fully
understands the communication process and the role that imagery plays
in this process, which is illustrated in Figure 7–1. As we mentioned
earlier, the communication process is rich with imagery. Words and
other forms of communication are symbols that evoke mental images.
In fact, communications is basically the management of symbols. It is
through the use of these mental images that we convey relationships
and promote understanding that generates the necessary action to accomplish organizational goals and objectives.

The process begins with the formation of a mental image. It may take
the form of a brilliant picture occurring in one's mind or it may manifest
itself in a feeling or a knowing sensation. Very seldomly, if ever, does
the image formation constitute a complete thought, therefore, time
should be spent nurturing the image into a clear thought. It is of little
value to try to communicate partial feelings or ideas that have not been

Figure 7-1
The Effective Communication Process Model

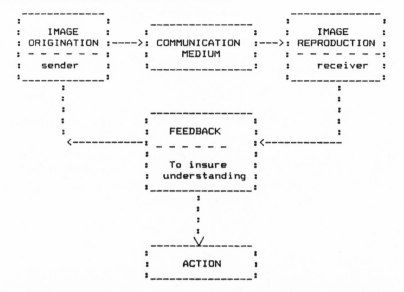

thoroughly planned. The old adage "THINK BEFORE YOU SPEAK" is definitely advice worth heeding.

After an individual has completely processed his or her imagery experience into a message, then it becomes necessary to envision how the message should be transmitted. If the message is quite critical in nature, and time is of the essence, then it might be appropriate to tell the person face-to-face. If distance is also an issue then telephoning or teleconferencing may be the most effective medium to employ. In a situation where time is not quite so critical and the message is very complex and intricate, then a very detailed letter might be more effective. With the advances of electronic mail, written communication can now be sent in almost the same time span as a telephone call, allowing for an adequate amount of time for composition.

Another facet of transmitting messages, which is as equally important to effective communication as is the selection of the medium, is the direction of the medium. An effective communicator will focus on the desired results of the message and then envision possible consequences to the direction of the message. For example, to accomplish a particular task, you might be well-advised to communicate the message upwardly into the organization in order to enlist the support of top management. In other situations it may be more prudent to communicate the message downward to one's employees in order to obtain the feasibility of accomplishing a particular task before approaching top managements being unprepared for their questions. In either case, it is advisable to spend a few moments envisioning possible outcomes in order that one might make the most effective decision.

After the medium and direction of the message have been selected, the sender then transmits the message. Upon receipt of the transmission, the receiver will then begin the image reproduction process. The effective communicator will not allow the communication process to terminate here. He or she will elicit feedback in order to ascertain to what extent the original image transmitted is the image that the receiver reproduced. This processing and reprocessing of feedback is an activity that requires some very well tuned behavior, sensitive skills, and a little more processing time than some managers are willing to give. However, the extra time spent here will pay dividends in time saved later on in not having to correct the problems that arise from ineffective communication.

To illustrate the art of eliciting feedback while still being sensitive to the listener, consider the following script.

> You are the personnel manager of the technical assistance department of a large electronic sensor manufacturing organization. The manager of one of your major manufacturing facilities has requested your help in establishing a training program for installing a new welding device. You are aware that the manufacturing personnel have gone on record stating that the new welder design is not appropriate for this type of manufacturing. In addition, you have worked with the engineering design group, and realize that this design is novel, however, once fully debugged, the new design should allow for some excellent technological advances to be made in the industry.
>
> You assign one of your most qualified training specialists to the task. You then envision your debriefing session with her. She is extremely bright and capable, but very proud of her own initiative. How can you ensure that the instructions you will give her are accurately received without her feeling you are talking down to her or being too authoritative.
>
> You see yourself bringing her up to date on the project. Because of the critical nature of the project you inquire if she has any questions. She does ask a couple of very intelligent questions of a technical nature, which indicates that, so far, the communication process is working. Then, just to make sure that the message has been received successfully, you make a point of the political nature of this problem and ask her for her suggestions on how the project should proceed. Being very appreciative that her thoughts are valued, she then proceeds to paraphrase the entire situation in her own words, adding her own suggestions for improvement. It is now quite apparent that the communication process has worked effectively and the likelihood of the project succeeding has now been greatly enhanced.

In this script, feedback has been asked for in an indirect way that did not belittle the receiver. In addition, the opportunity to make suggestions enhanced the receiver's sense of self-worth and provided some valuable new ideas. It obviously took more time on the part of the manager to envision the communication process in his mind, but the probability of success for the project has been dramatically improved.

Human Resource Role

As a human resource professional, one way you can help your organization increase its communication effectiveness is by conducting the following training session.

Step 1. Assemble small groups of six to eight employees of preferably the same organizational level and function.

Step 2. Have them relax and recall a recent experience in which they were required to originate the communication process.

Step 3. Ask them to recall what images raced through their minds as they decided what to say and how to say it.

Step 4. Have them envision their attempts to obtain feedback.

Step 5. Ask them to remember the consequences of their communication efforts.

Step 6. Have the group share their experiences and discuss what went right and what went wrong and why.

Step 7. After everyone in the organization has had an opportunity to experience the exercise, alter the group's composition first by function and then by level.

Here is a script you can use in this session:

> Remember the last time you were asked to give some directions to a co-worker. Try to recall how you felt when you were told to deliver this message. What images raced through your mind as you were trying to decide how to do it? Did you look forward to the interaction with this person because you normally enjoy their company? Or did the memory of prior unpleasant experiences with this person make you wish you did not have to do this?
>
> Recall the expression on their face when you delivered the message. Was it a smile or a frown? Now, try to envision what you did to ensure that your message was correctly received. Did you have this person repeat what you said? Did you have them paraphrase the message? Did the consequences to your message indicate that the communication process was successful?

This training program accomplishes at least two main functions. First, it makes people more aware of the communication process that, in and

Figure 7-2
Barriers to Effective Communication

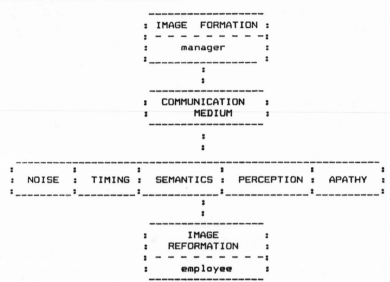

of itself, should have some impact on improving communication effectiveness. Second, it allows employees of differing functions and levels to appreciate the variation that occurs in the communication process as one moves across and up the organization.

BARRIERS TO EFFECTIVE COMMUNICATION

In addition to knowing exactly what to say before saying it, taking time to select the proper communication direction and medium, and in acquiring feedback the effective communicator must be aware of the barriers to effective communication. These are shown in Figure 7–2.

Semantics

The existence of multimeaning serves to make our language quite colorful and exciting. However, these same multimeaning words can also create a semantic barrier to effective communication. A word that conveys a certain image to the sender may evoke a completely different image in the receiver. To illustrate, consider the following script:

Imagine that you are a young management trainee recently transferred from a Midwest corrugated-carton manufacturing facility to a glass-forming operation on the east coast. As part of this company's training program, you are required to work in every manufacturing function for a short time in order to understand as much as possible about the total workings of the organization.

Today you are working in the glass-forming area. You see the forming machines revolving around the open forehearth picking up globs of molten glass in one revolution and ejecting glowing, hot, formed, glass bottles in the next revolution. You feel how terribly hot it is. You frequently wipe the sweat from your brow. You remember a foreman telling you that he was going over to the cafeteria and asking if he could bring you back a cold soda. Being from the Midwest, you shook your head no, wondering how anyone could enjoy a soda in such a dirty, hot environment. The foreman returns shortly with enough ice-cold-soda for everyone but you.

The communication barrier that was encountered in the above script was one of semantics. To a young, management trainee, the term soda conjures up images of a combination of ice cream and carbonation—not necessarily something one would enjoy in the smeltering confines of a glass-forming floor. To folks in the East, a soda is a soft drink that would be quite welcome anytime one was hot and thirsty.

Our language contains many words that have a multiplicity of different meanings. Consider such words as "run," "tip," "ball," "round," and "one." In addition, words take on different meanings depending on the situation. What may be a "fair" day's work to a union member, may not necessarily be a "fair" day's work to the shop foreman. In addition, words take on different meanings in different locations, as was the case in our script above. Extra attention must be given to semantics in order to enhance the communication process.

Noise

Noise is a communication barrier that can be either physical or psychological. Physical noise would consist of actual loud sounds that would impair the listener from receiving your message. Shouting instructions to an employee over the blasts of a large stamping die or trying to give directions to a subordinate as you board a jet with its engines roaring would constitute exercises in futility. The likelihood of you being heard, let alone understood, approximates zero.

Psychological noise consists of sounds in the listener's mind comprised of biases or attitudes that preclude the speaker from really being heard. The listener simply tunes the speaker out or only hears what he or she chooses to hear. In either case, the results are ineffective communication.

Of the two, physical noise is much easier to deal with. Just being aware of the noise level as one communicates and takes corrective action as necessary, should be sufficient. To overcome psychological noise requires much more effort. Care must be exercised when using emotionally charged words. Comments should focus on the work to be done and not on the individuals performing it. The benefits to be derived by the organization should be the ultimate driving force behind any communication action. And lastly, the effective communicator will envision several different outcomes to his or her communication in order to more successfully overcome the psychological noise.

Timing

To successfully play a piece of music, or tell a joke, or hit a home run off of a fast ball pitcher, one must execute good timing. The same is true in communicating. It is not so much a question of choosing the right time and the right place as it is a question of avoiding the wrong time and wrong place. For example, you are not going to get someone's undivided attention if they are running late for an important meeting. Giving a subordinate a lecture on tardiness will not produce the desired results if the subordinate is already emotionally upset over a major personal problem. Never try to communicate constructive criticism to a subordinate in the presence of another subordinate. Trying to communicate at the wrong time and wrong place not only results in miscommunication, but also normally results in exacerbating an already unpleasant situation.

To effectively overcome the communication barrier of timing, one must exercise patience. Even when you feel that you can't wait, if the timing is not right you are just wasting your time anyway. In your haste you will probably make matters worse. In addition, use your imagination. Try to envision the workday of the person with whom you must communicate in order to select just the right moment. By trying to envision the person's high and low periods, as well as their busy and slack times, you should be able to pick a good time and place in which to engage in communication.

Apathy

The communication barrier of apathy is experienced when the communicator fails to be empathic with the receiver. For the image that exists in the sender's mind to be successfully reproduced in the listener's mind, both parties must be on the same emotional level. For example, if the manager is excited about a new product being developed, he or she cannot instill the same enthusiasm to a subordinate if that person is quite momentarily depressed about losing a major contract.

When trying communicate instructions on how to operate a sophisticated piece of office equipment, he or she must realize that, while they might be the expert, the trainee is not. Chances are that the trainee is very nervous and intimidated by this electronic wonder. Therefore, if the trainer is going to communicate effectively the instructions, he or she is going to have to empathize with the learner and proceed patiently and ever so gently.

In any communication situation, if you want people to know where you are coming from, you have got to know where they are coming from. When you envision the communication process, always put yourself in the shoes of your receiver to make the process more effective. To help you become more empathetic with your audience we offer the following script:

> Imagine that you have been asked by your company to help write a letter that will be used in a major restructuring campaign for your company. This restructuring will cause many middle management jobs to be eliminated. You estimate that about one hundred managers are likely to lose their jobs. The product group where this restructuring is taking place has asked you for advice to construct the letter so that the message is communicated to those who will lose their job, but is done in a humanitarian manner.
>
> Even though you recognize that there are many individual differences among the hundred or so managers, you try to form a profile of the typical manager that will be affected—male, about fifty-five years old, with the company for twenty years, worked up through the ranks, mostly good, solid managers. You try to imagine how they will feel when they are informed of their options—early retirement, transfer, demotion, seeking work elsewhere. You think of your company's programs—early retirement counseling, job training, and outplacement assistance.
>
> You try to place yourself in their position. How would you feel if you received the letter you were being asked to write? How would you communicate to your family and friends that you had lost your job? What could you say in the letter to help them through the crisis? How can you provide emotional support and ego protection and, yet, still get the message across?

Imagery can help with the practice of empathy by allowing people to visualize what it would be like to walk in another person's shoes.

Perception

The communication barrier of perception results from differing values, affinities, and aversions that we all have. It can also result from cultural and societal differences. We see and hear the same thing differently because of these differences. To older individuals social security may mean financial independence for those who have worked hard all their lives. To a young couple it may be an added burden that is preventing them from affording the new home they want. Acid rain may be considered a menace to the environmentalist who is concerned about our country's wildlife. To the coal miner in West Virginia, it is only another reason for those bleeding heart liberals to try and eliminate his job.

Perceptual differences affect the way we interpret communication. The effective communicator will appreciate these differences and will tailor his or her communication efforts accordingly. The following script can be used with managers to help show how perceptual differences affect communications.

You are the supervisor of the copy production department for a medium-size advertising agency. You enjoy the excitement of this dynamic business and the freedom it allows you to demonstrate your creative abilities. You have recently graduated from college with your degree in communication and look forward to the day when you can become an account executive. Therefore you are very determined to demonstrate your abilities to upper management.

Late one afternoon you are asked by your manager if your department can complete a new ad campaign for a competitor's client. It would mean a chance to gain all of this new business if the campaign could be completed in the next couple of months. Your firm would definitely like to undertake this contract as it would mean gaining a competitor's business. However, since gaining all of this client's business is predicated on the performance of this campaign, upper management does not want to hire additional personnel and then possibly have to let them go if things do not work out. Your manager tells you that she must have your answer by tomorrow.

You put your feet up on your desk and try to envision how you can possibly accomplish the impossible. When you look at this through the eyes of your staff, things look bleak. You are already aware that you copy department is working at a maximum level. Asking them to take on more work without any more hiring will be a difficult task. They will think upper management is just trying to take advantage of them again.

When you view things through the eyes of upper management things look quite different. Here is an opportunity to gain incremental business with the prospects of gaining a brand new account. If only you could get your copy staff to view the new contract through the eyes of upper management.

To do this, you see yourself calling your staff together. You advise them of the new campaign and the extra hours that it will require. Since it might be a one shot deal you cannot hire more help. To counter their negative concerns you see yourself accentuating the positive side. If they pull it off there will be the benefits of the extra business this year. This department will demonstrate that they are a can-do group. And if the firm can gain all of this client's business, everyone will benefit.

In this script, the communication barrier of differing perceptions was overcome by bridging the gap. The big picture was presented, and the mutual benefits of gaining the extra business was the focal point. A definite win-win situation was used to make the communication process work.

OTHER ASPECTS OF COMMUNICATION TO BE CONSIDERED

Two other very important aspects of communication that must be considered if the communication process is to be effective are body language and the grapevine. While these aspects are not necessarily barriers to effective communication, they must be dealt with if we want to be successful in our communication activities.

Body Language

How many times have you heard, "It's not what you say, but how you say it that counts"? The use, or lack of use, of body language—gestures, facial expressions, etc.—is vital to the communication process. A frown on one's forehead denotes bad news. A lack of attentiveness to the speaker says that you are not interested. Constantly looking at one's watch is a cue to hurry the message. Not looking into the speaker's eyes suggests suspicion.

These examples may or may not be what is really the true situation, but to the party receiving the body language the message is the same. To become more aware of what you say with your own style of body language try to envision yourself in an everyday communication activity. Do you see yourself frowning quite often when you are really not down? Do you look others in the eye with the interest they deserve? Are you a watch watcher? Do you stand with your arms folded projecting an aloof image? Are you a hand waver? Do you speak with your hands in perpetual motion? Do you extend an open hand or hold up a clenched fist?

After you have used your imagination to determine what type of body language you employ when you speak, try to imagine what type of body language you would like to use. Mentally rehearse scenes where you are conducting meetings, giving presentations, or just having one-on-one conversations with your peers and employees. See yourself conveying your thoughts in the fashion that you want to convey them. See your posture. See your facial expressions. See how you use your hands. Try to envision the facial expressions of your audience. How are they responding to you? Is it the response that you want?

After sufficient practice you will notice a remarkable improvement in your communication style. Remember, a picture is worth 10,000 words, and your body language is a picture. Use your body language to your advantage in improving the communication process.

Grapevine

The grapevine is the informal communication network that exists in all organizations. It carries a lot of personal communication, mostly gossip, about who is seeing who, who is getting divorced, who is having financial problems, and so on. It is also a major source of rumor about what the organization may or may not be doing, which can result in a lot of headaches for your organization's management.

Remember that childhood game we played called "gossip," "telephone," or "whisper"? We would get into a line and someone at the end of the line would make up the gossip, normally a single sentence that would then be whispered into the ear of the next person in line. That person would then whisper what he or she thought they heard to the next in line until everyone in the line had passed the gossip along. It was very amusing to see how distorted the message would become by the time it reached the last person in line.

This is exactly how the grapevine works in an organization; but, unfortunately, the outcomes are seldom amusing. A lot of effort is expended in correcting problems that arise due to the existence of the grapevine. The grapevine, just like informal groups and conflict, was something that, for many years, managers spent vast amounts of time and energy trying to eradicate from the organization. Now we realize that the grapevine is here to stay and that our energies are more gainfully employed in attempting to manage the grapevine more effectively.

To accomplish this, you should try to envision how the grapevine works in your organization. Try to see who the main figures in the grapevine are and how the information flows. After you have gained a thorough understanding of how the grapevine works, use it to your advantage. First consider what happens, when your organization is making major decisions. Have all of your managers try to envision how and what kind of rumors your meetings are likely to generate. This will enable your organization to anticipate any problems that might arise. Second, have your managers imagine ways that the grapevine can be utilized to augment your formal communication channels in the desemination of information.

MONITORING PERFORMANCE

In order to ensure that his or her organization is on the right track in accomplishing its goals and objectives, the effective manager must monitor the performance of those in the organization. The monitoring activity involves seeking pertinent information by a continuous process of scanning one's environment and asking questions of one's managers and subordinates. By acting as a monitor, the manager seeks to be informed about the organization and its operating environment. Information is sought, both inside and outside the organization, in order to detect changes, to identify problems and opportunities, and to gain knowledge about the environment.

Many of the more contemporary management texts have popularized the "managing by walking around" technique. The key factor here is that the manager takes daily tours throughout the organization in order to maintain an awareness of what activities are taking place. This walking around is monitoring at its best. Being highly visible, so that you may be available for inputs from others, is extremely desirable if you want to stay on top of things.

Consider the following script for general managers:

You are the general manager of a very successful small appliance manufacturing business. You see yourself arriving at work one spring morning. You notice the surroundings. See the trees and other greenery around your building. You look at all of the other businesses in the immediate area. As you walk to the building, you can feel a bright sun shining in a very blue sky above you.

As you enter the building you are greeted by some of your workers. You smile and say "good morning." Before you begin your workday, you take your usual tour of the factory. As you walk along, you smile and greet members of your workforce.

You watch as the finished product comes off the assembly line. Notice how good you feel to know your company produces such a fine product.

You see yourself talking to your quality control manager. You are happy to hear how well a new quality routine has reduced scrap losses. As you continue your tour, your manager of manufacturing calls you over to where some new equipment is being installed. You and he discuss how much this new equipment will improve productivity by permitting the recycling of material.

You are paged by your personnel manager. She wants to know if you are still available to speak at the local chamber of commerce meeting. You tell her that you would not miss it. As you head back toward your office you walk into the administrative offices. The manager of marketing informs you that sales orders are ahead of schedule, and is the bet still on for who is awarded the salesperson-of-the-year award. You kid him back saying, "Of course, but at double the original stakes"! Your comptroller mentions that if this sales trend holds, it could mean the most profitable year your firm has experienced to date.

It is now late in the day and you are ready to go home. You are
tired but it is good tired feeling. As you leave, you realize how all
the years of hard work have finally paid off. Your firm makes a very
good product. You have a hard-working and loyal workforce and
your customers are satisfied with the high-quality standards that
you, personally, insist upon. Because of this you are able to generate
a nice return to your stockholders.

You feel very good inside as you leave for the day.

It is very likely that the success of the firm is attributable to the monitoring activities of the manager. By making the organizational tour a
part of his everyday routine, he is keeping open a major communication
channel. By using this information to the advantage of the organization
he is better able to monitor performance and direct the firm on a successful course of action.

IMAGERY AND SYSTEMS VISUALIZATION

By receiving communication in an organization we are normally
prompted into action. The majority of time this action necessitates further communication. For example, as a general manager you may be
approached by someone in marketing who is requesting that you tell
those manufacturing people that more product is needed. When you
do speak to the manufacturing personnel they advise you to inform the
marketing department that the constant changes in product demanded
by them is the real reason for insufficient inventory levels. So back and
forth you go.

It is, therefore, quite apparent that we must envision these communication and information patterns from a systems perspective. In one
case, the communication represents an input that is processed and
passed along as output to another party who in turn takes it as input,
processes it, and then passes it along as output. By better visualizing
the entire system of communications in your organization, you are better
able to manage it in order to achieve the desired effects.

To enable your entire organization to benefit from this system perspective of viewing communication activity, we suggest that you conduct
the following workshop.

Step 1. Using small groups of six to eight people, assemble them in a quiet and
comfortable setting.

Step 2. After a relaxation period have them try to envision the various sources
from which they receive communication.

Step 3. Ask them to see what actions they normally take after having received
the information.

Step 4. Have them see the individuals to whom they most often respond and what actions they requested. Allow them plenty of time to form images at each point. Here is a script you can use.

> Picture the information flows that occur among the people around you. Visualize this communication network as a spider's web. Where is the center of the web? In which directions do the threads of the web normally tend to go? Where are the thickest threads? Where are the thinnest threads? Where is the web attached? Is the web a strong web or does it need constant repairs. Is the web reliable in its purpose? Do you often get caught in this web or are you able to see it and avoid it?

Step 5. After the imagery session has been completed ask each person to outline the images they experienced in a system's design on large sizes of chart paper.

Step 6. Place the sketches on the wall and then allow each person time to explain their sketch.

Step 7. Resolve differences of perception or perceived blockages that occur.

The human resource manager should conduct this workshop with all key members of the organization. After this has been accomplished, take the sketches and summarize them by department or function. This will then yield a system schematic reflecting the flow of information in the organization.

These workshops, although very easy and simple to conduct, are very powerful training tools. They allow individuals to examine the sources and directions of their communications. It provides them an opportunity to see the actions and activities resultant from these communications. It allows them to see ways to make the communication process work more effectively. And, finally, the communication system flowcharts that are produced can become invaluable as a diagnostic aid in improving the communication process throughout the total organization.

IMAGERY AND INFORMATION MANAGEMENT

As we mentioned in the above discussion, there are many benefits that accrue to the organization when the communication and information gathering functions are managed from a system point of view. All of your managers are part of a total system of information management in your organization. They generate and receive information that makes your organization operate. Individually, they represent a communication and information processing subsystem. These individual subsystems, when viewed wholistically, comprise the total communication and information processing system for your entire organization.

For your organization to survive and prosper, this organization communication and information processing system must be effectively managed as a resource just like every other resource utilized by your organization. This total information management process, which is more often referred to as a management information system (MIS) includes more than hardware, software, telecommunication networks, and the systems people that make it all work. It includes every manager in your organization starting at the top and working down. By using the imagery techniques that we have been discussing, your managers can better see their roles in the management information system and greatly enhance their effectiveness.

The direction and control of any effective management information system must start at the top. First of all, it is of the essence that everyone on the management team know that the management information system is supported by top management. Second, strategic planning and other conceptual managerial activities, in order to be successful, must be conducted realizing that it will be necessary to enhance and expand the management information system accordingly. MIS projects should support the long-term goals and strategic plan of the entire organization. As top management envisions what the organization is to become, it is imperative that they envision the MIS needs that will be necessitated in order to support these future demands.

As other levels of management try to see how to accomplish shorter range goals, they should also try to envision what MIS projects are necessary to support the short-term goals of the organization. They need to see what projects should be integrated with ongoing systems and what other projects are necessary to result in an integrated system of information management that is designed around the fundamental activities of the organization. In order to accomplish these tasks, imagery sessions are quite helpful. These sessions will enable these managers to see what information needs are currently being served by the existing MIS and what MIS projects could be implemented in order to better meet their information requirements.

It has been said that the future will belong to those who will manage the information resource more efficiently. The technology in the MIS field is growing exponentially. The advances that will come from such sources, to name but a few—supercomputers, artificial intelligence, and optical processing technology—are mind boggling. In order to survive and prosper in this dynamic future, organizations must use all of the imagination and creativity they can muster to adequately serve their information processing requirements.

8

HOW IMAGERY CAN IMPROVE PRODUCTIVITY IN PROBLEM-SOLVING AND DECISION MAKING

Imagine this: you have just received notification from your supervisor that your unit will adopt a new computer system to manage the human resource function. While you are familiar with various computer approaches to human resource management (HRM), the new system is one that you are unfamiliar with...although you have been given full responsibility for implementing the system in the next thirty days...without the assistance of representatives from the computer leasing company. Thirty days seems like a long time, but you are also expected to continue your regular responsibilities during that period. What images come to mind as you ponder this problem set?

This is the type of problem where imaginal techniques can be applied to solve the dilemma better. Mental imagery and related processes can be quickly and effectively applied to the management of many types of problems within organizations. Human resource professionals can train employees to use imaginal processes to scan problem dynamics and to develop a rich list of alternatives to test for problem solution. While people sometimes resist using their imagery in problem-solving, once familiar with the techniques, they usually overcome their resistance. Just as is true in other applications within this book, trainer competency in the development and presentation of imaginal scripts and scenarios is critical in making imaginal techniques powerful tools in problem-solving and decision making.

This chapter provides information on and guidelines for the use of imaginal techniques in the problem-solving realm. Scripts show various ways that these techniques can be integrated with more traditional and rational means of problem-solving and decision making.

ANTICIPATING AND PREVENTING PROBLEMS

In today's turbulent societal and business environment, organizations face challenges and search for opportunities in their environments. Very few organizations are immune from influences of such things as the possibility of another fuel crisis, the federal budget deficit, international trade imbalances, the value of the dollar in reference to foreign currency, or the precarious geopolitical situation in the Middle East. Organizations that ignore these environmental realities, impact on their operations and strategies are suffering from a form of corporate myopia. Organizations that actively scan their environments, anticipate emergent problems and take advantage of opportunities that may arise over time. These are the organizations that will survive and prosper in the information age of the future. To survive, organizational members must be taught to appreciate and alter their mental models of the future so that surprises are prepared for before their impact on the organization.

Your organization's environment includes all of the political, legal, economic, international, sociocultural, value-based, technological, geopolitical, and demographic trends and changes that affect its ability to function effectively and efficiently over your strategic planning horizon. (See Figure 5–2.) Twenty years ago, there was more stability in this environment than there is today. As time passes, the social environment will become more complex and will present all organizations with novel problems that demand creative and anticipatory problem-solving skills. For example, we can no longer assume away the rest of the world economically. Most current business decisions are affected by international events; we truly live in a world economy.

One of the key functions of the HRM unit is to serve as a scanning unit that watches the environment for patterns of change that affect the organization. The HRM unit is in contact with many sources of current information about the future and the market place. This responsibility falls to the HRM unit because it works with the human dimension of organizational functioning. One creative way to accomplish the problem definition task is to use imaginal techniques to develop clear and explicit scenarios of the future as well as strategies your organization can apply to the hypothetical, but potential future environment. Further, you can share this expertise with other managers and planners, so that the total organization expands and articulates its visions of the future in preparation for that future.

For example, one problem that organizations will face in the future is the problem of recruiting qualified personnel. As the age of the population goes up, as the number of entering workers goes down, and as the technological sophistication of work increases, organizations will face the critical problem of finding, attracting, and maintaining competent work forces. If traditional manpower planning methods are used solely, one may find that these techniques don't function in the future environment defined by emerging trends. However, if HRM personnel are schooled in the use of creative, projective problem-solving, they can build scenarios of future conditions, how conditions will affect manpower planning over time, and how the organization can adapt its recruitment and selection techniques to accommodate these trends. In other words, imagery can be used to supplement traditional manpower planning, but not to replace it. In this example, the planning group would take part in a process that involves the following procedures (see Figure 5–1).

1. *Consensual Definition of the Problem*: Herein, the group discusses the nature of the problem that is anticipated and develops consensus about the dynamics of the problem. A suitable definition here would be: "How do we acquire talented and qualified employees in the future as the number of qualified applicants decreases and as the technological requirements of the workplace increase?" This definition presupposes that the HRM staff have prescreened the problem by using available forecasting and trend analysis information.

2. *Individual Problem Brainstorming*: After arriving at consensus on the nature of the problem, staff can be placed in a relaxed state and given imaginal cues to promote creative scanning of the problem and the potential ways that the problem can be solved. A possible script for this activity might go something like this.

> Take a moment now to close your eyes, stretch out, and let relaxation flow throughout your body. [Pause.] Become aware of any physical or emotional sources of tension or anxiety that you may be experiencing. [Pause.] As you scan your mind and body, imagine yourself converting negative or tense energies into black balloons—see yourself blowing these balloons up and watching them sail away from you, carrying both tension and routinized thinking with them. [Pause.] You are totally relaxed and open to using your imaginal and creative talents to handle the problem we are studying. [Pause.] Now envision yourself as adept and creative at problem-solving. See yourself as able to handle the most complex future problem in an intelligent and creative manner. See yourself as using your creative problem-solving skills to deal with our current problem. [Pause.]
>
> Now imagine that you're responsible for recruitment and selection of competent personnel five years from now. Imagine that you have carefully scanned the employment environment as you ponder how to attract and retain employees so that we remain effective and profitable in the future. [Pause.] Envision the types of employees

we will need to meet the challenges of this dynamic future. [Pause.] What types of skills and abilities will we need? [Pause]. What types of attitudes and characteristics will you be looking for in your employees?" [Pause.] What information sources and recruiting channels will you use to find potential employees who best fit the needs of the organization [Pause.] How will you influence prospective employees to see our organization as the type of place in which they prosper. [Pause.]

Take a moment now to reflect on your ideas and impressions. [Pause.] Try not to edit or screen any of your ideas. [Pause.] Where you have created an interesting idea, take some time now to play with the idea. [Pause.] Relax and let your creative powers help you further develop potential solutions to this future problem. View the problem as an opportunity for you to exercise your creative problem-solving skills on a challenge. [Pause.] That's good. Now, take another moment to collect your varied images and thoughts. [Pause.] Shortly we'll come back together as a group to look at the issue through the multiple and creative visions we have generated.

Be confident that your ideas will contribute to our overall problem-solving efforts. [Pause.] Once again, try not to edit or delete your thoughts. Imagine yourself as ready to record and share your good ideas. [Pause.] Imagine yourself writing your ideas down on a mental notebook for safekeeping and sharing." [Pause.]

This script gives personnel the opportunity to evaluate freely the problem from a variety of views and to share their ideas with others. It also gives them practice in reframing their conceptions of the problem and building freely creative depictions of potential solution paths.

3. *Reconstitution*: Herein, the group would come back together and share collective experiences, insights, and ideas generated during the imaginal script exercise. Someone in the group would record the ideas and at the close of this exercise would reiterate the ideas to the group. This reiteration would serve as the basis for the fourth step in this process. This process of "expanded effort" generates a great number of potential ideas that may be creative and feasible solutions' options. Research has shown that the more elaborate the information generation process, the greater the degree of creativity and originality that is promoted.

4. *Free Imaginal Excursion*: During this phase, staff uses the collective creativity of the group as a basis for further elaborating potential problem solutions. All staff have an expanded view of the problem from others' perspectives; they will use this broad-based cognitive structure to further study and solve the problem. A short, provocative image set allows staff to once again access and explore their creative ideas. Consider the following script.

Once again, take a relaxed attitude and posture. [Pause.] Place yourself in a creative state and review the materials we have just covered. [Pause.] You have expressed your ideas from the first script. Take a moment to review these ideas. [Pause.] Now take another moment to review the ideas of your colleagues. [Pause.] That's good. Now, once again, place yourself in the position of recruiting and selecting employees ten years from now. [Pause.]

Given all of the ideas that you have now experienced, how would you go about recruiting and selecting new employees for the firm in this dynamic future? [Pause.] Take a few moments now to develop a scenario for managing this problem. [Pause.] Try not to be limiting or judgmental in developing your strategy. [Pause.]

5. *Problem Elaboration and Solution*: After bringing staff back into the present and once again elaborating ideas, staff evaluates the various options that are present and develops an anticipatory recruiting strategy for dealing with work force changes of the future. Your strategies may focus on either training current personnel to be more adaptive in the future, or you may focus on an increase in manpower scanning efforts, which you decide is critical to recruitment and selection in the competitive future. The important process within this step is to consolidate the various perspectives on the problem and to generate strategies that take into account the dynamics that have previously been identified.

Problems can only be identified and proactively managed if they are anticipated by and considered within the mental models that organizational personnel hold about the future. These mental models are the recurrent images, depictions, and scenarios that we hold of our organizations and the action paths of these organizations. Mental models are highly imaginal in nature and can best be reviewed, modified, and improved by educating personnel to work comfortably with these models during imaginal practice sessions. If the mental models of personnel are overly focused on the short-term present, the likelihood that the organization can anticipate and manage very different future problems is greatly inhibited. Only by encouraging and rewarding people for envisioning the future can we actually begin to deal with the probable contingencies that will emerge.

Frequently, personnel are so tied to self-limiting and reactive future images of their organizations that little true anticipatory mindwork is done to prepare the organization for its challenges or its opportunities. In order to promote more long-term thinking, you can help educate other personnel in anticipatory-projective imaginal exercises that allow them to move beyond the routinized thinking that often governs many facets of organizations.

Our research has clearly shown that matching an inappropriate problem-solving approach with a creative or challenging problem leads to less productivity and creativity in problem-solving. If we are to adapt a method of preventative problem-solving in the future, we must activate the imaginal powers of personnel to depict, alter, and improve our organization's response to inevitable changes. Unique problems cannot be solved through retrospection or through routinization. Such problems are solved when individuals go beyond habitual thinking patterns. Problem-solving is a skill area. As with any other skill area, acquisition and use of sound methods in problem-solving occurs through practice.

The next section of this chapter looks at Creative Problem-Solving and ways to promote this within a firm.

CREATIVITY AND INDIVIDUAL/ORGANIZATIONAL PRODUCTIVITY

As with anticipatory and preventative problem-solving, creative problem-solving will be a characteristic process within the successful organization of the future. In fact, anticipatory problem-solving is closely related to the creative process, and allows the creative individual both to define the creative process and to define the problem more vividly.

Creativity seems a mystery to most of us. We often assume that only a very few talented people are fortunate to have this wondrous human capacity. We reward creativity with accolades and large paychecks. We all secretly wish that we were more creative. Many consulting organizations offer "surefire" programs and techniques that will enhance creativity in a two-day (or so) seminar. While all of this is understandable, it is unfortunate. Creativity is an innate cognitive process that is available to most healthy individuals when and it they choose to prioritize creativity as a skill area to be developed.

Mental imagery is an important component of creativity and a process that is available to everyone in order to recognize and apply in personal and professional activities. Recent research has shown that individuals who have vivid and controllable imagery also have higher degrees of creative expression than individuals with less vivid imaginal experiences. The ability to build and elaborate imaginal mindsets and scenarios is a learned skill for many people and something that they have consciously applied in their life. Research also shows that by merely telling someone that they either are creative (by reputation) or should "be creative" in a problem-solving context improves the number and quality of their ideas or problem responses. This suggests that even superficial manipulation of the creative self-image of an individual can have positive effects on creative performance. Finally, historical and anecdotal reports on the creative works of Einstein, Edison, Kekule, Wordsworth, Whitman, and many other artists, writers, and statespersons consistently indicate that they utilized and manipulated their imaginal processes to deal with problems that required creative or innovative solutions. These results are important to keep in mind, especially since we too often see creativity as a talent of the few rather than as a potential that most of us can have.

THE CREATIVE SELF-IMAGE

Enhancing creative problem-solving involves recognizing the importance of self-image to one's creative behavior. For instance, if you define yourself as a creative individual, you will eagerly undertake challenging tasks that allow you to become more creative and adept at flexible methods of problem-solving. Likewise, if you mentally model yourself as uncreative, you will avoid unique, novel, or challenging tasks and will rely on routinized problem-solving methods to solve a limited set of predictable problems. In other words, the self-fulfilling prophesy contributes to creativity. Recall at this point that a mental model is the depiction, mental picture, or image set that an individual maintains and uses as a reference guide for choice and action. One's self-image is the mental model of self that guides the individual in dealing with reality. Creativity is one aspect of this mental model that most of us define both from our own experiences and from the evaluations of significant others in our lives and work. By helping your organization's employees recognize and perceive their abilities to be creative, you help them to re-frame their self-images so that their problem-solving improves. Several examples of brief imaginal techniques are provided in the following examples to show how the creative self-image can be enhanced.

After inducing a state of relaxation in staff or trainees, the following script can be used to help them re-frame their internal imaginal models of self.

Now that you are relaxed and free of tension, you will explore your creativity. You will scan your past, your present, and your future to picture your ability to be creative. As much as possible, relax during these excursions and develop a picture of yourself as a creative and contributing member of our team. [Pause.] Think of how you've dealt with problems in the past. [Pause.] Envision how you wish to deal with problems in the future. [Pause.] That's good—you are relaxed. [Pause.] The ability to relax helps you be more creative. [Pause.] Try to remember to relax each and every time that you are faced with a task that requires creativity and innovation. [Pause.] Now it is time for us to begin our travels. [Pause.]

Take a moment and return to a specific point in time in your past when you accomplished something that made you feel especially creative. [Pause.] Take your time in locating this event or period— there is no hurry. [Longer Pause.] Have you found that event? Good. Take a moment and re-live that event or period in your life as vividly as you can. Place yourself in that timeframe and re-experience the actions, feelings, and consequences of your creativity. Envision yourself in that time and space demonstrating and using your innate creativity. [Pause.] As much as possible, recall all that you can of that experience. [Pause.]

Now that you have relived that event, how did you feel about yourself at that time? [Pause.] What did it feel like to be creative and innovative? [Pause.] How did you use your innate creativity? [Pause.] What were your personal and professional rewards for being creative? [Pause.] You have clear evidence that you have been creative in the past. Now we are going to change our focus to the present. [Pause.]

As you maintain a state of quiet relaxed attentiveness, begin to scan the challenges and opportunities that you face today. [Pause.] What tasks currently require your creative or innovative attention? [Pause.] Be specific in defining these tasks. [Pause.] Now select one of the most important and difficult tasks that you face today. Why is this your most important task? [Pause.] Why does this task require your creativity and innovation? [Pause.] How are you planning to manage this task? [Pause.] Now as clearly as possible, imagine yourself carrying out this task in a very creative manner. Actually rehearse how you will manage this task so that your creativity is applied to it. See and experience yourself analyzing the task [pause], thinking creatively about the task [pause], and acting in a creative fashion as you succeed in accomplishing the task. [Pause.]

That was good—you now have envisioned yourself behaving creatively in the present. What are the consequences of behaving creatively? [Pause.] How do you feel about yourself when you apply your creativity to problems? [Pause.] How do your feelings about and images of yourself change when you behave creatively. [Pause.] Now it is time for you to project yourself into the future.

During this exercise, it is important that you begin to see yourself as creative and flexible in your problem-solving and decision making. [Pause.] Your self-image—that mental picture you hold of yourself— influences your creativity. It is critical that you perceive yourself as creative in your thinking and actions. [Pause.] Creative individuals, like yourself, maintain a creative self-image. [Pause.] Now, totally relax. [Pause.] Imagine yourself as creative and innovative in the future. [Pause.] As vividly as possible, see yourself as able to access and apply creativity as you need it. [Pause.] Think of creativity as a big pot from which you can scoop with a ladle when you need to do so. Envision yourself as able to use your mental imagery to help you solve problems. [Pause.] See yourself as able to tolerate the frustration and ambiguity that often surrounds innovative tasks. [Pause.] Experience yourself as a flexible thinker [pause]—a thinker who can generate many ideas [pause]; a problem-solver who creates many unique ideas and solutions to problems [Pause]; an individual who can think in many categories. [Pause.] Begin to build a new self-image of creativity. [Pause.] Hold this image and return to build it often. [Pause.] Use new experiences as challenges to test your creativity. [Pause.] Build a clear picture of yourself as easily able to think and act in creative ways.

This script, of course, will not make an employee more creative. It will reshape and reframe the thinking and self-imagery of the individual so that he/she comes to think and act in ways that promote flexible, creative production. Such a script, or derivations of this script, would be used a number of times in imaginal practice contexts to help the individual with the reframing process. The key point to recall is that as an employee comes to see him/herself as more creative, he/she will begin to behave in ways that demonstrate more creativity.

This script uses several critical imaginal formats that are important not only to self-image enhancement, but to other training venues within your organization.

First, when you have individuals recall and depict past experiences, you are helping them use *episodic recall imagery*. Such memory recall and depiction provides a framework for the individual to use when dealing with present or anticipated problems. Usually, episodic recall allows the individual to specify instances that are analogous to the present context of problem-solving. By so doing, some of the strangeness or ambiguity of the current problem is reduced. Additionally, recall allows the individual to review past actions in relationship to the present so that potential courses of action may be transferred to the present. Episodic recall imagery is largely based on accessing and replaying details of experience from long-term memory.

Second, this script made use of *behavioral* or *covert rehearsal,* a technique that has been widely applied in both therapeutic and training realms. This technique involves cuing an individual to project him/herself into a future condition, state, or scenario and asking that they rehearse the best way to manage a problem. You also ask them to imagine the consequences of adapting the given behavioral or problem-solving approach. Such rehearsal generates productive awareness and readiness for problems and helps the individual stylize potential choice and action paths for the future.

Finally, this script provides a number of questions and suggestions to the individual. These cuing mechanisms influence the expectancies of the individual relative to the present and the future. Research continues to show that one's expectancies about an event or problem greatly influence the eventual success or failure of one's efforts. By shaping the self-expectancies of the individual, you can help bring about an image of him/herself as capable of dealing with problems in more creative ways. This, of course, contributes to reframing the individual's self-image.

Overall, to engender more creative behavior, a good starting point remains the self-imagery of your organization's employees. If they cannot come to see themselves as creative, it is highly unlikely that they will adapt creative and flexible means for managing problems. Such a program could then be reinforced with organizational reward and incentive systems that contribute to the development of a creative culture in the organization.

Figure 8-1
Modes of Thinking

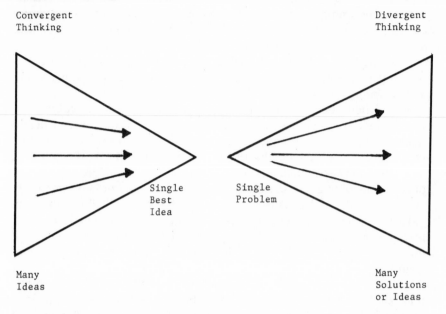

Convergent
Thinking

Divergent
Thinking

Single
Best
Idea

Single
Problem

Many
Ideas

Many
Solutions
or Ideas

DEVELOPING CONVERGENT AND DIVERGENT THINKING SKILLS

Two skill areas are critical in solving problems today—convergent and divergent thinking (see Figure 8–1).

Imagine this problem: how do we reduce our trucking costs from Orlando to Memphis by finding the route that is fastest, with cheapest fuel prices, and least patrolled by the police?

In this problem we are searching for the best solution to a problem that is defined by three conditions that must be met. Our solution must take into account these three conditions and is, in fact, boundaried by these conditions. We are working in a problem context of the type where IF fast, cheap, unpatrolled, THEN route A. We are seeking to reduce our options. We want the best logical solution. We use analysis, facts, and figures to draw our final conclusion. This type of problem requires *convergent thinking* skills.

Convergent thinking involves the ability to analytically and evaluatively view a dynamic problem to select or create the single, best solution or response. Herein, the individual converges on the solution that fits the demands of the problem (fast, cheap, unpatrolled). During convergent thinking, the analytical faculties of the individual are used to weigh the costs versus benefits or the threats versus *opportunities* that can result from a selected solution or action path. In this way, convergent thinking is consistent with logical, linear, or sequential thinking. This means of problem-solving and thinking is predominantly taught and used in American educational and business systems. It is an approach to problem-solving that works best in well-defined problem contexts where there is plenty of relevant information. However, with unique or novel problems where there is limited information, convergent thinking and problem-solving falters because it cannot accommodate a lack of rationality in the problem context. Further, convergent problem-solving, by nature, is reductionistic—it excludes facts and variables that are not immediately relevant or apparent to the development of the single, optimal solution.

Since the problems we will face in the future are likely to be unique and novel, convergent problem-solving skills may not be so useful as they have been in the relatively stable and predictable past. Convergent problem-solving may also lack power in the future because imaginal and intuitive processes are ignored in lieu of rational and empirical approaches to problem-solving. Since imaginal and intuitive processes are closely linked to creativity, the convergent problem-solver may be inhibiting his/her ability to think creatively.

Now, imagine this problem; how do we provide for the ongoing personal and professional development of our staff? In this problem, there probably isn't any one best way, since the needs of staff will vary as will their commitment to personal and professional development. Further, there is no single, time-tested method for evolving and promoting training and development. Lastly, the skills that are required of workers will change with increasing technological progress. Many skills that will be essential in the future do not even exist today. While the problem may seem deceptively easy to manage, it is one that many organizations will face in the future. To deal effectively with this problem, you must project yourself into a future context and imaginally evaluate the dynamics of the problem. This is a problem where *divergent thinking* skills are best applied.

Divergent thinking skills involve three basic abilities that can be taught. The first ability is *imaginal fluency*. Imaginal fluency involves the ability to use imagination and creativity to generate multiple potential problem responses, solutions, or ideas. Research has shown repeatedly that the individual who demonstrates imaginal fluency also demonstrates the second key area of divergent thinking, *originality*. Originality is what we often associate with pure creativity. It is the ability to develop unique or novel perspectives, solutions, or ideas. Finally, divergent thinking involves *flexibility* or the ability to think in many categories and to make shifts from one category of thinking to another in search of an idea, response, or solution to a problem. Fluency, originality, and flexibility lead to more adept and creative problem-solving.

Specified below is a script that can help you and your employees build scenarios to apply to this problem. This script promotes fluent, original, and flexible thought relative to the previously identified problem.

Now that you are relaxed and attentive, we are going to project ourselves into the future. We are going to place ourselves in this organization ten years from now. [Pause.] Take a moment now to re-orient your thinking to the future. You have done projective exercises before. Use your previous imaginal abilities on this problem. Take a moment now to establish a future mindset. [Pause.]

The problem we are considering is one that we have talked about often in staff meetings—how do we provide for the on-going personal and professional development of our employees in the future? This is a familiar yet difficult problem. It requires that we think in a long-term perspective. The script we will experience will help us do this and will help us generate many creative ideas about managing this problem. [Pause.] During the script, allow yourself to think flexibly. [Pause.] "Try to ignore any personal censorship you have about your ideas. When we are dealing with the future all ideas have value. [Pause.]

Imagine yourself coming to work ten years from now. Take a moment to scan your environment. What type of day is it? [Pause.] How do you feel about the day? [Pause.] As completely as possible, fill in the details of what it will be like for you to come to work ten years in the future. Envision what your office will look like. Think of the office machines you see. What will be on your mind as you come to work that day ten years from now? [Pause.] Take a moment now to build a scenario of this event. Sketch out in your imagination that day and your thoughts and feelings. [Longer pause.] That is good. You are ready to deal with the problem that has been mentioned. You will deal with it from a future perspective that you have created. [Pause.] Again, avoid censoring the ideas that come to mind—all ideas are appropriate. [Pause.] The problem our organization faces is how to provide relevant and meaningful training and development for our employees in the future. [Pause.] Allow your imagination to scan that problem freely for a moment. [Pause.] What ideas pop to mind? [Pause.] What spontaneous insights do you have? [Pause.] If none appear, relax and let your creativity come forward. [Pause.]

In order to meet the training needs of our employees in the future, we must know our employees. We are going to explore the needs, values, and skills of our employees ten years from now. Let your imagination place you in our organization ten years from now. [Pause.] In your own mind, imagine how the firm will look. [Pause.]

How will things be different from now? Take mental notes of your images and impressions. Take a moment to envision our workplace ten years from now. [Longer Pause.]

Now you have imagined yourself going to work and looking around the shop ten years down the road. Imagine that you are invisible to everyone in the firm. You can come and go as you please. [Pause.] This gives you great flexibility to observe and make mental notes on our future employees. [Pause.] You will take this opportunity to gather impressions of your firm's employees [Pause.] You will be asked to focus on several things during this experience. As much as possible, let your imagination direct your thoughts. Make mental notes of your impressions as they evolve. [Pause.] That's good, let's begin.

As you invisibly float through the organization, begin imagining that you encounter and observe various employees at work. As much as possible, use your imagination to answer the following key questions.

As you observe the operations in the firm, how are these future employees alike and different from current employees? [Pause.] Take a moment to imaginally develop likenesses and differences between today's worker and tomorrow's worker. Don't censor your thinking. That's good. Make mental notes as your impressions evolve.

This script would continue along these lines until your staff had imaginally developed impressions of the needs, values, skills, and attitudes of both new and continuing workers in the firm. By training your staff to break context and explore the long-term nature of this and other problems, you reduce their routinized problem thinking. You also increase the impressions that are relevant to developing programs for future training. A second script might focus on the evolution of programs that fit with the orientations of the workers. A short script of this follows. This script would, of course, be presented after impressions from the earlier script were aggregated.

Now that we have collectively envisioned the needs, values, skills, and attitudes of our future workers, we must build programs for them that sustain their motivation and development. [Pause.] This will be somewhat easier since we now have a clear vision of what our work force may be like in the future. We will use the information gathered in our previous script to build a potential programming strategy for the short-term and the long-term. [Pause.] Once again, use your imagination and creativity to build program ideas that address the needs, values, skills, and attitudes of our workers over time. [Pause.] Feel confident that your ideas are worthwhile.

Given our previous brainstorming, imagine and review our present programs and think of how these could be adapted to the future. [Pause.] Every idea is worthwhile—so eliminate self-censorship and make clear mental notes of your ideas. Try to develop as many ideas as you can. [Pause.] The first programming area you'll consider is career planning. [Pause.] Take a moment and think about our current program. [Pause.] What parts of the program are most valuable and should be continued? [Pause.] Likewise, what parts should be eliminated in the future? [Pause.] How should the program be adapted to meet the needs, values, skills, and attitudes of the future work force? [Longer Pause.] Take a moment now to scan the career planning realm. Develop as many ideas as you can to improve the effectiveness and relevancy of this area in the future. [Longer Pause.] That's good—make mental notes of your ideas. [Pause.] We'll now move on to recruitment and selection.

Relevant scripts, similar to the one in the above example, can then be written for recruitment and selection, compensation, training, performance appraisal, and the other functional areas of your HRM department. The key to writing these scripts is to encourage your personnel to apply information and impressions from previous scripts to the remodeling of the various areas. Varying the script approach for each area will reduce monotony. For instance, if you wanted to explore the area of an Employee Assistance, you might use a script such as this:

We will now turn to our employee assistance program. We have envisioned what our workers will be like in the future. We have a clear picture of their needs, values, skills, and attitudes. [Pause.] We also know that stress will increase in the future. Our current EAP program helps our employees work with to solve stress and other counseling problems. Take a moment to reflect upon our current program. [Pause.] What areas do you think are effective? [Pause.] What areas will need expansion or enhancement in the future? [Longer Pause.] As you think about this, envision the types of future personal problems our workers will have. [Pause.] As you generate ideas, also think of programs and activities that the EAP can use to meet these problems. [Longer Pause.] Don't constrain your thinking. [Pause.] "That's good, make mental notes of your impressions— we'll now share our ideas.

These scripts would promote fluency, flexibility, and originality of thinking. Over time and with increased exposure to imaginal techniques, your staff's ability to apply these processes to tough problems will grow. Convergent and divergent thinking abilities are both necessary for effective problem-solving. Both areas can be enhanced through a variety of imaginal scripts such as those above. Beyond this, one can use other techniques to enhance creativity and problem-solving effectiveness. We'll explore a few of these techniques now:

1. *Timeouts*: In lieu of coffeebreaks, you may want to introduce a timeout option in your firm. Evidence has shown that most employees spend only thirty-

five to forty-five minutes of productive activity per hour of work. Thus, within an eight-hour workday, approximately two hours are wasted. In order to gain back some of this precious time, you can set up one or two regular break periods during the day when employees can either listen to relaxation tapes or be involved in focused imagery exercises. In either case, employees will become more acclimated to imaginal processes and techniques as they are given opportunities to practice. Focused imagery sessions might deal with relevant topics such as career planning, stress reduction, dietary adjustment, or other areas that are relevant to members of your team.

2. *Idea Books*: One approach that has worked well in workshops that we have conducted is to train individuals in the "Journalizing" process. Most people are constantly encountering images, impressions, and ideas that may have future value even if perceived as irrelevant to current problems. Most of us let these ideas slip by and often later regret the fact that we had a good idea, but have now forgotten it. By helping staff to appreciate and record their images and impressions in notebooks, you encourage your personnel to accumulate a rich reservoir of ideas that are stored for later application. An alternative "journalizing approach is to encourage staff members to spend a small amount of time each day recording general ideas. Our experience has shown that employees will initially resist the journalizing process, although with exposure to the benefits of self-recording, resistances fall away. A second alternative in this area is tape-recording. For some people, the high-tech approach is more appropriate. We make it a habit to have either a tape recorder or notebook with us at all times. It is amazing how many ideas we captured out of the blue by simply being prepared to record them.

3. *Gaming*: A third way to promote general creativity and problem-solving effectiveness is through "gaming." This approach may take the form of transforming a problem into a distant but analogous context, or it may involve having employees work with various problems that demand creative fluency, originality, and flexibility. Several types of games can be used that involve reconceptualizing problems in terms other than those commonly used for problem definition. For example, one might envision the problem of recruiting as getting animals aboard the ark. The problem then becomes one that is out-of-context and open to new ways of viewing the situation. Thomas Gordon's *Synectics* has many transformational approaches to gaming with problems. Games may also take on the ambiance of a competition with the team generating the most creative yet feasible approach to a problem winning a prize. Creativity is often fueled by humor, and humor can often be promoted through generating a game atmosphere during serious problem-solving. Remember, creativity is not just an innate talent, it is a skill arena that can be recognized and improved through practice.

IMAGINAL APPLICATIONS IN CONFLICT AND NEGOTIATIONS

Conflict and negotiation events engender much stress in organizations. As the world becomes more complex and as individuals compete for fewer resources, the potential for conflict will increase within and between organizations. Social psychological research has long shown that when groups are in conflict, they tend to distort perceptions (or mental models) of themselves and their adversaries. In fact, these distortions of reality aggravate conflict situations and often inhibit attempts at negotiation and resolution. Various imaginal techniques can be applied within conflict situations to help competing individuals and groups: (1) correct distorted mental models; (2) re-envision relationships and interpersonal dynamics; and (3) develop strategies for conflict management and future cooperation.

An example from recent history may illustrate how conflict is difficult to handle in organizations.

The well-publicized demise of Frank Borman at Eastern Airlines represents the consequences of a conflict that was improperly managed because neither Borman nor the involved union officials could transcend their routinized images to develop a collaborative plan of problem resolution. When individuals and groups become stuck in dysfunctional thinking or mental modeling, functional fixedness exists. This kind of habitual, reactive, and stagnant thinking restricts the ability of competing parties to evolve win-win options for the management of conflict. Stale, archaic, and often adversarial warfare images dominate the thinking of competing parties and lead to an "I'm gonna win at any cost" mentality which ensures that neither party will benefit in the end.

As we can see with the Eastern situation, Borman's images appeared to freeze. It was as if he sought to protect the sacred managerial prerogative that is the cornerstone of much corporate image-making and strategy. Apparently, he had difficulty envisioning a more collaborative approach to conflict resolution. His image-making seemed to become insular and he may have excluded sound advice that would have altered the dynamics of the conflict. The same is probably true of the union. Negotiators for flight attendants and mechanics probably bore and generated extremely negative images of Borman and the managerial team at Eastern. In the imaginal scenarios that governed their negotiation choices and alternatives, the union representatives also decided that they wouldn't give in to Borman and his allies at any cost. What developed and was publicized was the adolescent "warmaking" of two groups that couldn't see beyond their mutually destructive and obsolete images to reframe alternatives in the best interests of both parties. In the end, both parties lost as Eastern was enveloped by Texas Airlines. It was the mental modeling of the two adversaries that spelled their mutual doom. This is often true in conflict situations, although it doesn't have to be this way. As noted earlier, there are at least three areas in which imaginal techniques can contribute to effective conflict resolution. We shall now provide examples of such applications.

CORRECTING DISTORTED PERCEPTIONS

In conflicts, competing groups distort their perceptions of themselves and their adversaries. Take a moment to think back to a recent conflict in which you were a part. This may have involved a conflict with another unit in your organization, a supplier, or a union. Recall and imagine the types of thinking that went on in your own group as you manipulated your images of your group and your conflicting group. If your group is like most groups in conflict, you probably developed highly positive, protective, and self-righteous images of yourself. You, in fact, altered perceptual reality so that you appeared in your collective mind's eye to be better than your competitors, but also more deserving of victory or favor and more in tune with positive motivations and agenda relative to the conflict. Your group developed an imaginal set that played out the theme: "We are really better than that other group." Now realize that the other group was doing exactly the same thing. They, too, were building inaccurate imaginal sets of their own goodness in reference to your group. A second imaginal alteration that occurs during conflict is that while we are improving our self-images, we increase the amount of fault-finding and derogation of the other group. We may actually fantasize and invent shortcomings of our adversaries. We may generate rumors about them and attempt to "negativize" their image in our own eyes and in the eyes of others. Both of these activities are largely mental in nature and involve distortions of reality. Both tendencies are also extremely common in conflicting groups. Finally, both activities make conflict harder to manage because these imaginal distortions contribute to greater adversarialism and pig-headed imagery between groups. While these distortions are detrimental to negotiations and conflict management, they can be overcome. Below is a script for use after a relaxation induction session that helps in this area:

> As you know, we are having some problems with _____. For the next few moments, we are going to study and evaluate the images that govern our thinking and action in reference to this group. As much as possible, free up your images and come to terms with your perceptions and misperceptions of _____. [Pause.] That's good, you are relaxed and ready to explore the perceptual dynamics of the current conflict. [Pause.] You are also ready to recognize and amend your images of _____ so that management of our existing conflict moves toward a win-win solution. To do so, old and obsolete images must be corrected and new images inserted into your thinking. [Pause.] Remember to take good mental notes of your impressions, as we will use these impressions to build new mental models of our relationship to _____. [Pause.]

Take a moment now to travel back in your memory to review the
past occasions that you have had to meet with the members of
_____. Think about the different individuals in the group. [Pause.]
Take a moment to review occasions when you have had positive
relationships with _____ members as individuals. [Pause.] As
much as possible, envision _____ not as group, but as individuals. [Pause.] Review your impressions of the individuals in that
group. What are some of the positive and negative impressions that
come to mind about these individuals? [Pause.] Don't edit your
thinking, let your impressions come forward freely. That's good. As
you recollect individual impressions built on previous interactions
with group members, how does this alter your mental model of that
group? [Pause.]

Now let's take a moment to envision how the members of _____
are similar to us. What likenesses in thinking and behavior do you
share with individuals in this group? [Pause.] Good—make a mental
list of these as you review your images of _____ members as
individuals. [Pause.] Now take a moment to review the congruence
between your current images of this group and your past impressions of them as individuals. [Pause.] That's good—make mental
notes of your impressions. These notes will help us build a more
productive picture of _____ so that we can better resolve our
conflict. [Pause.] Now take another moment to review your current
impressions and images of the individuals in _____. [Pause.] How
accurate are these images and impressions? [Pause.] Where there
are inaccuracies, how did they develop? [Pause.] How can you alter your impressions of _____ members so that we have grounds
for resolving our current conflict? How do negative or inaccurate
images contribute to the adversarialism we are now experiencing
with _____?

While this script won't cure the adversarialism between the groups, it
can reduce the impact of distorted perceptions and images and forge a
better overall picture between the competing groups. The script would,
of course, have to be applied to both groups, and both groups would
then discuss their collective impressions separately and later together
in order to build a common perceptual ground upon which to manage
the existing conflict. Any number of similar scripts can be built so that
distortions are minimized and likenesses are emphasized. As distortions
are normalized the emotionalization of conflict is greatly reduced.

Re-envisionment of Interpersonal Dynamics and
Cooperative Strategies

As distortions of perception are corrected, room develops for a reframing of the interpersonal dynamics between the competing parties.

In conflict situations, one cannot remedy the conflict by merely altering the mental modeling of perceptions between and within groups. Rather, this reframing must extend to the behavioral dynamics that govern interactions. As new attitudes are integrated through "re-envisionment" techniques, new behavioral mindsets can also evolve. The following script illustrates one approach to this.

> Now that you are relaxed, we are going to experience a trip into the future. You are to imagine yourself on a spacecraft traveling to Mars for the first landing of men/women on the planet's surface. [Pause.] Imagine that members of the crew include your own teammates and members of _____. [Pause.] In order for the mission to be successful, there must be mutual cooperation between the teams even though your individual team goals and values may be quite different. [Pause.] Think about the members of _____. How are their goals and values like and unlike your own team's values and goals? [Pause.] How are their team actions and strategies like and unlike your own team's strategies for reaching goals? [Pause.] Be certain to take good mental notes of your impressions as you imagine yourself having to work with _____ in order to succeed in your mission. [Longer Pause.] Imagine now that the interdependency of team interactions determines the success or failure of your mission. [Pause.] While you do have differences, you must forge a link of cooperation to achieve your mission and to survive. [Pause.] In your own mind, what would you do to change your current interactions with _____ to ensure that cooperation replaces competitiveness? [Pause.] How would you positively manage existing and emerging tensions that undermine interdependency? [Pause.] What kind of new relationships would be necessary if your mutual goal is to be achieved? [Pause.] What kinds of tactics and methods would you use on this mission to ensure the development of greater cooperation between yourselves and _____? [Pause.] What strategies can be used that your two teams can use to deal with conflicts and crises that arise? [Pause.] Open your thinking and allow good ideas to come forward.

As noted, changes of perceptions should be followed by changes in the actions and interactions between the teams. A first critical step here is to reframe current interactions in terms of future interactions of interdependency. While attitudinal changes may produce some behavioral changes, we must make certain that concrete behavioral strategies and new interpersonal dynamics are generated to reinforce new mental models within and between the groups. We wish to reiterate that first steps in the management of conflictual problems are to recreate and reframe the competing images of the involved parties. If these images are not revised, there is little likelihood that productive conflict management can evolve. In conflict situations especially, ideation (mental modeling) precedes and influences actions. Realistic and accurate modeling can reduce adversarialism that complicates the negotiation process.

REMOVING BARRIERS TO DECISION OR SOLUTION IMPLEMENTATION

A final area where imaginal techniques are helpful in problem-solving is in the management of change within an organization. Employees resist change for many reasons including fear for personal security, disruption of the status quo, anxiety about reduced status and power, and fear that new changes will be too difficult to learn or manage. Generally, these barriers are largely perceptual in nature. While change may, in fact, disrupt routines, it is the perception of this disruption that leads to crippling resistances that thwart progress. Since resistance to changes or decisions is rooted in the perceptual mental models of employees, these models are amenable to alteration through the use of imaginal techniques.

Vital to managing resistances is ensuring employees recognize that resistances exist. This may be accomplished through the following script, which focuses on the introduction of advanced computerization in a firm.

> Now that you are relaxed and attentive, you are going to explore general reactions you have to the introduction of the new computer systems. As you know the decision has been made to acquire and introduce the TM–650 system. This system will improve many of our operations and will allow for quicker and more accurate decision making throughout our firm. The decision to acquire and implement this system was an organizational one based on giving us a greater competitive edge. Reflect for a moment on your reactions to the process that was used to make this decision. [Pause.] Are there things that bothered you about how the decision evolved? [Pause.] If so make some mental notes of these factors. [Pause.] We will discuss them later. Do not edit your thinking or your reservations. [Pause.]
>
> Now we are going to shift focus. Perhaps there were things about the decision that bothered you. That is okay. Keep those factors in mind for later reference; but, for the time being, you are going to project yourself into your job and evaluate how the new system will affect you in a number of key areas. [Pause.] The more that you can picture the impact of the system, the better you'll be able to identify the positive and negative reactions that you have to the system. [Pause.]
>
> First, take a moment to think about your job and your job's function in the recent past. [Pause.] What things do you like about your

job? [Pause.] What things do you dislike? [Pause.] Take a moment to weigh the pros and cons of your job. [Pause.] Now focus your attention on only the information processing aspects of your position. How have you traditionally dealt with information processing problems and channels? [Pause.] What do you like and dislike about the ways in which information is used within your unit? [Pause.] Imagine yourself drawing up a balance sheet of the positive and negative aspects of information management within your unit. That's good. Now, envision the ways that you think the new computer system will impact your work and your job. [Pause.] Envision both the positive and the negative consequences. [Pause.] What makes you feel comfortable about this change? [Pause.] What makes you uncomfortable about the introduction of the system? [Pause.] What does this change mean to you personally and professionally? [Pause.] If you had your choice, how would you like to see this change handled—be specific, and come up with suggestions that can be discussed later.

Such a script can help employees focus on the resistances that they have to a new program, and can give management clues as to how to best implement a change agenda within the firm. All too often, new technologies and methods are introduced without their impact on the personal and professional consequences of change being considered. When this is the case, management will face stalling, resistance, and even sabotage as new approaches are integrated into the existing organizational culture. To deal effectively with resistances, you must know what they are so that you can clarify the eventual consequences of change, while also helping your workers deal with the anxiety that comes up when change occurs. A second example shows how you might help your employees come to terms with the personal relevance of change. This script would, of course, be presented after you and your employees had candidly looked at the issue of resistance and had consented to deal with resistance within the implementation program.

For the next few minutes, you are going to build a scenario of the future. You will be using your creativity and imagination to project the various impacts of the new system on different aspects of your work. By envisioning what you think the likely consequences of implementation will be, you can establish how you wish to respond positively to the new system as an individual and as a member of the team. Take a moment and relax. Open your mind to the future and place yourself in this organization one year from now. [Pause.]

As you think about your unit and your job one year from now, take a little time to study your impressions about several areas. Each of these areas may have changed in the future as a result of the system implementation. It is your task to project and predict what types of changes are likely in each of these areas. The clearer a picture you can build, the better. Let's see what your images tell you.

The first area you will scan is the area of personal relationships within your unit. Think of the people you work with at this time. Think about how they will react to the changes that are taking place with the introduction of the computer system. [Pause.] From your impressions of their current attitudes, how will they adjust over the next year to the new system? Who will be most amenable to change and who will tend to resent the change? [Pause.] How will your interactions with your personnel and colleagues be affected as a result of this change? [Pause.] Be as specific as you can in building this picture of future relationships after the introduction of the computer system. That's good.

Next, try to envision how the new system will impact your personal performance in the unit next year. [Pause.] How will your ability to lead be either improved or hampered by the system? [Pause.] Can you envision yourself as able to manage the new technology effectively? [Pause.] Try to build an image of competency. [Pause.] See yourself as able to adapt to the new system and as able to model new behaviors for your staff. [Pause.] The more that you can lead by example, the better for you. [Pause.] Your employees will follow your lead and will adapt attitudes about the system that are a reflection on your own. [Pause.] Build a comprehensive model of how you want to see the staff use the new system. [Pause.] Build an ideal scenario for application to your unit. [Pause.] That's good.

Again, such scripts won't eliminate resistances, but they can help get primary issues of concern on the table for discussion. Further, projective scripts can help personnel develop strategies for the introduction of a change agendum in the firm. In the imaginal realm, these scenarios can be manipulated safely and inexpensively so that problems are anticipated and dealt with in advance of their arising. As with all problem-solving, this ability to project and anticipate the dynamics of the problem increases the likelihood that the problem can be managed in an effective manner. Problem-solving fails when people go into problem events with habitual and reactive thinking. Effective efforts at problem-solving occur when personnel are able to move beyond reactivity. Imaginal techniques can, in fact, provide this opportunity to members of your firm.

CONCLUSION

Outlined in this chapter are just a few of our ideas about imagery applications in organizational decision and problem-solving processes. Your ability to apply such technologies is only limited by your own creativity and willingness to experiment with non-traditional approaches to organizational effectiveness. As has been previously emphasized, creativity and effective problem-solving emerge from concerted practice in these skill realms. Commitment to the use of imaginal or envisionary technologies will not of itself solve your problems more easily. Rather, the introduction and use of these technologies gives you tools to use to enhance the efficacy of your personnel in the evermore complex discipline of decision making.

9

HOW IMAGINAL TECHNOLOGIES CAN IMPROVE THE PERSONAL EFFECTIVENESS OF YOUR EMPLOYEES

One of the most troubling experiences in managing others is having to deal with the chronically tardy, stressed-out, procrastinating employee who is unable to organize him/herself. Every firm has individuals who operate from this chaotic mode. Often these people have a great deal to offer, but because they are so disorganized themselves, their potential is squandered. Take a moment to think about such an employee within your firm. Imagine how this individual complicates work for everyone else and causes others stress, forcing them to waste time. Imagine how this individual manipulates and controls others through his/her own procrastination. Recall and experience the feelings that you have about this individual. Did your blood pressure go up? Maybe so—people who cannot manage themselves are burdens to your organization. While the quick fix solution to this dilemma is to fire them, there are other ways to manage wayward employees. This chapter will focus on self-management—a goal that you should have for yourself and should engender through the HRM function in all your employees.

Imaginal techniques, again, are powerful tools to help people gain greater control of themselves and their agenda. In this chapter, we will review the ways in which imaginal technologies can be applied to improve the overall employee self-confidence, time, and stress management efforts, and career development. It is our opinion that an effective manager of others is first an effective manager of self. If you cannot manage your own affairs in an organized and efficient manner, you will be less likely to manage others effectively, especially when they are looking to you as a role model.

As a human resource professional, you set the tone for your unit and for the organization. By helping yourself and your personnel become more effective, you increase the probability that satisfaction, motivation, and positive performance will permeate your work unit. Again, we do not espouse a quick fix approach to personal effectiveness. Becoming effective involves prioritizing time and energy to the tasks of goal, time, and stress management. While imaginal technologies are fine tools with this process, self-management is a tough process. It demands personal discipline to become as effective as one can. However, the long-term consequences of positive self-management are cumulative and can enrich one's personal and professional life.

BUILDING SELF-EFFICACY IN YOUR ORGANIZATION

Self-efficacy is a concept that was developed by social learning psychologist Al Bandura during the late 1970s. The concept is closely allied with the idea of self-confidence, although self-efficacy is a more complex, cognitive self-attribution. Self-confidence involves the popularized can-do attitude. While a can-do attitude is important, especially when managing challenging assignments, one must have both defined expectancies and skills, which establish behavioral performance. A can-do attitude unsubstantiated by skills and abilities represents wishful thinking, and is indicative of the swagger before substance mentality of much organizational training today. This approach involves flash and image management, creating an erroneous impression that somewhere beneath the fluff there must be something of value. Such a mentality is in the vein of positive thinking and is of limited value in complex organizational environments where attitudinal change must be supplemented with existent skills.

Self-efficacy is based in substance before swagger bias, and involves at least three components of individual functioning: (1) realistic positive attitudes about self and others; (2) expectancies consisting of the projective images we hold of self and our abilities to manage future challenges; and (3) demonstrated skills (see Figure 9–1). These arenas are closely interrelated. If you have positive attitudes about yourself and others, you utilize positive imaginal scenarios of yourself in reference to your work. These positive scenarios will reinforce your expectancies about your ability to accomplish significant goals, individually and collaboratively. These positive attitudes and expectancies, while imaginal in nature, influence how you use existing skills and /or learn new skills to become a more effective individual. Self-efficacy evolves in response to your experiences in challenging situations. Everyone can learn to

Figure 9-1
The Self-Efficacy Triangle

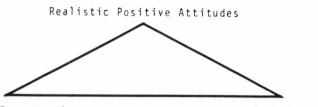

become more self-efficacious within the limits of their existing and potential abilities.

Generally speaking, we build strong imaginal sets about our capacities
and our strengths as well as our weaknesses. Further, we learn to attribute our successes and failures to either our own efforts or to extra-
neous factors such as fate, chance, or God. As a self-attribution, self-
efficacy is an imaginal reference cue for all choices and actions that we
make.

Self-efficacy is important to effective management because individuals
with positive self-efficacy images and expectations are more productive
employees, who are willing to take risks in pursuit of challenging goals.
While self-efficacy is learned via experience, it can be amended through
a variety of imaginal techniques, which allow the individual to reframe
both his/her self-imagery and his/her expectations regarding the future.
The imaginal techniques that are used depend on which area you wish
to develop in the holistic self-efficacy that leads to self-management.
Scripts can be created to improve attitudes, to enhance expectancies
about future goals, or to reinforce skill learnings and performance. It is
important to remember that all three areas must be addressed if you are
to improve your self-efficacy.

Three brief script excerpts are provided demonstrating how attitudes,
expectancies, and skills can be improved through imaginal techniques.
Keep in mind that changing the imaginal mindset of an individual
doesn't directly produce more effectiveness. Rather these techniques
reframe the inner stage upon which we establish our options before
acting. This reframing contributes to more motivated performance, more
creativity and risk-taking, and more ability to develop skills. Many types
of topically specific scripts can be created to help your personnel build
general and specific self-efficacy mindsets and expectancies. Often, these
self-efficacy scripts are best applied with other training materials in a
skill-specific learning methodology such as teaching more effective problem-solving. Thus an individual will be simultaneously gaining skill-
relevant information and practice, while building a new set of positive

self-images regarding his/her ability to acquire, use, and apply new skills. Consider this self-enhancement script:

> During this imagery session, you will review attitudes that govern your life and work. Let your mind exist in the scenarios that are described. You will confront things you like and dislike about yourself. This can be difficult. Imagine yourself doing a self-audit. [Pause.] Imagine that you have two sides to your personal balance sheet: positive attitudes that contribute to your effectiveness [Pause] and negative attitudes that deter your success. [Pause.] Your attitudes affect both your expectancies about the future and your ability to apply your skills to the challenges you face. [Pause.]
>
> Rather than focusing on your own views, you will step outside of yourself for a moment. [Pause.] Try to place yourself in the following situation. [Pause.] Take a moment to bring to mind the image of your best friend. [Pause.] Is this individual a man or a woman? How long have you known him/her? [Pause.] Why is this individual your best friend? Why do you trust this individual as you do? [Pause.] Now imagine that you are about to meet your friend for lunch. [Pause.] During lunch, you will carry on an important conversation with this individual. [Pause.] As much as possible, place yourself in this conversation—make mental notes of what your friend shares with you. [Pause.]
>
> Imagine yourself asking your friend the following question: _____, "I'd like you to tell me frankly what you like and dislike about me. Don't worry about what you say. I need your feedback to help me adjust my attitudes." [Pause.]
>
> Now imagine yourself listening to your friend's response. [Pause.] What does he or she say that is positive? [Pause.] Take mental notes of his/her remarks. [Pause.] What does he/she say that is negative? [Pause.] Take a moment to imagine this conversation. [Pause.] Let your imagination fill in the details. [Pause.] Make this experience as vivid as possible. Take clear mental notes of the positive and negative impressions that are generated. [Pause.] Good. You will use these notes to build a more positive attitude. Take a moment to think about what you have just learned. [Pause.] We'll now change our focus somewhat.
>
> In your mind, identify a fellow employee you do not like. Bring that individual's image into focus. [Pause.] Recall your past interactions with this individual. [Pause.] Consider why your relationship is negative. [Pause.] That's good—as much as possible tune-in to your images of this individual. [Pause.] Now, imagine that you are to have lunch with this individual. During that lunch, you ask this question, "_____, we have known each other for some time now. I know that you don't like me and I'm not crazy about you either— that's a given. But I need to know what you think of me—positively

and negatively. So, if you don't mind, I'll listen." [Pause.] Imagine
that this individual delivers a response. What does she/he say? Listen
carefully in your mind to hear the response. [Pause.]

Note: At this point you may ask the participants to make mental or
written notes of their experiences and impressions within the script. We
have consistently found that cuing people to make mental notes or to
write down their impressions improves their recall and use of imaginal
learnings.

This script is then processed so that you categorize both the positive
and negative attitudinal factors that you think others hold of you. These
external image references help you define what is appropriate and inappropriate about your attitudinal set. They help you see yourself as
others see you and thus better understand both your positive and negative characteristics. This type of self-awareness serves as the foundation
upon which you begin the self-management process.
    A second script will focus on developing positive expectancies of your
ability to manage future challenges. This script will focus on the past
and the future.

In your mind, imagine that your life is like a map. You visit different
countries and encounter different challenges as time goes by. In this
session, imagine that you are a mapmaker who must chart your past
and your future. [Pause.] Take a moment to imagine yourself sitting
before a great oak table in a dimly lit room, with candles. [Pause.]
Imagine that there are writing implements and a large scroll before
you. [Pause.] Imagine that you must chart your past and your future.
[Pause.] Imagine that you can do this in any way you wish, although
you must identify the positive and negative situations you have
encountered in the past. [Pause.] Further, you must inspect and
predict the future directions that your life may take. [Pause.] First,
you will draw a map of what the past five years have been like for
you in the firm. [Pause.] Think of the positive experiences that you
have had; imagine yourself drawing in these experiences in a symbolic or figural form that will help you remember them. [Pause.]
Imagine that you are drawing positive milestones along the road
you have traveled. Identify and record positive achievements you
have accomplished. [Pause.] Now, on that same road map of the
past five years, identify the positive relationships you have started
and built. [Pause.] You will also want to focus on the significant
negative experiences in the past five years. [Pause.] Diagram or draw
these on your road map of the past five years. [Pause.]
    That's good. Take a moment now to fill in any gaps that you
overlooked the first time around. [Pause.] You will now shift your
focus to the future. Many of your future goals are based on your
past experiences. Imagine that you are in a time machine that allows

you to make excursions into the future. [Pause.] See yourself becoming comfortable in your seat as you prepare to map out your
future goals. [Pause.] You will not only travel into the future, but
you will also identify the goals that are most important to you over
that timeframe. [Pause.] Think about your goals for the future.
[Pause.] Before you begin your envisionary travels into the future,
make certain you specify your goals and the timeframe for these
goals. [Pause.] Now, place yourself in your time machine and prepare for your departure into the future. As much as possible you
will envision both the goals you have for the future and the ways
in which you will achieve these goals. [Pause.] Additionally, you
will note these goals on your roadmap, which you carry with you
in the time machine. [Pause.]

This script, while indirect, allows an individual to do both retrospective and prospective work related to expectancies. The events that appear
during this scenario have importance to the individual and can be used
as data for helping him/her identify circumstances and attitudes that
lead to positive outcomes. Within this set of images, the individual can
identify how and when she/he best responds to challenges and what
personal approaches lead to the best results.

Our third example and excerpt deals with the critical behavioral realm
of performance appraisal. Before developing the script, we'll provide
some context. This skill area is essential for all managers, yet many are
hesitant to take decisive action, particularly with troublesome employees. Consider this scenario.

Imagine that you are facing the uncomfortable experience of having
to terminate a popular but mediocre employee who habitually does
sloppy work. Suppose that you are a manager who has low or negative self-efficacy expectations. You are generally hesitant to take
decisive action even in safe situations because you believe that any
action path is fraught with uncertainty and potential danger. You
especially like to work in predictable situations and, in this case, you
have limited projective images about the consequences of any decisive action—particulary the termination of this popular employee.
You are generally tentative and evasive in your managerial actions.
You believe no action is preferable to decisive action. In other words,
you're hesitant to act. Given your fixed expectancy mindset, you
don't act in this situation, hoping that it will either go away of its
own accord or someone else will make the decision for you. These
are choices of the low self-efficacy manager. Have you ever found
yourself responding in this manner? If so, identify the situation and
make mental notes of relevant circumstances. Think about situations
similar to this one and how you have reacted similarly in the past.

If not, make some mental notes of the ways that you generally handle negative situations. [Pause.] What skills or abilities do you apply in such situations? [Pause.] How do you manage your emotions at such times? [Pause.]

If you haven't found yourself in this type of situation, think of someone you work with who did or does behave reluctantly in such situations. [Pause.] What situations have you noted that are similar to this one? [Pause.] How did he/she manage the situation? [Pause.]

At this point, you would shift gears and provoke more positive and effective imaginal scenes related to the same topic area.

In contrast, you're a manager with high and positive self-efficacy. Having confronted and managed similar touchy situations in the past, you have positive past imagery to think of in dealing with this situation. You recall how you have managed difficult situations in the past and you have the confidence to work with this situation until it is resolved. Rather than hesitating, you call the employee in and inform him that a continuation of counterproductive or sloppy work behaviors will lead to a termination. You behave decisively, based on your expectancies that this is the right way to manage and you leave nothing to chance in the situation.

An example of this is provided below in the area of performance appraisal. This script should be presented during the training session and could be modified or reiterated as needed during learning and acquisition phases of skill development.

An ancillary method here might be to have your employees participate in videotaped mock interviews with a variety of employee types of problems. Research shows that videotape feedback is a very effective means for helping people adopt new skills and recognize dysfunctional habits or behaviors. Such feedback can also help them develop clearer images of themselves. Consider this script, which is presented under the assumption that such pretraining has occurred.

Now you are going to imagine yourself applying the skills that you have just learned during training. You have watched a videotape of yourself using these skills in a mock performance interview. Now, visualize yourself applying these same skills in the scenario that will be described. [Pause.] As much as possible, be in this situation and rehearse your use of these positive appraisal skills. [Pause.] I will review these skills for you now. As I do this, imagine yourself exhibiting the skills; they include: (1) active and attentive listening (see yourself as able to attentively listen to others); [Pause]; (2) a positive, open, relaxed posture (see yourself as relaxed, leaning forward, and showing an open posture); [Pause]; (3) giving supportive feedback

to your subordinate (see yourself as appreciating and acknowledging
your subordinate's perspective, especially where you may disagree);
[Pause]; (4) developing a collaborative partnership with your subordinate (see yourself as non-adversarial with your subordinate and
open to using his/her ideas about performance enhancement); and
(5) exhibiting a non-defensive attitude when receiving negative feedback (see yourself as relaxed and able to listen to both the positive
and negative comments of your subordinate). [Pause.] Now that you
have envisioned yourself applying these skills, you'll place yourself
in a simulated appraisal situation and rehearse the event.

This script could then be elaborated so that trainees mentally walk
through a performance appraisal. The rationale for using these covert
rehearsal strategies is based solidly in research. If an individual is able
to imagine her/himself performing a behavior or skill, he/she will be
more able to perform the behavior or skill in real-life contexts. Mental
rehearsal reinforces both new learnings and the application of these
learnings to new situations. Combining mental rehearsal with skill practice, role-playing, and simulations is an economical means of improving
both the skill development and the self-efficacy of employees.

A combination of positive attitudes, realistic and appropriate expectancies, and skills will enhance the self-efficacy of personnel.

TIME MANAGEMENT

In today's hectic world, effective managers are the managers who
realize that time is their greatest asset. These proficient self-managers
use time wisely to optimize both their personal and organizational
achievement. As with many areas, time management is a fad area with
many consultants providing the quick fix approach to time efficiency.
Quick fixes don't work any better in this domain than in any other critical
management realm. Before an individual becomes an effective time manager, he/she must reconceptualize his/her images of time and time efficiency in order to prioritize time as a critical resource to success. Too
often individuals freeze their conceptions of time and fall into habits of
excuse-making, withdrawal from responsibility, and procrastination. In
the short- and long-term, this unwillingness to reframe the import of
time will lead to lower levels of personal and professional development.
It is obvious that the individual who cannot manage his/her own time
efficiently will have great difficulty directing and organizing the work
of others.

First, imaginal techniques can be used to help people recognize and
change their resistance to time management. Resistance, herein, often
involves excuse-making about why one is not organized. This excuse-
making is then habituated into a work- and lifestyle that is based on

procrastination. The individual may develop an attitude of learned help-
lessness. The following excerpts from a conversational script of a pro-
crastinator may illustrate the types of excuse-making and rationalization
that characterize poor time managers.

> Well, I wish I could be organized, but I'm just not that type of person.
> Organization restrains my creativity. I'm more a free-flow person.
> Sure, I don't get some things done, but that's no big deal. If I don't
> get something done, its probably not worth doing, anyway. I guess
> this whole thing started when I was in college and I waited till the
> last minute to get things done. Usually when I did this, I got good
> reinforcement . . . I mean, I got good grades. Why should I change
> when I work best under pressure? After all, only nitpickers plan
> every day and every week according to a schedule. Not me, though.
> Its just not my style.

In this script one can see that the individual is building a case to support
his position. Before an individual can deal with this mindset, he/she
must recognize the negative consequences of poor time management.
This recognition will unfreeze some of the resistance that the individual
exhibits and will start him/her on the road to more productive time uses.
A brief script is given below that has frequently been applied in workshops on procrastination.

> You are relaxed and ready to look at time as a resource in your life.
> [Pause.] When you hear the word "time," what images come to
> mind? [Pause.] Do images of clocks come to mind? [Pause.] Is time
> like a calendar or is time like a bank account from which you make
> withdrawals? [Pause.] Not only try to identify spontaneous images
> that you have of time, but recognize the emotions that you attach
> to the concept. [Pause.] Do you feel positive or negative about time?
> [Pause.] Is it something that you control or is it something that
> controls you? [Pause.] Let those images develop fully. What feelings
> and thoughts come to mind as you ponder time? [Pause.] That's
> good—time is a critical resource. [Pause.] How well do you use your
> time? [Pause.] Do you optimize your use of time? [Pause.] Recall
> periods in your life when you effectively managed time—bring these
> times into clear focus. [Pause.] How did you feel about yourself as
> you managed your time effectively? [Pause.] What were the personal
> and professional consequences of good time management for you?
> [Pause.]
>   Now think about how you manage time in the present. How much
> control do you now have over your time? [Pause.] When you think
> of your current time management ability, what images come to
> mind? What are the present consequences, personal and profes-
> sional, of your ability or inability to manage your time. [Pause.] How
> would your life and work be better if you were able to get more

control of your time? Build some concrete images of how your life would improve.

This script will help one consider both effective and ineffective time management strategies and, more important, the consequences of either style. The inability to manage time usually contributes to increased stress and reduced goal achievement. As an individual confronts inappropriate time management strategies, he/she can clearly envision how more effective management contributes to effective self-management. Once an individual has done this, he/she can adopt any of the numerous scheduling and prioritization techniques that are typically used in time management workshops.

Imaginal techniques can then be used to help employees imaginally frame their responsibilities so that a mental template is created each day. This template conceptualizes the ideal day in the individual's mind and serves as a guide for managing both expected and incidental activities. The individual can then transfer this qualitative image of time allocation to a hard schedule. As with many imaginal techniques, this allows the individual to form an internal reference, which is then reinforced by definitive action. An example of a time-related template is your vision of the schedule you face each day at work and/or the ways in which you envision your leisure time. While you may keep a hard-copy calendar of events, you also carry around with you a mental calendar, to which you make reference periodically to make sure you have not missed an important event or meeting. Most of us have time templates of the weekend that involve images of cookouts, relaxation with friends, travel, or hobbies. Again, these templates allow us to frame our time in terms of the activities we prioritize.

Time management is, finally, a matter of personal self-discipline. If one is unwilling to spend time each day for envisionment and scheduling practices, one should not be surprised when he/she doesn't achieve as much as others who are more organized. Paradoxically, to manage time, one must set aside time for time management every day. A general guideline that we share in our time management seminars consists in picking a consistent time each day when you shut out all of your responsibilities and work on both calendar and mental scheduling for both the next day and the week in which you are operating. You should make the determination as to what time is best, but our experience with many people indicates that either early morning after arriving at your job or late afternoon are good times for planning. Failing to do this reduces the likelihood that an individual will maximize opportunities, while at the same time it increases the probability that goals will be squandered and stress will chronically accumulate. Specified below is a short personal time management script that can help you during planning sessions. You would, of course, use this script after a brief period of relaxation.

> I am going to think about what my day will be like tomorrow. I am going to identify the critical things that I must accomplish within my professional and personal life. I am going to use this time to better manage my tomorrow's time. I see myself rising tomorrow morning. As I envision myself dressing, what priorities run through my mind as I envision my day? [Pause.] What things do I wish to accomplish above all others? [Pause.] What things do I wish to delay or exclude from my activity schedule? [Pause.] What people will I interact with during the day? [Pause.] What types of interactions do I wish to have with them? [Pause.] If I could have the perfect day, how would it evolve? [Pause.] As I think about my morning, how do I want things to go? [Pause.] With meetings, what are my goals? [Pause.]

You'll notice that this is a self-directing script in which you give cues to yourself and then build your time template for the given day. Obviously, the script can be adapted for presentation to others by simply changing the future. Consistent practice of such a script during a prioritized planning time can be of great benefit to you and others in your time management efforts.

STRESS MANAGEMENT

As with time management, stress management is a tough assignment for most of us. We must, again, create time each day to manage the ever present stress, personal and professional, that impacts on us. Talking about stress management will accomplish little. As a human resource professional, helping managers and employees to manage stress is an important component of your job. To manage stress, people must make both lifestyle and personal management changes that allow them to work at a high level of positive arousal without undergoing burnout. Stress management also involves taking responsibility for identifying the causes of the stress that impacts on us and for making lifestyle and habit changes that reduce the negative emotional and physical consequences of stress. However, you cannot accept responsibility for managing others' stress—they must do this themselves.

In Chapter 2, we showed you a model of how stress affects performance (see Figure 2–1). As stress increases your emotional and physiological arousal also increase. This positive arousal, eustress, allows you to perform at high levels of both attention and motivation. Eustress is not a problem. Stress becomes problematic when we cross out personal stress tolerance threshold and experience distress. This threshold will

vary for each individual, but each of us does have a limit on the amount
of stress that we can manage. When this threshold is reached, distress
begins and accelerates. As distress increases with increasing arousal,
our performance, our motivation, and our attentiveness drop significantly. Unless stress is managed so that it is kept in the range of eustress,
eventually, the performance and commitment of an overstressed employee will suffer. That's the bottom line—either manage your stress or
suffer the negative personal and professional consequences of chronic
reduced performance and emotional instability.

Imagery can be used as a technique for both assessing the stress factors
in your life and as a direct intervention technique for stress management.
Perhaps there in no other area of personal development where imagery
has been more applied than in the stress management realm. Below are
two script excerpts. The first deals with assessing stressors in a systematic way and the second is a brief stress reduction scenario that has
frequently been used in our workshops.

> You are relaxed and attentive. You are ready to use your imagination
> to do self-evaluation. The focus in this session will be on identifying
> primary stressors that impact on you. Further, you will imagine how
> these stressors impact on you. You will also think of ways that you
> might handle stress better in each area. We will begin with stressors
> in your personal life. [Pause.] As we identify these areas, envision
> each arena as vividly as possible—looking for the stressors that im-
> pact upon you. [Pause.]
>
> You will now think about your personal life. To help you do this,
> I will give you cues to envision different areas of your lifestyle.
> [Pause.] As you build a picture of each arena, think about things,
> people, or situations that cause you stress. [Pause.] Also think about
> how these factors affect you. [Pause.] Finally, for each arena, en-
> vision what you might do to reduce stress where stressors are iden-
> tified. [Pause.]
>
> Envision your relationships with others. [Pause.] Think about re-
> lationships in your family, with friends, with co-workers. [Pause.]
> Who are these people? [Pause.] As you think about them, envision
> their faces and your latest interactions with them. [Pause.] You may
> with to think first about your family members or very close friends.
> [Pause.] That's good. Envision interactions that you have found
> yourself engaged in with people recently. [Pause.] When you de-
> velop a negative picture of an individual, identify why this is the
> case. [Pause.] As you think about this negativity, imagine how stress
> develops from your interaction. [Pause.] How does this stress affect
> you. [Pause.] What does the individual do that bothers you? [Pause.]
> What do you do that makes the relationship negative and stressful
> for yourself and the other individual. [Pause.] What can you do to
> change the interaction? [Pause.] Now change your focus and envi-

sion your relationships with co-workers. [Pause.] Call to mind the faces and actions of the people with whom you work. [Pause.] Now think about and envision how each of these individuals contributes to or helps you reduce your job-related stress. That's good. [Pause.] Where you find a troubling relationship, what are you doing about it? [Pause.] If you are doing nothing to alleviate stress between yourself and others on the job—what could you do? [Pause.] Think of ways that you could change either your attitudes, thoughts, or behaviors toward troubling co-workers. [Pause.] Develop a strategy to reduce the impact of these individuals on your life. [Pause.]

This script could then continue by focusing on personal and professional arenas where stress-provoking behaviors and interactions are likely to be present. In the personal realm, this imaginal scanning includes the areas of fitness, diet, time management, goal achievement, spirituality, and personality. In the job-related realm, you want the individual to investigate and identify stressors related to supervision, workload, time demands, role conflicts, job ambiguities, and the overall psychological climate in the organization. As one becomes more acquainted with the variety of stressors that are present at home and work, one is more likely to adopt some form of routine and regular stress management discipline to cope with stress. In the future, stress will increase and it will be those who cope with stress who succeed in the face of spiraling pressures.

Below is an imaginal scenario we often use to induce relaxation in our trainees prior to actually taking them through an imaginal script experience. Relaxation must be paired with imagery sessions to allow participants to focus internally and vividly on their mental life. However, this and other scripts can easily be used as stress management devices to help your personnel tune in to a quiet place where relaxation helps them better manage their stress. After the script, some other types of relaxation practice will be illustrated.

For the next few minutes, you are going to travel to your favorite place in the world. Without hustle or bustle, you will use your imagination to transport you to this place. [Pause.] As you make your journey, your imagination will be the cloud upon which you ride to get from here to your favorite hideaway—that place where you are at peace and are totally relaxed. [Pause.] For you this place may be at the beach [Pause] . . . or in the countryside [Pause] . . . or in the mountains [Pause] . . . or somewhere special that only you know about [Pause]. Wherever your quiet place is, climb aboard a cloud and imagine yourself floating there—gently soaring above the earth [Pause] . . . totally relaxed, totally at peace, totally in control. [Pause.] Imagine yourself soaring in a bright blue sky above and beyond the stress and troubles that sometimes bind you. [Pause.] See yourself trailing a string of balloons from your cloud. [Pause.]

> Each balloon is a stressor that you are letting go. [Pause.] As you
> sail to your favorite place, imagine that you are inscribing these
> balloons with the things that cause you stress. Let these balloons go
> and totally relax as you float above the earth or sea. [Pause.] Now
> imagine yourself making a gentle and relaxing descent to that haven
> where you feel most comfortable. Imagine your touch-down.
> [Pause.] Imagine that you have arrived at your favorite spot and are
> going to relax and let all tension flow from your body. [Pause.]
>   As you imagine your favorite spot, what sights come to mind?
> [Pause.] What sounds do you hear in the background? [Pause.] What
> colors surround you as you survey the landscape that surrounds
> you? [Pause.] What movement are you aware of as you relax and
> take in the natural beauty? What feelings do you have as you relax
> and let your worries subside? [Pause.] Let yourself totally relax as
> you enjoy your favorite place. [Pause.]

This script would continue for a total of about twenty minutes, during
which the individual would project him/herself into various expansions
of this favorite place scenario. Such expansions might include scenarios
related to my favorite people, my favorite past vacation, or my fantasy
vacation. The key here is that the individual imagines vividly that place
and the physical and emotional dynamics of relaxation. With practice,
your personnel can use such scripts on a regular basis to reduce stress
and to regain perspective on the challenges that occupy their time.

This is not the only type of script that you can create. Many relaxation
scripts simply involve playing gentle classical or soft jazz music in combination with cues that instruct the individual to either flow with the
movement of the music or become the music and experience the spontaneous images that arise. Other scripts may focus on what is called
"progressive relaxation." This long-popular technique involves cuing
the individual to imagine the various major muscle groups of his/her
body, tightening these muscle groups (either actually or imaginally),
and then relaxing then. This is done progressively from the toes to the
top of the head, and usually is accomplished through directive imaginal
cues that lead the individual from one body region to the next in a
sequential manner. Excerpted below is a short portion of a progressive
relaxation script:

> Now that you are stretched out on the floor, you are going to focus
> your attention on major muscle groups within your body. Please
> close your eyes. That's right, relax and close out distractions. We
> will start at your feet. Point your toes downward as hard as you
> can. That's it—straighten those toes and hold for the count of five
> ... one ... two ... three ... four ... five. That's very good. Now re-
> lax your toes. Feel warmth and relaxation flowing through your feet.
> [Pause.] Now focus your attention on the calves of your legs. These

are very strong muscles. Tighten your calves as much as possible.
That's it . . . and hold to the count of five . . . one . . . two . . . three . . .
four . . . five. Good, now relax your calves. Excellent, feel the flowing
warmth or relaxation in your calves. Tension is falling away and you
are beginning to feel very relaxed.

This script would continue to include the knees, thighs, hips, trunk,
abdomen, chest, shoulder, neck, head, and face of the individual. At
each point the individual tightens the identified muscle groups for five
seconds, then releases the tension. This technique is so effective that
many people often fall asleep during their first experience of the script.
Still other scripts may involve projection of the individual into a specific
and well-defined scenario, which he/she is asked to experience as vividly
as possible. Such a script might involve placing the individual in the
mountains, at the beach, or in some pastoral setting. In such a script,
you would address all the senses and help the individual be there as
much as possible. Regardless of the type of script you develop, the most
important aspect of relaxation/stress management efforts is regular and
systematic practice of a routine. It is our opinion that identifying stressors
and taking proactive steps to act rather than just to dwell on stress leads
to greater capacity to manage stress. Individuals who deny or ignore
stress and its manifest physiological and emotional symptoms are setting
themselves up for future trouble as well as for eventual declines in
performance and motivation on the job.

CAREER PLANNING AND DEVELOPMENT

Recently, more and more organizations have introduced formalized
career development programs into their human resource departments.
In fact, within the past ten years, career development has become an
extremely hot topic. Organizational leaders now recognize that effective
career development programs allow an organization to attract, encourage, and retain committed employees who have a balance between the
interests of the organization and their own interests. There are many
areas in which mental imagery techniques have importance in career
development of your employees. Afterall, most employees have future
visions of both where they wish to go within an organization and what
the best paths to get to these goals are. These career schemata serve as
templates for choice and action related to career and all other aspects of
organizational behavior for the individual. The employee with a vivid,
realistic, and attainable template is more likely to be both satisfied and
productive than the employee with a less clarified or inappropriate template or schema. Imaginal techniques can assist employees in creating
their personal roadmaps for organizational success and can serve the

organization by helping it clarify its own hierarchical succession pictures for the future.

In this section, we will offer ideas for the application of imaginal techniques in important career development areas including organizational socialization, career transitions, career pathing, and outplacement. Several brief scripts are presented.

In the area of organizational socialization, you are concerned with the fit between the individual and the organization. A lot of money and time is wasted when this fit is bad or when potentially productive employees bail-out during the early days of their career experience with your firm. The key area where imaginal techniques can help in this realm is in harmonizing the ideational expectations of the new employee with the realities of your organization's culture. Socialization doesn't come to pass frequently because this potential mismatch is either ignored or passed over during the early days of an employee's career. Ideational expectations are the images and imaginal scenarios that the individual has about his/her first job experience and the ways that your organization will function. Often these expectations are unrealistic and incongruous with what he/she will experience as a new member of the firm. You can adjust these expectations by providing both realistic job previews in advance of employee selection and by leading new employees in imaginal scripts that depict the typical day (as will be noted in a restaurant script in Chapter 10), pro and con, within your firm. These imaginal renditions of your organization's reality can then be compared to the ideational expectations of that young, aggressive employee, so that greater harmony is encouraged in this area. While we don't want to quell the dynamic ambitions of talented new workers, neither do we want them believing in a view of organizational reality that is a fantasy. Sometimes this process of matching will lead to resignations. We feel this is good for both the individual and the organization. Hangers-on usually cause more problems than they are potentially worth, and it is far easier to change the mental models of an employee than it is to change the culture of your organization. Attention will now turn to the area of career transitions.

While mid-life crisis is a cliché in our society, it is obvious that most of us encounter several transitional crises during our personal and professional lives. Any time that we encounter change or novelty in our roles and responsibilities, as well as in the mental models that govern our choice and behavior, we will experience stress, potential trauma, and crisis. Typical crises that most of us have or will experience are (1) organizational socialization, where our grandiose expectations meet reality; (2) job change, internally or externally, where we must adopt to a change in the routines that have governed our workstyles; (3) mid-life crisis, both for men and women, where we do both retrospective evaluation and future projection related to our lives; (4) outplacement, where we are fired or laid-off; and (5) preretirement and retirement anxiety where we sever lifelong connections and identity with a firm. Any and all of these transitions will shake up our self-images and our images of ourselves in relationship to our work and lifestyle. Clearly, a great deal of both functional (projective ideation) and dysfunctional (retroactive ideation) mental scripting occurs for the individual during a crisis confrontation. How well an employee manages a crisis is often directly related to how he/she manages the ideational/imaginal mental modeling that accompanies a crisis. Below is an example of a script for the employee who is facing retirement.

> Now that you are relaxed, you are going to travel both into the past and into the future. [Pause.] You are going to access and use your memory to recall the significant events that have occurred during your _____years with our firm. As much as possible, recall these events and relive them—emotionally [pause] and behaviorally. [Pause.] Many things have occurred to you during your tenure with our firm. It is time for you to replay these events so that you can appreciate the many changes that you have made during your time here. [Pause.] Go back to the days when you first entered the firm. [Pause.] Who were the significant people who influenced your development here? [Pause.] How did they influence your development? [Pause.] How did they affect your later career? [Pause.] As much as possible, recall your interactions with significant others and replay your positive experience with them. [Pause.] Think back over your years with the firm and identify the critical events that shaped your performance here. [Pause.] What were your greatest achievements or satisfactions as an employee? [Pause.] How did these experiences shape your relationships with others in the firm? [Pause.] Think about your supervisors. Who were the men and women who most contributed to your development? [Pause.] Where are they now and what are they doing? [Pause.] What kinds of contact will you have with them after you leave the firm? [Pause.] Who will be your subordinates that you most miss? [Pause.] How will you contact them in the future? [Pause.]

This script could then be elaborated to help the individual imaginally articulate his/her positive and negative history with the firm. This scripting could be framed in terms of early, middle, and later career periods, and gives the individual the opportunity to do an important career review that reconciles one's past experiences in reference to the future. This historical context allows the individual to build a coherent model of his/her experiences in the firm in relation to his/her projected separation from the firm. The next script excerpt would follow this history-taking and would ask the individual to project what difficulties, changes, and planning strategies he/she would use upon departure from the firm. This allows the individual to schematize the future and survive the separation crisis with some framework for action.

> Now that you have reviewed your rich experiences with our firm, you will turn to the future and the ways that you will spend your time after retirement. By building a clear picture of the potential future, you can anticipate adjustment problems you may encounter and plan for changes that need to be made as you adjust. Further, you can evolve strategies for dealing with your time, your new roles, your finances, and your skills during a period when you will have great autonomy.
>
> First, it is important to admit the anxieties that you have about retirement. [Pause.] Call to mind images you have about the wrong way to retire. [Pause.] Use the experiences of people you know to build your images of negative retirement. [Pause.] Articulate as much as possible what you don't want to see happen in the future. [Pause.] Take mental notes of your impressions and images about a negative future. [Pause.]
>
> Next, envision the things that you have always wanted to do. [Pause.] All of us have fantasies that we'd like to experience. [Pause.] Identify some of the fantasies you have that may come to pass during your retirement. [Pause.] Keep note of the images that come to mind. [Pause.] These images will serve as guides for time usage in the future. [Pause.] You will also envision your hobbies. [Pause.] How do you plan to expand or change these hobbies in the future? [Pause.] What new hobbies or activities might you develop that would challenge and motivate you?

This script would continue until the individual had a pretty clear picture of a potential positive image of the future as compared to a potential negative image of the future. This imaginal contrast allows the individual to move toward positive adjustment activities and away from counterproductive rumination about the future. Here are some additional script excerpts.

> Now that you have a clear picture of your past, a clear ideation of how you don't want to retire, and a clear ideation of the positive options that are open to you, you will build your perfect retirement day. [Pause.] From this perfect day, you will eventually build your perfect week. [Pause.] From your perfect week, you will build your perfect year. [Pause.] Building a positive retirement future begins with building the ideal day. [Pause.] Let's begin. [Pause.]
>
> Imagine yourself waking up two years from now. [Pause.] Where will you be living at that time? Look around your home. What do your furnishings look like? [Pause.] Look out your window. What type of day is it? [Pause.] What type of surroundings do you envi-

sion? [Pause.] Who are you spending time with these days? [Pause.]
What is on the plan for that day? What do you wish to accomplish?
Who will you be with during your activities? [Pause.] As clearly as
possible, imagine what you would do on that positive, productive
day two years from now. [Pause.]

This script could be expanded to further elaborate the future options of
the individual. Again, the clearer the individual visualizes the possibilities, the more likely that he/she will develop and follow a positive and
adaptive course of action. This and related scripts could be applied to
almost any transitional state that employees normally encounter. It
should be noted that these scripts should be reinforced with paper and
pencil planning and brainstorming sessions that articulate past, present,
and future dynamics of any given transition. This, in fact, is what we
suggest with most imaginal techniques. They work best when they are
coupled with other tools for personal development and planning.

A final area where imaginal techniques apply in career development
is career pathing and supervision. In path-goal notions of leadership,
the motivated, performing employee is the individual who has clear
personal and career goals and who is supported and guided by a supervisor who helps him/her reach those goals within the organization's
goal framework. Employees become thwarted and discontent when they
don't reach goals or when the paths to career and personal achievement
are closed or reduced. Envisionary career projection involves helping
the individual sculpt a realistic future path within the firm. Much guided
imagery involves an emphasis on cues provided by a trainer or facilitator.
With envisionary projection, the individual fills in much of the script
him/herself by (1) identifying his/her needs; (2) specifying his/her goals
within the organization; and (3) building strategy models of action to
reach these goals. He/she then shares this information with a supervisor
who helps him/her adjust these schemata in a realistic manner to the
possibilities that exist within a firm. Career envisionment is an excellent
supplementary technique to use after socialization techniques, because
it keeps an employee on-track with the changes in the career opportunities of the organization. The more congruent the employee's projective
career path images are with the career ladder and advancement opportunities within the firm, the more likely that you will have an employee
who is striving for optimal performance. Consider the brief career path
script below:

It is critical that you develop a plan for your career. One way to do
this is to envision a path that you wish to take within the firm.
[Pause] That path serves as your guide for career planning. While
it is a guide, it is flexible. Given changes in your own preferences
or those of the firm, you may find yourself branching out into new

areas. Allow yourself this flexibility for change. [Pause.] Before you begin your travels down your career path, call to mind a picture of the organizational chart we use. [Pause.] Review in your mind the various levels of management in our firm. [Pause.] Envision the people that currently hold those positions. [Pause.] Can you see yourself holding a particular position? [Pause.] If so, why is this position of interest to you? How can you improve the nature of that position? [Pause.] In what timeframe can you realistically accomplish promotion to the position that you aspire to achieve? [Pause.] What impasses or barriers might you face in your aspirations? [Pause.] What types of experience and training will you need to get to where you wish to be? [Pause.]

Now that you have looked at our firm and the options that are open to you, let's build a career path for the next five years. [Pause.] Imagine, once again, the organizational chart. Imagine titles by each of the levels of management that seem attractive to you. Where do you picture yourself in one year from now? [Pause.] What steps will you take on your path to get to this point? [Pause] Imagine in your mind that you are erecting a sign beside a country path. On this sign is your goal for a year from now. [Pause.] Now that you have that goal, what steps will you take to reach that milestone in your path? [Pause.]

There will be occasions when problems occur in finding your career path. At those points, supervisors can intervene to help the individual adjust his/her career images or counsel the employee to find an alternative path where a better fit exists between the needs and goals of the individual and the talent requirements of the firm.

CONCLUSION

Each of the areas discussed in this chapter is directly related to the professional and personal development of your employees. Once organizations were less concerned with development than we are today. We now realize that we improve both the talent pool of our employees and the culture of our organizations when we invest in employee development. The employee who can successfully manage time, who can cope with stress, who holds a positive self-image, and who has clear visions of his/her career future is the type of employee all organizations will pay gold to hire and retain. However, it is naive for us to believe that such employees are born—they are crafted by intelligent, envisionary managers who know that the effective individual is the effective employee. Holding this image may help you as you seek to improve the personal and professional competency of your employees.

In the next chapter, we see how these ideas can be extended to create a synthesis between imagery, performance, and productivity.

10

IMAGERY, PERFORMANCE, AND PRODUCTIVITY: A CREATIVE SYNTHESIS

Many of our actions that involve the imagery part of our brain are undertaken with little conscious forethought. We daydream, perform a routine skill (like tying shoes), or hold a routine conversation without necessarily forming a mental image of what we are doing. Whereas at one time we may have used imagery to learn or perfect a skill, now we often carry out an action without thinking about it. We act on the basis of habit, routine, and convenience. We automatically perform many functions without thinking because they are so familiar to us that we feel entirely comfortable with them. These actions are second nature to us.

This unthinking routinizing behavior occurs because it simplifies our life. We do not need to think about performing countless everyday actions. Yet there is a great danger here. Precisely because we do not think about these actions we cease to learn. We no longer look for ways to change and improve these actions. We take the status quo for granted.

One of the most interesting aspects about Frank and Lillian Gilbreth, two early time study engineers, is that they applied time and motion study principles to everyday, routine actions. As depicted in both the book and film *Cheaper by the Dozen*, they both performed various tasks such as bathing or dressing while being checked by a stop watch to see if there was a way to perform the task more efficiently. (With a dozen children to raise, and with two careers, time saving, efficient methods were absolutely critical!) Invariably, they would develop a faster more efficient way to do such everyday chores as clearing the table, washing the dishes, or mopping a floor. Though the Gilbreths made a conscious effort to examine existing methods in order to improve efficiency, most of us do not make such concerted effort in any daily lives unless a major change occurs. It often takes the birth of our first child, a divorce, the death of a loved one, or a serious illness to cause us to re-examine our daily routine. Then we may undertake action to improve or change the mental scripts and templates we unthinkingly follow.

The scripts and templates in our minds, which we follow every day at work, also provide us with a work routine based largely on a set of habits. Most of us do not systematically question these routines to see if they can be improved or if they are even necessary. Again, just as in our personal lives, this does not happen unless we face a serious crisis or major problem that is disruptive. Important deadlines are missed, a key employee quits, we are promoted, or we get a new boss. These situations usually will cause a rethinking of our normal work routine. We will question our present scripts and templates and devise new ones if necessary. Sometimes we try to change or interpret events to make them fit our existing templates. The key for productivity improvement, however, lies in making improvement changes before the crisis hits. That is where imagery can have its greatest impact.

HUMAN RESOURCE PROFESSIONALS—THE CATALYSTS

Human resource professionals in all areas of human resource management—training and development, recruiting and hiring, wage and salary administration, and so on—are in a unique position in most organizations. They are concerned specifically with making the personnel resource more productive. Consequently, human resource professionals should play a role in bringing about productivity improvement by challenging the existing way of doing things. They need to get both line managers and operational employees to think about their effectiveness and productivity. Human resource professionals should be the catalysts that challenge the status quo.

> One of your authors once worked with a large electrical utility, which was striving to adjust and become more competitive under deregulation. Regulated utilities tend to prefer the status quo and established routines. When deregulation hits regulated industries, it is very difficult to get people to change behavior. They are comfortable with the old behavior, yet it soon becomes evident that new forms of behavior are required to survival in a newly competitive environment. These companies face this critical question: How can we get our managers and employees to re-examine their present work routines, question those that need to be changed, and establish new more effective and productive behaviors?

In this electrical utility the personnel manager and training and development director established a series of workshops that examined the essential management skills of planning, problem-solving, communication, and leadership. In a seminar format, groups of managers were asked to review and evaluate their performance of these skills. Imagery exercises were used to help with the evaluation and with establishing new work routines using these skills. As a result of this nine-month program, a new strategic planning and a new performance appraisal process were adopted.

The significant aspect about this example is that the questioning or unfreezing of behavior was initiated by the two key human resource professionals in the company. Of course they had to sell the president on the idea of change. Once the CEO was sold, however, other managers accepted the need for the examination and change.

Catalytic involvement of human resource professionals in the change and productivity enhancement process puts a new slant on an old technique known as organizational development. Integrating human resource professionals into the productivity enhancement efforts of companies by using imagery ties both imagery and organization change and development efforts to the bottom line of productivity enhancement. Since the practice of imagery is skill-specific, emphasis is placed on improving various work routines so that new (and more productive) skills can be practiced.

In basketball a free-throw shooter who hits nine out of ten throws is more efficient and productive than one who hits six out of ten. By the same token, a manager who conducts an effective, worthwhile performance appraisal interview contributes more to organizational productivity than one who bumbles through such an interview. Imagery enhances managerial skill in conducting such an interview, and human resource professionals enhance the use of imagery.

How Can Human Resource Professionals Become Productivity Catalysts?

The first step is achieving and maintaining credibility. Human resource professionals will not be listened to unless they are viewed as a credible source of ideas. This is not the place to go into methods to enhance credibility. However, by properly using techniques that work—such as imagery—credibility can be enhanced.

The second step is appropriateness. Imagery should be suggested only for areas where appropriate. These are areas of management that are skill-specific and exist where skill enhancement will improve productivity, like those discussed in this book. Imagery, like any management technique, is not a panacea.

The third step is articulateness. Imagery, as a technique to enhance productivity, must be presented in a clear, straightforward manner. Enhancing productivity and the bottom line, rather than making people feel good, must be stressed; backup documentation illustrating such productivity successfully enhancing sports, counseling, and business should be presented.

The fourth step is patience. To many people, imagery sounds like a far-out method. Of course it is not, but patience is required when explaining the technique over and over again.

Fifth, follow up is necessary from two standpoints. First, in selling the idea, and second, in evaluating its results. It may be necessary to offer the suggestion several times when selling the idea before the organization decides to buy it because the initial reaction is often one of unfamiliarity and skepticism. After imagery sessions are conducted, follow-up evaluation as to its effectiveness must be conducted. This includes participant evaluations immediately at the conclusion of a session as well as evaluations several weeks later to see if the technique is being used and if it is enhancing productivity. Success breeds success so it is especially important that the initial sessions go well. This means careful planning and script writing as well as rehearsal on the facilitator's part.

Finally, and perhaps most important, the CEO and corporate officers must eventually be sold on the idea and become visible role models. Noel Tichy et al. point out that no fundamental change in a corporation's approach to business will likely occur until these individuals become involved.[1] He describes how training has been used successfully at General Electric to bring about changes in leadership styles. Tichy et al. reason that most corporations support benign management development activities out of fear that truly effective programs will create leaders who will rock the boat. Corporations encourage survivalist cultures. Any radical change could result in the people in power losing their jobs. Consequently, getting the people in charge to support any new program is essential. By being credible, articulate, using appropriate imagery applications, and by practicing patience and follow-up, human resource professionals can win this support.

EXPANDING BRAIN POWER: HOLISTIC MANAGEMENT

Since World War II, managers of organizations have been drilled in the hard, quantitative issues of managing. Subjects such as finance, economics, operations research, simulation, and so on have dominated business school curricula both at the credit and non-credit levels. The soft issues of values, culture, vision, and human relations have not received so much rigorous attention. These soft areas are harder to teach and learn. They are difficult to quantify and research in a systematic way compared to the hard areas. This overemphasis on the hard issues has highly rationalized business decision making and management.

The overemphasis on quantification of variables ignores those elements that do not lend themselves to easy quantification. Yet it is precisely these elements of vision and values that a true leader exemplifies. Achieving this holistic management approach is necessary to improve productivity. Emphasizing the quantitative measures at the expense of the soft measures is a left-sided approach. A holistic approach that uses the whole brain is needed instead. Imagery is a systematic way to engage the right side of the brain to achieve this holism. The argument is not to replace the hard with the soft, but to use both. Imagery supplements but does not supplant rigorous, logical analysis.

Let's look at some examples. First, consider a plant location decision. This decision lends itself to a high level of quantification. Land costs and taxes, prevailing wage rates, transportation costs, road configurations, construction and leasing costs, delivery times, port and rail capacities, cost-of-living indexes all can be quantified. Yet some of the most important factors cannot. These include quality of schools and neighborhoods, the cultural environment, the quality of the work force, and other issues such as restaurants, shopping, community spirit, traffic congestion, climate, and so on. Yet these so called soft factors have as much to do with a plant location decision as do the hard factors. So the dilemma involves how to systematically consider these factors.

To some extent they can be quantified. Funding spent on education, mean high and low temperatures, and the number of restaurants and malls in the community all help to give a picture of many of the soft variables. But the use of imagery can add to the understanding of these variables. For example, people who will be asked to move to the new plant can be asked to imagine what it would be like to live in different cities under consideration. A script of living a typical day in Atlanta could be compared with that of Denver, Tallahassee, Little Rock, or Minneapolis if those are the cities under consideration for the new facility. This will enable the people to vicariously experience a typical day in the new city helping them to better understand what it would be like to live there. (Of course this should be a realistic presentation of a typical day, rather than a chamber of commerce city promotion.)

Another example where imagery can be useful in helping to understand an event from a more holistic view is in employment recruiting and selection. Much has been written about realistic job previews where job applicants are given a more balanced picture of working in a particular job.[2] Typically, the employer only presents positive aspects of employment to job candidates while ignoring the negative. In a realistic job preview both are presented.

Of course there are many quantitative factors that are presented to a job applicant: wage or salary, vacation days, holidays, sick leave, insurance benefits, seniority rights, production or sales standards, and so on. But many important factors in weighing a job decision cannot be quantified. This is where imagery applies. It can be used to highlight such important but non-quantitative issues as job pressure, potential job satisfaction, corporate culture, job morale factors, job duties, and other important hard to quantify factors. This will help the candidate decide if the job is right for him or her. Here is an example of how imagery can be used to provide a realistic job preview for a cook in a restaurant:

Script for Realistic Job Preview for Restaurant Cook

You will be working under the supervision of Chef Vito along with three other cooks. Your job will be to cook all of the sautéed dishes on a gas stove. All of our dinners are prepared fresh to order so this means you will sauté items freshly prepared, not frozen.

The pace of your work will depend on the pace at which the prep cook can prepare the items. His work is determined by the number of sautéed items turned in by the waiters with their orders.

The kitchen is hot and crowded. Six of you will be working in a ten-by-twenty-five-foot space. There is much movement as all the cooks work very quickly to fill and put up orders. From 7 P.M. to 9:30 P.M. the pace is especially hectic. People yell for items, grab items, rub shoulders. The floor becomes wet and slightly slippery. Steam rises off the water bottles. Even with adequate ventilation, the temperature will rise to 90 degrees in the winter and to 105 degrees in the summer. The humidity usually runs at 90 percent. Under these circumstances Chef Vito will yell at you to perform various duties. He may even call you names.

You are expected to clean up the kitchen once the restaurant closes. This means washing large pots and pans, wiping down counters, mopping the floor, and emptying garbage.

Even though you will work five evenings per week, you may be expected to come in on an off night at very short notice if one of the other cooks takes ill or is otherwise unable to come in. Sometimes you will need to work when we are short-handed with help in the kitchen and will need to double up with your duties so as to help others. This means, for example, that from time to time you will need to do your own prep.

The above script gives a potential job applicant a pretty clear idea of what the job is like. Some people disagree with using a realistic job preview such as this by arguing that it makes the job more difficult to fill. Yet it is better to fill the job with someone who has clear expectations and knows what to expect than to fill it with someone who does not know what to expect and cannot work under the job conditions. It is better to hire someone who will stay at the job and perform the duties than to hire someone who quits or has to be fired. Both a disgruntled employee and the turnover rate are very expensive for any organization.

Let's look at one final example where mental imagery can be used to supplement quantitative analytical techniques in order to achieve a holistic approach. One area of significant research for most companies is consumer or market behavior. Systematic research of market and consumer behavior is a must today for any company that wishes to remain competitive. Even governmental agencies, such as the city of Tallahassee, annually conduct resident opinion surveys both to assess citizen evaluation of government services and to obtain input on future services.

Market and consumer research is highly quantitative and well it should be. A host of demographic factors for a market or potential market can readily be obtained today from the U.S. Census Bureau, private demographic companies, or original survey research conducted by the company or consultant. These demographics include such easily qualified factors as age, gender breakdown, median family income, family size, occupational breakdown, educational level, neighborhood location, and so on. Even such factors as number of automobiles owned, number of bathrooms, ownership of particular appliances such as televisions or VCRs can be obtained. But what is more difficult to quantify are the psychological and social reasons why people buy or don't buy a product. These often are as important if not more so than the easily measurable demographics.

While is is true that demographics are often used to represent psychological factors (e.g., families with teenagers have a need for saving for a college education), actual measurement of psychological factors can be difficult. How do you measure a person's need for luxury or status in making an automobile purchase decision? Self-report measures are used (e.g., "rank your need for status on a one-to-five scale"), but these have many inherent biases and inaccuracies. Indirect measurements are also sometimes used (e.g., "rank the factors in order of importance that most people consider in buying a new car"), but these may not apply to the motivation of the particular respondent.

Therefore, imagery can be used to help get a better picture of market and consumer behavior. We have used imagery in two different ways to help better understand consumer behavior. First, we have asked representative sample groups of present or potential consumers of a certain product to experience an imagery session. Second, we have asked key decision makers to experience an imagery script from the point of view of the customer. Let's look at each of these scripts.

First, let's consider the script that we used with key decision makers of a mail order catalogue house. The objective of this script was an attempt to get them to see their product and service from the eyes of the customer. Go through the script after a relaxation excercise.

Mail Order Catalogue Customer Script: Company Key Decision Makers

Now imagine that you are a woman who has just arrived home from work at about 5:30 P.M.. You pull the mail out of your mail box. As you glance through it, you notice a couple of bills, a letter from an old friend and two catalogues. One of the catalogues is from _____.
You casually look at the cover of each catalogue and place them along with the rest of the mail on the kitchen counter. As you hang up your coat, put away your purse, and change into something more comfortable, you think about fixing dinner. But first you read the letter from the old friend and place the other mail, including the catalogues, on an end table.

You fix and eat dinner, and later that evening pick up the catalogues. (As a regular catalogue shopper, you receive an average of two or three catalogues a week and usually look through them.) As you glance at the pictures of the fashions in the _____ catalogue, you admire how nice the clothes look on the models. You casually wonder about price, ordering information, refund policy, etc.

The phone rings and you answer it after placing the catalogue down on the sofa. Soon after the telephone call, one of your favorite TV shows comes on, so you watch it. While watching it you glance again at the catalogue. You see something you might want to order but your attention is distracted by the television. At that point your husband arrives home from work late and wants to talk with you about his day. You close the catalogue and place it in the magazine rack with about a dozen other catalogues.

Okay, come back to the present. take a few minutes to jot down the observations you have that would help your company better make a sale to that particular person.

The above script experience attempts to place the executives of the company in the actual position of the customers, including the context of the situation in which the customer considers the product. Too often key decision makers of a company lose sight of what it feels like to be a customer. Imagery can help them to live that experience vicariously. In the example above, as a result of the imagery experience, the catalogue company decided to do the following:

1. Make a brightly covered catalogue;
2. Place ordering information and a toll free number on the front *and* back of the catalogue;
3. Follow up with a post card mailing one week after mailing the catalogue to remind the customer to relook at the catalogue.

Now, let's look at how imagery can be used to achieve a more holistic approach in understanding the consumer, only this time using a customer focus group. In this case we used a representative cross-sample of eighteen customers of a major bank. After explaining the purposes of our research and putting them through a relaxation exercise, we used the following imagery script:

Focus Group Script

> Imagine that you are driving in your car on your way home from work when you realize that you still have several checks in your wallet that you have forgotten to deposit this week. You wish to deposit these checks and keep a portion in the form of cash. Immediately you think of the location of the bank you usually patronize as well as both close by branches and Automatic Teller Machines (ATMs). As you decide to drive to your normal banking location, what do you think about? [Pause.]
>
> Once you arrive at the bank, you notice long lines at the drive-through bays so you pull into the lot and park. You then leave your car and walk into the lobby. What do you think about now? [Pause.] While standing in line you notice a sign advertising a home equity line of credit (second mortgage) account. Does this interest you? Why or why not? [Pause.]
>
> Finally, you have your turn at the teller window. What comes into your mind as the teller greets you? [Pause.] You finish your transaction and turn to walk out of the lobby. How do you feel? Do you decide to investigate the home equity account now? At a later time? Never? [Pause.]
>
> You notice the ATM as you leave the bank and think about using it next time. You also hope the drive-through lines are not so long. You also consider banking by mail.
>
> As you get into your car, start it, and begin to leave the parking area, what are your thoughts about your banking experience? [Pause.] Please jot down all ideas that come to mind.

This script resulted in several findings for the bank.

1. ATMs were not conveniently located.
2. Customers were afraid the ATM would make a mistake.

3. Customers dreaded the crowded traffic and parking in and around the bank.

4. Customers disliked the long lines at teller windows and had difficulty choosing the right line.

5. Customers did not want to take the time to learn more about home equity accounts when they made a routine visit to the bank.

As a result of these findings, the bank made several changes in its ATM locations, parking configuration, hours of operation, and teller line queuing.

Both of these examples on how imagery can better help a company understand the customer show that imagery can do much to supplement the hard data gathered about a firm's customers or clients.

This section emphasizes a more holistic approach to management and operations. By using imagery, the so-called soft aspects of decision making can be systematically tapped to be used with the more rigorous analytical numbers side.

ENHANCING CREATIVITY IN THE CORPORATE CULTURE

Many people are afraid to be creative. Being creative means trying something new. Trying something new involves the unknown. Risk is present. Many people are risk averse. They prefer to stick with the tried and true. There is comfort and security in certainty. To them nothing ventured, nothing gained becomes nothing ventured, nothing lost.

As we saw in Chapter 8, creativity is critical for effective problem-solving; but it is more pervasive than this—it is virtually critical in every area of management from planning to rewarding through controlling. World competition in virtually all markets requires creative management. Human resource professionals have an obligation to help their organization's managers become more creative in all aspects of management. As we saw in Chapter 8, this can be done in problem-solving sessions. But it needs to be incorporated into other areas of management training and development.

In addition to problem-solving, we have seen in this book how imagery can be used in strategic planning, leadership, interpersonal relationships, communications, and personal effectiveness. These are critical managerial functions and imagery can have a major role to play in enhancing the practice of these functions in organizations. But the application of imagery goes beyond its application to specific managerial functions. It can be used to change and enhance the *organization culture* where management is practiced.

Various companies such as 3M, IBM, Apple, and Dana Corporation have become known for the sense of innovation and entrepreneurship that has been instilled in their respective corporate cultures. This is not an easy task to accomplish since large established companies act like bureaucracies when it comes to change and innovation—they often very strongly resist it. (Small companies resist change too.) Yet it is this change in culture that not only permits but encourages innovation, which is required in today's worldwide economy.

Imagery can help transform a company's culture. By focusing on ways to unleash the creative spirit in most people, imagery can encourage people to dream and to express those dreams without fear of reprisal.

Imagery works three ways to infuse an organization's culture with innovation and creativity. First it can be used to help people get a reading on the present status of an organization's culture; second, it can be used to initiate change in the culture; third, it can be used to solidify a new culture in place. Let's see how imagery can be used in each of these three steps.

Assessing Corporate Culture

We have used the following script to help people better depict the present state of their organization's culture. Use it after a relaxation script.

Imagine that you are a cultural anthropologist from the People's Republic of China. You have never visited the United States before and are unfamiliar with its corporate form of organization, yet you are trained in anthropological techniques and methods. You plan to spend a month virtually living in _____. During this time you will work alongside operational and managerial employees in each of the firm's offices and divisions. You will have many conversations as you try to determine the cultural makeup of the company.

Often spending several days talking with a munber of employees, you begin to form an idea of the primary values the company seems to believe in as seen from the eyes of the employees. You write these down. [Pause.] You also note little incidents, stories, and historical anecdotes the employees frequently tell you. You write down a few notes describing these. [Pause.]

Next you begin to draw some conclusions about how the employees work. You note their work habits, their views toward quality, punctuality, service, cooperativeness, neatness, and so on, and you jot these down. [Pause.]

As time goes on you begin to work with the company's managers more and more. You begin to see the primary values the company believes in from the eyes of management. You jot these down. [Pause.] You see how similar or different this list is compared to the employees' perception of company values. [Pause.]

You notice the stories managers tell about the company and you write down a few notes describing these. [Pause.]

As time passes, you notice various symbols that seem to have meaning in the company. These include office location dress, lapel pins, and the like. You note which symbols seem to be most important and why. [Long Pause.]

You observe how well management and employees work together and note those areas where they cooperate the best [pause] and areas where they fail to cooperate properly. [Pause.] You try to get a sense or feel for the teamwork displayed by employees working with other employees [pause] and managers working with other managers.

You listen to what people say about one another behind their backs and jot down common comments people make about others in the organization. [Pause.]

You listen to what people say about the company and their jobs. You note the frequency and types of their complaints. [Pause.] You note what they are most proud of and jot these down. [Pause.]

As a foreigner you are both impressed and shocked by what you have learned about the organization's culture. You make a list of the things which most impress you [pause] and those things which shock you the most. [Pause.]

The above script has been used with both large and small organizations in business and the not-for-profit sectors. It is effective in helping members of an organization describe the culture of the organization. The discussion after the imagery session usually results in a broad-based consensus as to the present culture of the organization.

Changing Corporate Culture

The next step to enhancing creativity and innovation in the culture involves initiating changes in the corporate culture. Changing culture is very difficult. One of the functions of culture is to add stability to any social system. Culture builds slowly over time and has its roots in tradition.

However, there are several ways to change culture. The classic case is Lee Iacocca's work at Chrysler Corporation. Here a dynamic, aggressive, and charismatic CEO was appointed to Chrysler by the board of directors and told to remake the company. Since the company was on the verge of bankruptcy, Iacocca had the very real leverage of survival as the impetus to change and success.

Of course, many organizations do not find themselves in this situation and still need a major change. Yet a company should not wait until it is on the verge of bankruptcy before initiating cultural change. By then, it is too late sometimes, as we saw with the once popular, high flying

Air Florida situation. The television broadcast of the rescue effort of passengers after one of their airliners crashed in the Potomac River in Washington, D.C., in 1982 was the final blow to the company's survival.

So our question of focus is how can imagery be used to initiate change in an organization's culture? Here is a script we have found useful with a variety of organizations. Use it after relaxation exercise.

> Imagine that you are the CEO for your organization. You have the power to institute whatever changes you desire in your company. Think about your organization's culture. Think about those things that need to be changed the most. [Pause.] Now assume that you can make these changes. Pick the most important aspect of culture that needs to be changed. Mentally jot down the steps required to bring about the change. [Pause.] Now think about the next most important aspect of culture that needs to be changed. What steps need to be followed to bring about this change? [Pause.] Now move to the third area of cultural change that is needed. Mentally list the steps required to make this change. [Pause.]
>
> Even though you are the CEO and have the power to institute these cultural changes, you know that there will be barriers, resistance, and objections to some of the changes you want to institute. What three most critical barriers are you likely to face? [Pause.] What people are most likely to resist your desired cultural changes? [Pause.] What will be the objections of these people? [Pause.] What are some things you can do to overcome these objections? [Pause.] How long do you think it will realistically take you to put in place the new culture? Who will help you establish your new culture? [Pause.] Do you actually see these people helping you?

Establishing the New Corporate Culture

The third step in the process is to solidify or establish the new culture in place. The members of the organization should adhere to the new culture as if it were second nature to them. This will take time. Yet a clear picture of the desired culture is necessary if people are expected to adopt and adhere to it.

Since a new corporate culture is like a mosaic, we have found the following imagery experience to be helpful in establishing the new culture. Use it after relaxation exercise.

> Imagine that you are putting together a large multipiece jigsaw puzzle. All of the pieces are scattered in front of you on a card table. You are sitting in a chair while you look at all the pieces. The jigsaw puzzle represents your new corporate culture. Your job is to put the pieces together to form the desired picture of the culture you want.
>
> You look at the picture of the puzzle seen on the box. You see

white-capped mountains, a blue sky with white puffy clouds, a green meadow in the foreground with white and yellow flowers blooming. The picture is calm, restful, beautiful, yet powerful and complete.

How are you going to put the pieces together into the desired picture? Where will you start? At the corners? Which corner will be done first? How will you examine each piece to see where it fits? Imagine picking up a piece, looking at it, and fitting it into the puzzle? Do this again [pause] and again. [Pause.]

Now you begin to see your puzzle taking shape. You see a small part of the sky, mountains, and meadows. It is time-consuming and painstaking work, but slowly you see it beginning to take shape. You complete all four corners. Now the left side is completed, then the top side. Finally, all four sides are completed. You have the parameters done. You begin to fill in the middle. The job becomes easier as you solve the puzzle. You have fewer pieces with which to work. Finally, there are just a few pieces left. Quickly, you pick them up, fill in the last few holes, and complete the puzzle.

You feel proud. The puzzle is even more beautiful than the one in the box.

Now, imagine that this puzzle represents your new corporate culture. You know what you want your new culture to look like— you have the picture on the box—but you see many pieces lying in front of you. Each piece has an important role to play. The puzzle will be incomplete if any one piece is missing. Where do you start? Which pieces do you work with first? How do you establish the corners and sides of your new corporate culture? How long will it take you to complete the corporate culture puzzle? What will you do if you get stumped in one area? To what area will you move next? How will you keep someone from coming along and bumping the table while you are working on the corporate culture puzzle? What will you do at night to protect the part of the puzzle you have together from being disturbed until you can get to it the next day?

Now imagine that you finally get to the last few pieces. What do you see? What will be the last piece to fall in place in your corporate culture puzzle? How long do you think it will take you to put the puzzle together? Will it look like the picture on the box? If not, how will it differ? Will this difference matter? Can you do anything about it? Should you? How easy will it be to keep the puzzle together? How will you keep people from bumping the card table and upsetting the puzzle? How will you keep the completed puzzle from becoming dirty and grimy? What will you do with the puzzle if you need the card table for a party?

The establishment and maintenance of a new corporate culture is not easy. It requires time and attention to detail. The pieces do not automatically fall into place, and, once in place, do not automatically stay there. The corporate culture imagery exercises will help your organization's managers see this and better understand how creativity and innovation can be built into the corporate culture.

The Brain and Problem Solving

As we age we tend to cease experimenting. We use the tried and true when we face problems. We reach into our mental hat and pull out a solution that has worked for us in the past. We feel comfortable and confident in using this approach to solving problems. It's fast and it helps us cope.

However, there are two major drawbacks to this approach. First, we may misdiagnose the problem and, consequently, use a good solution, but on the wrong problem. We put a new engine in our car when it is the transmission that really needs fixing. Or we have the problem right, but use the wrong solution. We really do need a new engine, but the one we put in is as defective as the one we are replacing.

Accurately diagnosing the problem and coming up with the right solution can become more difficult with time. We can overrely on our experience and underrely on our creativity. Instead of relying on the tried and true, maybe we should go for the untried and new in order to be creative in today's highly competitive environment. This means releasing the creative forces that each of us has in our brains. It means we need to tap our right side as well as our left side when we face a problem.

Avoiding the Mental Trap

Because things are changing so quickly, no problem today is exactly like the problem of yesterday, although it may be similar. GM must compete with Hyundai as well as Nissan. Reading the problem of today and assessing its similarities and differences compared to similar problems of yesterday is an important skill. Competing in worldwide automobile markets today is different from what it was in the late 1970s. There are more foreign competitors (Hyundai, Yugo, etc.) who have a larger share of the U.S. domestic market. Foreign companies such as Nissan, Toyota, Honda, and Mitsubishi have either wholly owned or joint venture plants in the United States and more are expected to be built. U.S. labor unions in the automobile industry have less power today than in the past. These very real differences mean that U.S. auto makers face a different set of problems with respect to competition today than they did in the late 1970s. Therefore, to call on the solution set of that time period even if those solutions worked then—and there is much disagreement as to whether they did—would be inappropriate. Different, yet similar, problems require different solutions.

The reason we get into this mental trap is because we fail to see the differences. We see a few surface similarities to past problems and we immediately jump to the conclusion that the present problem is, therefore, the same. We don't ask enough questions. We satisfy too easily. We are no longer a child asking the question "Why?" and thus we err on the side of familiarity.

Here is an imagery exercise that can help in diagnosing a problem from a new and fresh perspective. Use it after a relaxation exercise.

Think back to your childhood days. Go back to when you were four, five, or six years old. Remember the home and neighborhood where you lived. [Pause.] Remember your parents, brothers and sisters, and playmates. [Pause.]

Now think of a time when you faced a very perplexing problem at this age. It may be one that frightened you or one that simply made you extremely anxious. Perhaps it dealt with your first day at school or a new toy, or a serious disagreement with a friend, parent, or sibling. Perhaps it dealt with a major disappointment or with a family crisis. Perhaps it was simply a problem of curiosity—such as why the sky was blue or why butterflies flew. Take a moment and pick and focus on this problem. [Pause.]

Remember how you felt in trying to understand this problem. [Pause.] Remember the questions that went through your mind. [Pause.] Remember how you felt when you finally started to get answers that made sense and you finally began to understand the problem. [Pause.] Think back to how long it took you to understand the situation. Your sense of curiosity led to frustration, but also to eventual enlightenment.

Now think of a problem you now face at work. It may be personnel, interpersonnel, a project deadline, or another problem. [Pause.] Focus on that problem. Now pretend that you are a child of six again. You think like a child. You know nothing of the problem or of your company. [Pause.] Yet you encounter this problem and it raises your curiosity. Think of the questions you would ask as a six year old. [Pause.] Think of the answers you would seek in language that you could understand if you were that age. [Pause.] Ask the question "Why?" as does a child. [Pause.] What answers do you hear? Are you satisfied with them?

Thinking like a child allows us to take nothing for granted. Everything is new. We question everything. We are unfamiliar with problems we encounter. Next time you face a problem at work, try this approach. Next time you help your organization's managers in a problem-solving exercise, try the above script.

Building New Mental Templates

As we go through our organizational life, we need new mental road maps as benchmarks and pathways change. As a child we continually were building new road maps as part of the growing and learning process. As an adult, we may cease to do this. We must be careful not to claim twenty years of experience when what we have is one year of experience repeated twenty times.

Imagery can help here by creating opportunities to learn from new experiences. This new learning serves as the foundation for new road maps. We gain insight—we see—and we form new templates of understanding.

Certainly a conscientious program of reading, studying, training, and attending conferences and seminars can all help us to learn. But we must ensure that we actually take in and process the new information presented to us. It is easy to let our perceptual screens and biases—our comfortable ideas—prevent us from learning. However, through imagery we can relax these biases and screens so that we are more receptive to new information. We can use this new information to build new road maps. Here is an imagery experience to help reduce perceptual screens. Try it after relaxation exercise.

> You are standing in the middle of a mountain meadow. You are surrounded by knee-high grass and wildflowers. It is a bright sunny day. There is a gentle cool breeze blowing against your face. In front of you off in the distance are snow-capped purple mountains. The sky is deep blue with white fluffy clouds. You take a deep breath and smell the grass and wildflowers. The air is fresh and clean.
>
> Around you, you hear the buzzing of bees. You watch the bees as they move from flower to flower. You also see butterflies. You watch them intently, noticing the vivid colors and markings on their wings.
>
> You hear birds chirping. You listen to the various types of chirps and calls of the birds. You spread a blanket out and lie down on it. While lying on your back, you watch the clouds drift by. You notice their shapes and patterns. Some are larger than others. Some are darker than others.
>
> You take all this in—the clouds, the sky, the gentle breeze, the smell of the grass and the flowers, the sound of the bees, the chirping of the birds, the feel of the grass through the blanket under your back. You notice and listen intently to everything.

Here is another imagery exercise for use after a relaxation exercise, to help us better learn to be sensitive to experience.

Mentally count the number of windows in your home. [Long Pause.] Now choose a room in your home. Stand in the middle of it. Notice the ceiling. Notice the carpet. Now look at each wall. What do you see? Notice colors, furniture arrangement, pictures, mementos. Dwell on these for a minute. [Pause.]

Now move to another room. Look at the ceiling. Look at the floor. Look at each wall. [Pause.] Again, notice the colors, pictures, furniture, and mementos.

Now move to another room. Look at the ceiling. Look at the floor. Look at each wall. [Pause.] Again, notice the colors, pictures, furniture, and mementos.

Finally, move to one more room, look at the ceiling. Look at the floor. Look at each wall. [Pause.] Again notice the colors, pictures, furniture, and mementos.

Now think what you have just seen in your mind. Did you notice some things that you had not seen for a long time? [Pause.] Were you happy with what you saw? The next time you are home compare the rooms with the pictures you had formed in your mind and notice any differences.

These imagery experiences help to train us to be open and receptive to the experiences around us. Too often we look but we do not see, we hear but do not listen, and we receive but do not understand. Developing new mental road maps begins with awareness of what is happening around us. To be aware we must reduce our filtering screens.

Here is an imagery experience that can help managers build new road maps. First, complete a relaxation exercise.

Think about the people you interact with at work. First, think about your subordinates. Think of each of their faces. Now, mentally draw a line between you and each subordinate. Let the thickness of the line represent the amount of interaction with that subordinate. [Pause.] Are you happy with the thickness of each line? Should you be reacting more with some subordinates and less with others?

Now think about your boss. Draw the mental line between you and your boss. How thick is it? Is it too thick? Too thin? Should anything be done about it?

Now think of others in your organization at your level with whom you interact. Mentally draw a line to each of them [Pause.] Again let the thickness of the line represent the amount of interaction. [Pause.] Which lines are too thick? [Pause.] Which ones rate too thin? [Pause.]

Now think of others with whom you interact at all levels in your organization. These may be other bosses besides your own as well as other subordinates. Mentally draw a line to each of these people. [Pause.] Which lines are too thin or too thick?

Now think of those with whom you interact outside of your company. These might be customers [pause], suppliers [pause], distributors [pause], government regulators [pause], the media [pause], or your competitors. [Pause.] Think about the thickness of each line. [Pause.] Which lines would you like to change?

Now mentally picture all of these people with whom you interact. Draw a line from you to each person. Now on a sheet of paper with you in the middle draw lines to each person as you would like interaction to be. Let the thickness of each line represent the frequency of interaction. Where you are now interacting but no longer wish to be, X over the line. [Pause.] How similar is this new interaction map to your old interaction map? What can you do to achieve the new interaction map?

This experience can help to formulate a new interaction road map for managers at work.

Improving Productivity

The base line reason for using imagery, or any management techniques for that matter, is because it improves individual and organizational productivity. The use of imagery in your organization should be sold on this basis. As a human resource professional, you need to convince your organization's managers that careful and disciplined use of imagery will make them more effective managers. It allows them to rehearse mentally key skills. This practice allows them to improve performance just as it helps athletes who use imagery to improve their performance. It expands their horizons by allowing them to use their imagination in a constructive and disciplined way. New horizons lead to new visions and new goals.

In an intensely competitive worldwide environment there is a place for a dreamer—especially one who tempers dreams with reality. Imagery, this new management technique, is a key tool, which can be used to use the resources of our mind better. Imagery helps us to see better that which needs to be seen, hear that which needs to be heard, and to act upon that which needs action. As the Reverend Martin Luther King, Jr., once said, "I have a dream. . . . "

NOTES

1. Noel Tichy et al., "Strategic Human Resources Management," *Sloan Management Review* 23, no. 2 (1982): 47–61.

2. James A. Breaugh, "Realistic Job Previews: A Critical Appraisal and Future Research Directions," *Academy of Management Review* 7 (1982): 570–578.

BIBLIOGRAPHY

Abbs, P. Education and the living image: Reflections on imagery, fantasy, and the art of recognition. *Teachers' College Record*, 1981, *82*, 475–496.

Abselson, R. P. Psychological status of the script concept. *American Psychologist*, 1981, *36*, 715–729.

Adams, J. L. *Conceptual blockbusting: A guide to better ideas.* San Francisco: Jossey-Bass, 1986.

Agor, W. H. *Intuitive management.* Englewood Cliffs, N.J.: Prentice-Hall, 1984.

Ainsworth-Land, V. Imagery and creativity: An integrating perspective. *Journal of Creative Behavior*, 1982, *16*, 5–28.

Anderson, C. A. Imagery and expectations: The effect of imaginal behavior scripts on personal intentions. *Journal of Personality and Social Psychology*, 1983, *45*, 293–305.

Anthony, W. P. *Participative management.* Reading, Mass.: Addison-Wesley Publishing Company, 1978.

Anthony, W. P. *Managing your boss.* New York: AMACOM, 1983.

Anthony, W. P. *Practical strategic planning: A guide and manual for line managers.* Westport, Conn.: Quorum Books, 1985.

Anthony, W. P., & Maddox, E. N. The use of guided imagery techniques in management education and training. Proceedings, Southern Management Association Convention, New Orleans, November 1984.

Anthony, W. P., Wheatley, W. J., & Maddox, E. N. Better management through the mind's eye. *Association Management*, 1985, *37*, 86–90.

Arieti, S. *Creativity: The magic synthesis.* New York: Basic Books. 1976.

Assagioli, R. *Psychosynthesis.* New York: Penguin Books, 1965.

Bandura, A. *Social learning theory.* Englewood Cliffs, N.J.: Prentice-Hall, 1977.

Bandura, A. The self-system in reciprocal determinism. *American Psychologist*, 1978, *29*, 344–358.

Basadur, M., & Thompson, R. Usefulness of the ideation principle of extended effort in real-world professional and managerial creative problem-solving. *Journal of Creative Behavior*, 1986. *20*, 276–282.

Betts, G. H. The distribution and functions of mental imagery. *Teacher's College Contribution to Education*, no. 26, 1–99.

Bracken, J. The historical development of the strategic management concept. *Academy of Management Review*, 1980, *5*, 219–224.

Breaugh, J. A. Realistic job previews: A critical appraisal and future research directions. *Academy of Management Review*, 1982, *7*, 570–578.

Brown, A. Everywhere, planners are in pain. *Long Range Planning*, 1983, *16*, 18–20.

Brown, D. A. A life-planning workshop for high school students. *Vocational Guidance Quarterly*, 1980, *29*, 79–83.

Bry, A. *Visualization: directing the movies of your mind*. New York: Barnes and Noble, 1979.

Cartwright, D., Jenkins, J. L., Chavez, R., & Peckar, H. Studies in imagery and identity. *Journal of Personality and Social Psychology*, 1983, *44*, 376–384.

Cautella, J. R., & McCullough, L. Covert conditioning: A learning theory perspective on imagery. In J. L. Singer & K. S. Pope (eds.), *The power of human imagination*. New York: Plenum Press, 1978.

Cerio, J. E. The use of hypnotic elements and audio recordings with fantasy relaxation technique. *Personnel and Guidance Journal*, 1983, *7*, 436–437.

Certo, S. C. *Principles of modern management: Functions and systems*, 3rd ed. Dubuque, Iowa: Wm. C. Brown Publishers, 1985.

Chandler, A. D. *Strategy and structure*. New York: Doubleday, 1962.

Channon, J. Visions of the future: Forscum 1990. *OE Communique*, 1982, *2*, 14–22.

Churchman, C. W. *The systems approach*. New York: Dell Publishing, 1968.

Currant, N. Expanding learning through mazes and visual imagery. *Academic Therapy*, 1982, *17*, 529–536.

Dauw, D. C. *Creativity and innovation in organizations*. Dubuque, Iowa: Kendall Hunt Publishing, 1976.

Davis, T., & Luthans, F. A social learning theory approach to organization behavior. *Academy of Management Review*, 1980, *5*, 282–290.

DeWitt, D. J. Cognitive and biofeedback training for stress reduction with university athletes. *Journal of Sports Psychology*, 1980, *2*, 228–294.

Dilley, J. S. Mental imagery. *Counseling and Values*, 1975, *19*, 110–115.

Drucker, P. *Management: Tasks, responsibilities, practices*. New York: Harper and Row, 1973.

Dyson, R. G., & Foster, M. J. Making planners more effective. *Long Range Planning*, 1983, *16*, 68–73.

Edwards, B. *Drawing on the artist within: A guide to innovation, invention, and imagination*. New York: Simon and Schuster, 1986.

Emshoff, J. R., & Mitroff, I. I. Improving the effectiveness of corporate planning. *Business Horizons*, 1978, *21*, 49–60.

Epstein, M. L. The relationship of mental imagery and mental rehearsal to performance of a motor task. *Journal of Sports Psychology*, 1980, *2*, 211–220.

Ernest, C. H. Imagery ability and cognition: A critical review. *Journal of Mental Imagery*. 1977, *2*, 181–216.

Fombrun, C., Tichy, N., & Devanna, M. A. (eds.). *Strategic human resource management*. Reading, Mass.: Addison-Wesley, 1984.

Forshiba, B. C. Mental imagery and creativity. *Journal of Mental Imagery*, 1978, *2*, 209–238.

Friedman, J. S., & Krus, D. J. Imagery and success: Are dimensions of mental imagery valid predictors of the accumulation of wealth? *Educational and Psychological Measurement*, 1983, *43*, 557–562.

Galton, F. Statistics of mental imagery. *Mind*, 1880, *5*, 300–318.

Galyean, B. The effects of a guided imagery activity on various behaviors of low achieving students. *Journal of Suggestive-Accelerative Learning and Teaching*, 1980, *2*, 87–97.

Galyean, B. Guided imagery in the curriculum. *Educational Leadership*, 1983, *40*, 54–58.

Gavel, R., Lemieux, G., & Ladouceur, R. Effectiveness of a cognitive behavioral treatment package for cross-country ski racers. *Cognitive Therapy and Research*, 1980, *4*, 83–89.

Gazzaniga, M. S. The split brain in man. *Scientific American*, 1967, *217*, 24–29.

Ghiselin, B. *The creative process*. New York: New American Library, 1952.

Ginter, P. M., & White, D. D. A social learning approach to strategic management: Toward a theoretical foundation. *Academy of Management Review*, 1982, *7*, 253–261.

Gioia, D. A. & Poole, P. P. Scripts in organizations. *Academy of Management Review*, 1984, *9*, 449–459.

Gluck, F. W., Kaufman, S. P., & Walleck, A. S. Strategic management for competitive advantage. *Harvard Business Review*, July-August, 1980, *80*.

Goldsmith, R. E., & Matherly, T. A. The two faces of creativity. *Business Horizons*, 1986, *43*, 8–11.

Gowan, J. C. Imagery, incubation, and creativity. *Journal of Mental Imagery*, 1978, *2*, 23–32.

Grayson, J. B., & Borkover, T. D. The effects of expectancy and imagined response to phobic stimuli on fear reduction. *Cognitive Therapy and Research*, 1978, *2*, 11–24.

Gurman, H. A. Using mental imagery to create therapeutic and supervisory realities. *American Journal of Family Therapy*, 1982, *10*, 68–72.

Hargraves, D., & Bolton, N. Selected creativity tests for use in research. *British Journal of Psychology*, 1972, *63*, 451–562.

Harrell, T. H., & Beiman, I. Cognitive-behavioral treatment of the irritable colon syndrome. *Cognitive Therapy and Research*, 1978, *2*, 371–376.

Havens, R. A. The mind uncaged. *Management World*, 1982, *11*, 26–29, 34.

Hazler, R. J., & Hipple, J. E. The effects of mental practice on counseling behavior. *Counseling Education and Supervision*, 1981, *20*, 83–89.

Heinrich, R., & Fuller, M. *The use of guided affective imagery in the control and modulation of pain in selected chronic pain patients*. Abstracts for the First World Congress on Pain, Florence, Italy, 1975, p. 110.

Hershey, M., & Kearnes, P. The effect of guided fantasy on the creative thinking and writing ability of gifted students. *The Gifted Child Quarterly*, 1979, *15*, 91–102.

Hickman, C. R., & Silva, M. A. *Creating excellence: Managing corporate culture, strategy, and change in the new age*. New York: New American Library, 1986.

Holt, R. R. Imagery: the return of the ostracized. *American Psychologist*, 1953, *19*, 254–264.

Horowitz, M. J. Image formation: clinical observations and a cognitive model. In P. Sheehan (ed.), *The function and nature of mental imagery*. New York: Academic Press, 1972, 281–352.

Hunt, M. *The universe within: A new science explores the human mind*. New York: Simon and Schuster, 1982.

Hussey, D. E. Strategic management: lessons from success and failure. *Long Range Planning*, 1984, *17*, 43–53.

Isaksen, S. G., & Parnes, S. J. Curriculum planning for creative thinking and problem-solving. *Journal of Creative Behavior*, 1985, *19*, 1–29.

Jarviven, P. J., & Gold, S. P. Imagery as an aid in reducing depression. *Journal of Clinical Psychology*, 1981, *37*, 523–529.

Jenkins, J. A. *Creating the future*. Bureau of National Affairs, 1979, 22–29.

Jung, C. G. *Psychological types* (H. G. Baynes, trans.). New York: Harcourt, 1926. (Originally published, 1921.)

Kanter, R. M. *The change masters*. New York: Simon and Schuster, 1985.

Katz, N. W. Hypnotic inductions as training in cognitive self-control. *Cognitive Therapy and Research*, 1978, *2*, 365–370.

Kaufman, G. Mental imagery and problem-solving. *International Review of Mental Imagery*, 1986, *1*, 65–105.

Keegan, W. J. *Judgements, choices, and decisions: Effective management through self-knowledge*. New York: Wiley & Sons, 1984.

Khatena, J. Major directions in creativity research. *The Gifted Child Quarterly*, 1976, *20*, 216–228.

Khatena, J. Identification and stimulation of creative behavior. *Journal of Creative Behavior*, 1978, *12*, 30–38.

Klinger, E. *Structure and function of fantasy*. New York: Wiley and Sons, 1971.

Kniker, N. Strategic planning. *OE Communique*, 1980, *2*, 154–158.

Kolb, D. A. Problem management: Learning from experience. In N. S. Srivasta (ed.), *The executive mind*. San Francisco: Jossey-Bass, 1983.

Kosslyn, S. M. *Ghosts in the mind's machine: Creating and using images in the brain*. New York: W. W. Norton, 1983.

Lazarus, A. *Seeing with the mind's eye*. New York: Wiley & Sons, 1984.

Leuner, H. Guided affective imagery: A account of its development. *Journal of Mental Imagery*, 1977, *1*, 73–92.

Leuner, H., Horn, G., & Klessmann, E. *Guided affective imagery with children adolescents*. New York: Plenum Press, 1983.

McWhirter, J. J., & McWhirter, M. Increasing human potential: Relaxation and imagery training (RIT) with athletic and performing arts teams. *Personnel and Guidance Journal*, 1983, *62*, 135–138.

Manz, C. C., & Sims, H. P. Vicarious learning: The influence of modeling on organizational behavior. *The Academy of Management Review*, 1981, *6*, 105–113.

Meier, D. Imagine this. *Training and Development Journal*, 1984, *38*, 26–29.

Miechenbaum, D. *Stress reduction and prevention*. New York: Plenum Press, 1983.

Mintzberg, H. Planning on the left side and managing on the right. *Harvard Business Review*, 1976, *76*, 49–58.

Mitchell, T. R., Rediker, K. J., & Beach, L. R. Image theory and organizational decision making. In H.P. Sims and D.A. Gioia (eds.), *The thinking organization: Dynamics of organizational social cognition*. San Francisco: Jossey-Bass, 1986.

Morris, P. E., & Hampson, P. J. *Imagery and consciousness*. London: Academic Press, 1983.

Naisbitt, J., & Aburdene, P. *Reinventing the corporation*. New York: Warner Publication, 1986.

Neurenberger, P. Mastering the creative process. *The Futurist*, 1984, *17*, 33–36.

Nezu, A. M. Cognitive appraisal of problem-solving effectiveness: Relation to depression and depressive symptoms. *Journal of Clinical Psychology*, 1986, *42*, 42–48.

Noddings, N., & Shore, P. J. *Awakening the inner eye: Intuition in education*. New York: Teachers College Press, 1984.

Parnes, S. Learning creative behavior. *The Futurist*, 1984, *17*, 30–32.

Parnes, S., & Meadow, A. Effects of brainstorming. *Journal of Creative Behavior*, 1977, *11*, 1–11.

Pavivio, A. *Imagery and verbal processes*. New York: Holt, Rinehart, and Winston, 1971.

Perkins, D. N. Reasoning as imagination. *Interchange*, 1985, *16*, 14–26.

Peters, T. J., & Allen, N. *Passion for excellence: The leadership difference*. New York: Harper & Row, 1985.

Peters, T. J., & Waterman, R. H. *In search of excellence: Lessons from America's best-run corporations*. New York: Harper & Row, 1984.

Porter, M. E. *Competitive strategy*. New York: The Free Press, 1980.

Pulvino, C. J., & Post, P. B. The use of mental imagery in small groups. *Journal for Specialists in Group Work*, 1979, *4*, 216–221.

Rhodes, J. W. Relationships between vividness of mental imagery and creative thinking. *Journal of Creative Behavior*, 1981, *15*, 90–98.

Samuels, M., & Samuels, N. *Seeing with the mind's eye*. New York: Random House Bookworks, 1981.

Sarnoff, D., & Reiner, P. The effects of guided imagery on the generation of career alternatives. *Journal of Vocational Behavior*, 1982, *21*, 229–308.

Schendel, D. E., & Hofer, C. W. (eds.) *Strategic management: A new view of business policy and planning*. Boston: Little, Brown and Company, 1979.

Sheenhan, P. W. A shortened form of Bett's questionnaire upon mental imagery. *Journal of Clinical Psychology*, 1967, *23*, 386–389.

Sheikh, A. A., & Sheikh, K. S. *Imagery in education: Imagery in the educational process*. Farmingdale, N.Y.: Baywood Publisher, 1985.

Shelton, T. O., & Mahoney, M. J. The content and effects of "psyching-up" strategies in weight lifters. *Cognitive Therapy and Research*, 1978, *2*, 275–284.

Shepard, R. N. The mental image. *American Psychologist*, 1978, *33*, 125–127.

Shepard, R. N. Ecological constraints on internal representation: Resonant kinematics of perceiving, thinking, and dreaming. *Psychological Review*, 1984, *91*, 417–447.

Simonton, O. C., & Simonton, S. Belief systems and management of the emotional aspects of malignancy. *Journal of Transpersonal Psychology*, 1975, *7*, 29–48.

Singer, J. L. *The inner world of daydreaming*. New York: Harper & Row, 1966.

Singer, J. L., & Pope, K. S. (eds.). *The stream of consciousness: Scientific investigations into the flow of human experience*. New York: Plenum Press, 1978.

Singer, J. L. & Switzer, E. *Mind play: The creative use of fantasy*. Englewood Cliffs, N.J.: Prentice-Hall, 1980.

Somner, R. *The mind's eye: Imagery in everyday life*. New York: The Delacorte Press, 1978.

Sproull, L. S., & Hofmeister, K. R. Thinking about implementation. *Journal of Management*, 1986, *12*, 43–60.

Starling, G. *The changing environment of business*. Boston: Kent Publishing, 1984.

Steiner, G. A. *Strategic planning: What every manager must know*. New York: Free Press, 1979.

Steiner, G. A., Kunin, H., & Kunin, E. Formal strategic planning in the United States today. *Long Range Planning*, 1983, *16*, 12–17.

Toffler, A. *The adaptive corporation*. New York: Random House, 1986.

Van Grundy, A. B. *Training your creative mind*. Englewood Cliffs, N.J.: Prentice-Hall, 1982.

Veron, P. E. *Creativity*. Baltimore: Penguin Books, 1970.

Wheatley, W. J. Maddox, E. N., & Anthony, W. P. *Enhancing strategic planning through the use of imagery*. Paper presented at the Annual Meeting of the Academy of Management. New Orleans, November 1987.

Wilson, I. Futures research in an age of uncertainty. *Los Angeles Business and Economics*, 1981, 22–29.

Wilson, W., & Eddy, J. Guided imagery in career awareness. *Rehabilitation Counseling Bulletin*, 1982, *25*, 291–295.

Witmer, J. M., & Young, M. E. The silent partner: Uses of imagery in counseling. *Journal of Counseling and Development*, 1985, *64*, 187–189.

Woodman, R. W. Creativity as a construct in personality theory. *Journal of Creative Behavior*, 1981, *15*, 43–66.

Worthing, E. L. The effects of imagery content, choice of imagery content, and self-verbalization on self-control of pain. *Cognitive Therapy and Research*, 1978, *2*, 225–240.

Yankelovich, D. *New rules: Searching for self-fulfillment in a world turned upside-down*. New York: Random House, 1981.

INDEX

About the Authors

WILLIAM P. ANTHONY is Professor and former Chairman of the Management Department of the College of Business at Florida State University. He conducts seminars, workshops, and conferences with a wide variety of private, governmental, and military organizations throughout the United States on such topics as strategic planning, managing change, participative management, upward management, and managing problem employees. Among his eleven books are *Practical Strategic Planning: A Guide and Manual for Line Managers* (Quorum Books, 1985), *Managing Your Boss, Managing Incompetence,* and *Management: Competencies and Incompetencies.* He has published over thirty-five articles and papers on various subjects in the fields of management, personnel, and strategy in academic and professional journals.

E. NICK MADDOX, Assistant Professor of Management, currently teaches behavioral science courses in Management in the School of Business Administration at Stetson University, Deland, Florida. He also works as an independent human resource/development consultant in the central Florida area.

WALTER WHEATLEY, JR., is a member of the Department of Management at the University of West Florida. He has several years of industrial experience as a financial manager and trainer with General Electric. He has authored several publications involving the utilization of mental imagery.